Manpower ECONOMICS

THE IRWIN SERIES IN ECONOMICS

Consulting Editor
LLOYD G. REYNOLDS
Yale University

Manpower
ECONOMICS

LOWELL E. GALLAWAY
Professor of Economics
Ohio University

1971

Richard D. Irwin, Inc.
HOMEWOOD, ILLINOIS 60430
IRWIN-DORSEY LIMITED, GEORGETOWN, ONTARIO

FIRST PRINTING, JUNE, 1971

Library of Congress Catalog Card No. 72–153167
PRINTED IN THE UNITED STATES OF AMERICA

Preface

THIS book attempts to accomplish two things: (1) the presentation of my view of what a course in "manpower economics" or the "economics of the labor market" should be and (2) the integration of approximately a decade of my own research into labor market phenomena. In both respects what is presented here has been extensively pretested, both in the classroom and in the world of academic publication. In the course of that pretesting I have become a firm believer in integrating the theoretical aspects of economics with the empirical testing of the hypotheses that the theory generates. My classroom experience leads me to believe this is sound pedagogy. Presenting the economic theory of the operation of labor markets without empirical evidence strikes students as being a sterile exercise; offering them just empirical evidence without a theoretical focus seems to produce an aimless, relatively undisciplined approach to problems.

Somewhere between these two extremes lies an avenue which not only permits the student to relate the material of the course to actual labor market problems and data but requires that he do so in the context of the formal apparatus of economic theory. To my mind, the end result is a better appreciation of both the nature of the problem under discussion and the contribution that economic analysis has to make to understanding the world around us.

Fortunately, this approach to presenting labor market problems in the classroom is consistent with my own notion of what constitutes sound research methodology. Consequently, I have attempted in this volume to relate some 10 years of research to a variety of problems to provide a systematic overview of the performance of labor markets in the United

States in allocating manpower resources. The end result is an image of American labor markets which emphasizes their basic capacity to perform the tasks assigned them by formal economic theory—that is, if they are given half a chance. There is a fundamental theme to much of what emerges from this book, namely, that market mechanisms *will* work effectively.

One other aspect deserves mention. There is a basic public policy orientation to what is presented. The ultimate objective of the discussion of various labor market phenomena is the development of recommendations with respect to public policies that might be adopted to deal with certain crucial problems. This is reflected from time to time in the several chapters of the book, but the bulk of the public policy discussion is concentrated in the concluding chapter entitled, "Public Policy Considerations: How Well Do American Labor Markets Work?" In that chapter I attempt to summarize in a concise fashion the public policy implications of the analysis contained in the previous 14 chapters and to lay out the various policies I would follow "if I were king." That discussion contains a sizeable subjective component. This is unavoidable in a treatment of policy matters since certain rather critical judgments must be made as to what the objectives of public policy should be. I have attempted to make clear what my judgments are and, consequently, the material presented in Chapter Fifteen should provide a basis for a rational and intelligent treatment of public policy matters even though there might be disagreement as to the proper objectives of those policies.

May, 1971   LOWELL E. GALLAWAY

Acknowledgments

WHILE there is just a single author listed on the title page, it will be apparent as one reads the book that numbers of other people have contributed in substantial ways to its contents. How many hours of discussion with colleagues, how much work by undergraduate and graduate student research assistants, and how much technical assistance has been provided by various universities and government agencies would be difficult to estimate. However, I shall attempt as comprehensive a list of credits as possible. Perhaps at the top of the list should go Ohio University, which has provided for me an academic environment that has been most conducive to the conduct of the necessary research which has gone into the work presented in the pages that follow. My gratitude to the University is substantial and especially to Burton DeVeau, who has been exceedingly patient with my idiosyncrasies and has done as much as was in his power to create a favorable set of conditions for carrying out serious research. Also, the University contribution to my efforts in the form of virtually unlimited access to the facilities of the Ohio University Computer Center is immeasurable. In the same vein, I should also note that some of the calculations which are presented were conducted at the University of Pennsylvania Computer Center to which I also express my indebtedness. Certain of the data at my disposal were provided by the Social Security Administration while I was in their employ. In this regard, I am particularly grateful to Ida C. Merriam for her efforts in helping to develop these data and making them available to me to be analyzed.

Next, I must mention a number of colleagues and friends whose contributions to the volume are reflected in many ways. Some have actually been co-workers in the sense of our producing a joint research product and have graciously authorized me to report our findings in this volume. In those cases, I have attempted to make this clear in the footnote citations in the various chapters. Among these are (listed alphabetically) Zachary Dyckman of the Center for Naval Analysis, Rajindar Koshal of Ohio University, Gerald Scully of Southern Illinois University, Sebastia Svolos formerly of the Social Security Administration, and Richard Vedder of Ohio University. Other colleagues and friends have contributed their time and efforts in the form of conversations and discussions as well as helpful remarks on various drafts of manuscripts as they have appeared. Among these are (again listed alphabetically) Robert Aronson of Cornell University, Oswald Brownlee of the University of Minnesota, Gene Chapin of Ohio University, Malcom Cohen of the University of Michigan, George Hildebrand of Cornell University, Selig Lesnoy presently with the Social Security Administration, Robert Raimon of Cornell University, and Vishwa Shukla of Ohio University. I should also thank the numerous referees and editors of academic journals whose suggestions are frequently reflected in the final product which has emerged. By way of acknowledgment, certain passages of the volume draw rather heavily on my own material which has appeared in the following academic journals: *American Economic Review, American Journal of Agricultural Economics, Journal of Economic History, Journal of Human Resources, Quarterly Review of Economics and Business, Southern Economic Journal, and Western Economic Journal.* Earlier, I briefly mentioned that a number of graduate and undergraduate students had assisted at various stages in the work. Among these are Walter Bowman, Michael Hamant, William Karis, John Kern, Kenneth Lowe, Charles Marshall, and Walter Stewart. To this list should be added my daughter Kathleen. Of course, none of the people or institutions I have mentioned to this point bear any responsibility for the views I have expressed. They are mine and mine alone, and I must take the credit or the blame, whichever may be appropriate.

Finally, it behooves me to recognize two rather general sources of encouragement. First, I would be quite remiss if I did not note the contribution of Alma Herbst, a grand lady now deceased, who did much to enable a young graduate student to continue his academic career. My debt to her is immense. And second, I must acknowledge the patience and understanding that my family has given me over the years. They have quite readily tolerated the absent-minded behavior, crossness, and strange hours that seem to accompany my working habits. Thank you Gladys, Kathleen, Michael, and Ellen.

May, 1971   LOWELL E. GALLAWAY

Contents

chapter ONE

The Significance
of the Labor Market

In the past 20 years the American economy has experienced almost the full gamut of possible labor market conditions. Commencing with the Korean War episode and its accompanying inflationary pressures, we have moved through a period in which there have been, first, a steady secular drift upwards in unemployment rates in the economy; second, a concerted use of fiscal policy to "beat down" unemployment; third, the reemergence of inflationary pressures as the result of the combination of the use of monetary and fiscal policy and the increasing commitment of military power in Vietnam; and, finally, a movement toward higher unemployment rates at the beginning of the 1970's. Thus, we have gone from what is popularly called "high" full employment during the Korean War to less than full employment during the late 1950's and early 1960's, to "low" full employment in the mid-1960's, back to "high" full employment in the late 1960's, and then a return to less than full employment.

Not surprisingly, this great variation in labor market conditions has been accompanied by a considerable amount of controversy with respect to the desirability of one policy measure vis-à-vis another. As cases in point, one need merely recall the "growthmanship" issue of some 10 years past, or the argument with respect to whether the upward drift in unemployment rates from 1957 to 1963 was caused by "structural" change or "a deficiency of aggregate demand," or the present concern of policy makers, viz, how to limit inflationary pressure while maintaining satisfactory levels of growth and unemployment.

1

As if this assortment of policy problems with labor market overtones were not sufficient, the immediate past has seen the addition of questions such as the relationship between economic opportunity and the presence of poverty and the broad issue of the Negro's position in the labor market. These latter problems, of course, reflect the recent emphasis on facilitating the elimination of poverty in the economy as well as the society's concern with providing equality of economic opportunity to its citizens regardless of their race.

I. THE LABOR MARKET AND UNEMPLOYMENT

To this point it has simply been asserted that problems such as the level of economic growth, unemployment, inflation, poverty, and the economic status of the Negro have significant roots in the way in which labor markets in our economy function. In some cases this is self-evident. For example, the matter of the level of the unemployment rate is rather obviously related to the manner in which labor markets perform the task of bringing jobless workers in contact with available jobs. In its simplest form this merely involves whether the labor market is able to equate the quantity demanded of labor with the quantity supplied. If these two magnitudes are not equal, the result is unemployment. Such a view of the labor market is a gross oversimplification in that it compresses the great diversity of American labor markets into a single generalization. Rather than there being one broad market for labor there are a great many smaller markets which interact with one another to produce an exceedingly complex set of labor supply and demand relationships.[1]

For example, if unemployment develops in one region or one industry, the unemployed workers in that market may seek employment elsewhere and an adjustment process is set in motion. If that process functions smoothly, unemployment will be gradually eliminated through unemployed workers in one sector finding jobs in other areas. Whether all the unemployment disappears as the result of movement of this sort depends upon not only the efficiency of the adjustment process but the degree of flexibility of wage rates throughout the economy. If wages are relatively inflexible, job opportunities may not be available in suffi-

---

[1] There is a great variety of evidence relating to the diversity of American labor markets, evidence which has sometimes been interpreted as indicating that the generalizations of conventional economic theory may be of limited usefulness in dealing with labor market phenomena. One of the earlier suggestions along this line may be found in Cairnes (25), in which the concept of noncompeting groups in the labor force is developed. For a latter-day treatment of this matter, see Kerr (99).

cient quantities in other sectors to absorb the initial unemployment.[2] Of course, implicit in the assumption of an original amount of unemployment in a particular market is at least temporary wage inflexibility in that sector. Otherwise, the adjustment to unemployment could presumably be made within the sector itself through downward movements of wage levels.[3]

Moving to the level of multiple labor markets alters things only slightly. Regardless of whether the labor market is viewed as a simple or complex arrangement the overall level of unemployment is integrally related to the effectiveness of the labor market adjustment process. The linkage may take one of two forms. First, in the case of a general decline in aggregate demand in the economy, such as that which accompanies a downturn of the business cycle, the responsiveness of labor markets in general to the presence of unemployed workers has an influence on the general level and duration of unemployment. If these markets respond to unemployment by exhibiting flexible money wages,[4] some or all of the impact of the decline in aggregate demand may be absorbed. However, if in general, money wage rates are inflexible downward, little of the unemployment generated by the downturn of the business cycle will be eliminated. Thus, the effectiveness of labor markets in adjusting to the presence of unemployment has a significant effect on the severity of cyclical unemployment.

In addition to its impact on the level of cyclical unemployment the nature of the labor market adjustment process also has an effect upon the amount of unemployment which is observed during periods of what we choose to call full employment. At any point in time displacement of workers is occurring due to dynamic changes in the economy. Shifts in consumer demand and technological innovations introduce random shocks which generate unemployment which puts pressure upon labor

---

[2] It has been argued by Keynes (**100**) that flexible money wage rates may not be sufficient to produce labor market equilibrium in the aggregate. The crux of this argument is the matter of interdependencies between wage rates, aggregate demand, price levels, and costs. For a treatment of this subject in the literature, see Bronfenbrenner (**19, 20**); Junk (**94**); Rothschild (**162, 163**); and Weintraub (**212, 213**). My own view on this matter is that the Keynesian contentions are valid logically under certain assumptions but that the assumptions are not likely to be realized.

[3] When discussing a single sector of the overall market for labor the aggregation problems indicated in footnote 2 can be disregarded with relative safety as long as the sector in question is small relative to the entire market for labor. When this is the case the effect of the interdependencies which create aggregation problems is in large part "washed out."

[4] The question of how much and how rapidly the impact of declining aggregate demand will be absorbed by flexible money wage rates depends on the impact of the various interdependencies referred to in footnote 2. In short, it depends upon the validity of Keynes's (**100**) basic argument that flexible money wage rates may not be sufficient to produce an aggregate labor market equilibrium.

market adjustment mechanisms. To the extent that such unemployment is absorbed rapidly by labor markets in other sectors of the economy the level of unemployment associated with full employment is reduced. In effect, the ability of labor markets to react to such changes determines in fact what may be thought of as a normal minimal level of unemployment in the economy. This is commonly thought to lie in the range of from 3 to 4 percent for the United States, a part of which, perhaps 2 percentage points, can be viewed as minimal "frictional" unemployment where frictional unemployment may be thought of as unemployment resulting from the lapse of time required for workers to change jobs in the economy under "true" full-employment conditions.[5] The remainder represents the contribution made to normal unemployment by the inability of labor market mechanisms to shift workers between jobs in the time required in a true full-employment situation. Of course, the matter of what constitutes the normal length of time for job changing under full employment is a question of judgment.[6]

II. THE LABOR MARKET AND ECONOMIC GROWTH

It follows quite naturally and rather obviously that if the labor market mechanism has a significant impact on the overall level of human resource use, i.e., on the unemployment rate, it also has an effect on the process of economic growth in an exchange economy, for one of the major determinants of levels of economic activity is the extent to which an economy's human or labor resources are used. The effect of the functioning of the labor market on economic growth can take one or both of two forms. First, it may alter the growth rate of an economy by means of a "once-and-for-all" or "one-shot" type change. An example of this would be some alteration in the circumstances of the labor market sufficient to produce a permanent shift in the level of human resource use. Such a shift might have the effect of reducing the labor force participation rate in the economy or it might alter the intensity or degree of labor force participation of those still active in the labor market. Both of these are exemplified by the reaction of workers to the availability of retirement benefits of either a public or private character. The provision of such benefits operates through the labor market both to shift older workers out of the labor force and to reduce the amount of labor force participation among those older workers who remain in

---

[5] Simler (173) estimates that if long-term unemployment (15 weeks or longer) were eliminated, the residual amount of unemployment would be about 2 percent. In a crude sense, this may be thought of as "frictional" unemployment although I would regard it as a maximum estimate.

[6] In the previous footnote I have implied that a normal length of time for job changing under "true" full employment is less than 15 weeks. If such a definition is accepted, the Simler estimate of 2 percent unemployment with zero long-term (15 weeks or greater) unemployment measures frictional unemployment.

the labor force.[7] Such shifts have the effect of deterring economic growth during the period in which they occur. However, if they represent merely a transition from one set of retirement institutions to another, once the transition is completed the negative impact of the labor force changes on economic growth will no longer be felt although the economy will be operating at a lower level of measured real output than previously.[8] Thus, an alteration of labor market conditions of this type merely shifts the economy from one growth path to another without necessarily affecting its growth rate other than during the period in which the shift occurs.[9]

By contrast, there are aspects of the manner in which labor markets function which have a direct bearing on the size of the long-term growth rate of an economy. For one thing, the ability of an economy to grow is dependent on its capacity to adjust to the technological changes which are vital to increasing productivity and output. One aspect of this ability is the ease with which workers who are displaced as the result of an altered technology are absorbed elsewhere in the economy. If such absorption takes place relatively rapidly, unemployment among displaced workers is minimized and, more important, the society's willingness to accept and incorporate technological change is in all probability enhanced. Historically, there has been substantial opposition among workers to the introduction of laborsaving machinery.[10] Admittedly, such

---

[7] For a discussion of various aspects of the labor market response of the aged to retirement benefits, see Gallaway (71).

[8] Such a transition does not imply a lower level of social welfare even though measured output may have declined because of it. What has happened is that increased leisure has been substituted for goods and services which are priced by the market mechanism. However, leisure is not priced in this fashion and, according to our income accounting conventions, consequently, is not included in measured national output.

[9] It is possible for shifts of this sort to have a permanent effect on the economy's growth rate if it results in changes in the quality of the labor force. For example, if the general level of adaptability of the labor force to economic change is altered due to shifts in the composition of the labor force that result from the types of movements discussed here, the result may be a permanently changed growth rate for the economy.

[10] It would require a lengthy tome to chronicle all the examples of such opposition. One of the most famous, though, is the Luddite riots in England in 1830. However, this is not the first of such happenings. The following citation from Herbert Heaton (85) is illustrative:

"Popular or state opposition was easily aroused against any invention that threatened to injure some strong vested interest, or to reduce the demand for labor and thus cause more people to need poor relief. At various times mobs destroyed sawmills, ribbon looms, and knitting frames. Guilds condemned equipment or methods that gave one member an advantage over his fellows. The city of Danzig forbade the use of a loom which wove several strands of ribbon, and suffocated its inventor (1586). Charles I of England ordered the destruction of a needle making machine (1623) and banned the casting of brass buckles (1632) on the ground that six casters would endanger the livelihood of six hundred guildsmen who were making buckles in the old way."

In more recent times the so-called featherbedding controversies are reminiscent of this type of opposition.

efforts have not been able to permanently forestall the introduction of
new techniques with their accompanying contribution to increasing economic growth. However, it may well be that the rate of technological
progress has been slowed at certain times by efforts to protect workers
from the rigors of the ensuing adjustment process. In fact, there are
indications that this very thing may be occurring to some extent in
the contemporary United States. Increasing emphasis in collective bargaining negotiations on smoothing the technologically displaced worker's
transition to other employment at the expense of the introducer of the
new technology has the effect of increasing the cost of such changes
to the producer. In a market economy this results in a slowing of the
rate of adoption of technology due to the reduced level of profitability
produced by the higher cost of introduction. Consequently, if the pressure
for such cost increasing arrangements is reduced by the presence of
a smoothly functioning labor market mechanism, economic growth is
encouraged and facilitated.

In addition to its impact on private devices for dealing with the
problem of workers who have been displaced by technological change,
the effectiveness of labor market processes in producing necessary adjustments may also significantly influence public policy with respect to the
introduction of technological change. For example, labor markets that
produce a relatively inefficient adaptation to advancing technology may
engender public policies such as those adopted in France where significant
restrictions are placed upon the rights of employers to displace workers
from their existing employment.[11] Not all public policy measures dealing
with problems of displaced workers have to take the form of restricting
their movement out of or between jobs but public figures seem to have

---

[11] The following citations from Organization for Economic Cooperation and Development (145) are illustrative of the types of control which government instru-
mentalities may exercise in France:

(1) "By law the public authorities enjoy the most extensive privileges on the
     labour market, since their authorisation is required before any recruitments
     or dismissals in industry or commerce can take place." (p. 13)
(2) "In the matter of collective dismissals, . . . authorisation is given only if
     it can be proved that the dismissals are justifiable, either because of a real
     reduction in activity or in the development of new production methods,
     or because of the company's obligation to cut down overhead expenses."
     (p. 13)

In addition, approval is required of the Labour Inspector before overtime work
can be undertaken and the courts have ruled in some cases that "workers whose
dismissal has been brought about through the inefficient management of the enterprise could also suffer 'direct and special prejudice of sufficient gravity' to demand
legal redress." (p. 14)

No matter how loosely administered such an environment can hardly be conduc-
tive to the implementation of new technology.

an unfortunate predilection in that direction.[12] Consequently, an ineffective labor market adjustment mechanism is more likely than not to produce public policies which aim at limiting worker movement rather than encouraging it. And, if this does happen, the impact is apt to be a diminution in the rate of economic growth for the system.

III. THE LABOR MARKET AND INFLATION

The discussion of the relationship between the nature of labor market mechanisms and the problems of unemployment and economic growth suggest that these two phenomena are quite clearly interrelated. Unemployment levels affect economic growth and the manner in which growth is generated influences unemployment levels. And, of course, both are greatly affected by the way in which labor markets function to produce the adjustments required by both growth and the presence of unemployment. This pattern of interrelationship is repeated when the connection between the labor market and the phenomenon of price inflation is considered.

Price stability, or its inverse—price inflation—has been a constant source of concern in the United States over the past quarter century. Commencing with World War II there have been few periods in which the fear of substantial upward movements in the price structure was not present. And, in those instances where such fear did not manifest itself, unsatisfactorily high levels of unemployment were generally present. This suggests the existence of a basic conflict between the policy objectives of full employment and price stability in our economy. The empirical evidence on this count rather clearly indicates that this is the case. For example, a comparison of unemployment rates and increases in the price level for individual years can be summarized in the form of what has come to be called a Phillips' curve.[13] The Phillips' curve is a conceptual device for expressing the "tradeoff" between the unemployment rate and the rate of price inflation that exists in an economy and takes the general shape shown in Figure 1–1. That particular delineation of a Phillips' curve is taken from a 1960 paper by Paul Samuelson and Robert Solow and roughly approximates the relationship between the unemployment rate and the rate of price inflation for the American

---

[12] In general, public officials seem to be reluctant to encourage individuals to migrate from the areas which they govern. I first encountered this phenomenon when writing a doctoral dissertation on the subject of the economic problems of depressed industrial areas. See Gallaway (66), for a summary of my conclusions at that time.

[13] The concept of the Phillips' curve arises out of the work of Phillips (152).

economy in the post-World War II world.[14] Of particular interest is
the negative slope of the Phillips' curve in Figure 1–1 for this negative
slope reflects the basic conflict between the policy objectives of full employment and price stability. In effect, the relationship shown in Figure
1–1 says that it is only possible to obtain lower unemployment rates

FIGURE 1–1

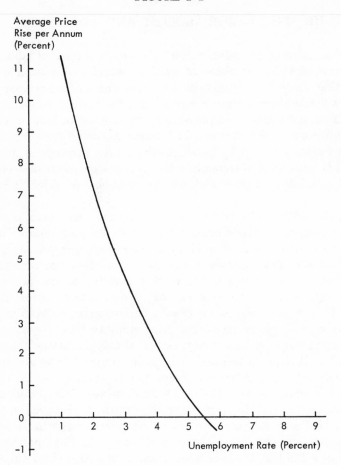

at the expense of greater price inflation or price stability at the expense
of higher unemployment rates. Thus, it depicts what is sometimes a
painful choice for a society that on occasion seems to have a rather

---

[14] See Samuelson and Solow (168). More recent views of the Phillips' curve
suggest that it is essentially a short-run phenomenon. This is argued by Friedman
(54) in his presidential address to the American Economic Association of December
1967. Essentially, what is argued is that in any model of the economy which
incorporates expectations, the Phillips' curve relationship is not stable over time.

low tolerance for price inflation. The choice shown here is made all the more painful by the fact that price stability may also be incompatible with high real growth rates for the economy as a whole. It is rather obvious that the conflict between full employment and price stability must be carried over at least in part to the relationship between the growth rate and price stability. But, the conflict extends even beyond this rather straightforward linkage, for it is quite clear that a rapidly growing economy is more likely to put greater demands on its resources and thus generate the increases in prices that we call price inflation.

The dilemma presented by the conflict between the various policy alternatives that face the economy has part of its roots in the operation of the economy's labor markets, for there are some clear relationships between the way in which these markets function and levels of economic growth and unemployment. Interpreted in the context of the Phillips' curve discussion, a more efficient labor market mechanism implies a more favorable relationship between the rate of unemployment and the rate of price inflation. This follows from the fact that at a given level of aggregate demand a more efficient labor market will produce a lower level of unemployment and, presumably, a higher level of output and a lower price level. Consequently, the particular workings of the labor market have a substantial impact upon the position of the Phillips' curve for the American economy and the set of policy alternatives which are available to the society. The more efficient the labor market the less painful the choice that has to be made between full employment, economic growth, and price stability.

IV. POVERTY AND THE LABOR MARKET

After observing a slackening in the rate at which poverty was being eliminated in the United States in the late 1950's and early 1960's, a number of people have argued that there is some fundamental shortcoming in the economy as it now stands which seriously limits the ability of individuals with extremely low levels of income to move to a non-poverty level of income.[15] As usually defined this means an inability to obtain a level of money income in excess of approximately $3,000 per year (in 1957–59 prices) but this definition is somewhat flexible.[16]

Those who are dissatisfied with the performance of the contemporary American economy in eliminating poverty usually argue that certain groups in the society are relatively isolated from its normal market processes and, consequently, do not share fully in the largesse generated

---

[15] See, for example, Harrington (83) and Galbraith (56).

[16] A more sophisticated set of definitions of poverty which takes into consideration varying family size has been developed by the Social Security Administration. See Orshansky (147).

by the system. Implicit in this position are some very clear attitudes with respect to how labor markets in the United States function, for a very substantial source of the economic isolation that is claimed for some portions of the population must lie in a lack of full contact with those labor markets. In fact, some argue rather specifically that for many this isolation from the economy's labor markets is so complete that normal measures to stimulate economic activity, such as monetary-fiscal policy, will prove quite ineffective in eliminating their poverty.[17]

Specific reasons for the relative isolation of certain groups from the mainstream of American economic life vary, but, in general, they seem to focus on a lack of marketable skills among these groups, either because of those skills being rendered obsolete by the process of technological change or because the skills were never acquired to begin with due to lack of educational opportunity and the like. Examples of the first type would be individuals with marginal labor force skills who are displaced by the introduction of laborsaving machinery and find themselves unable to locate another job over a protracted period of time. Obviously, this case is almost identical to that treated in the discussion of the significance of the labor market for the level of growth in the economy. However, when the displacement from employment becomes protracted true isolation from the labor market process can develop. To begin, after a substantial lapse of time without work an individual may become "discouraged" and simply stop looking for work, i.e., he may withdraw from the labor force.[18] Further, as he is divorced from work activity for longer and longer periods of time the possibility of erosion of his already meager labor force skills cannot be ignored.[19] Thus, a sequence of progressive isolation from the labor market may develop in situations such as this.

The process by which individuals may be progressively isolated from the labor market is somewhat similar for those who have never acquired skills of any particular significance. People in this category are more likely to undergo protracted periods of unemployment which in turn may lead to labor force withdrawal, erosion of what little skill they may have had and, finally, a settling into a permanent life of poverty. The possibility of large numbers of individuals slowly slipping into an economic way of life that leaves them without meaningful access to

---

[17] An exploration of this thesis on an aggregative level may be found in Gallaway (69); Aaron (1); and Gallaway (70). On a much more disaggregated level, see Anderson (125); and Gallaway (68).

[18] A good deal of recent research on the "discouragement" effect has been reported. See Barth (5); Bowen and Finegan (15); Dernburg and Strand (37); Strand and Dernburg (181); and Tella (185, 186). An excellent summary of much of this research is provided by Mincer (137).

[19] Simler (173) develops a full theory of long-term unemployment which incorporates the phenomenon of skill erosion explicitly.

the economy's labor markets and, consequently, relatively untouched by the normal processes of growth that characterize this economic system is not a pleasant one. However, it is certainly not clear that this type of isolation from the labor market mechanism occurs in quantitatively significant numbers. For one thing, the concept of skill is a variable thing. With low levels of aggregate demand in the economy and low levels of employment employers can afford to be quite selective in their hiring practices. For example, with an abundance of workers (a "loose" labor market) it may be feasible to insist on a credential, such as a high school diploma, before employing someone in a relatively unskilled job.[20] On the other hand, if the economy is operating with high levels of aggregate demand and a tight labor market, employers begin to find that such credentials are not necessary to carry out that particular job and, in general, there is an upgrading of skills as the labor market tightens. Such upgrading does reach down into the lower levels of the skill hierarchy but whether it reaches far enough to break down the isolation of many individuals from the labor market can only be answered in an empirical fashion.[21] Regardless of the nature of that answer it is clear that the manner in which labor markets function is an important aspect of the poverty problem.

V. THE LABOR MARKET AND THE NEGRO

The recent civil rights revolution has projected the economic status of the Negro into the forefront of discussions of contemporary American life. Such discussions have been quite varied ranging from esoteric treatments of the theory of economic discrimination[22] all the way to the most naïve form of casual empiricism. However, irrespective of the quality of the discourse, it has been characterized by an emphasis on the Negro's labor market position relative to that of whites. A number of statistical measures suggest a basic weakness in that position.[23] Unemployment rates among Negroes are larger than those of whites by approximately a multiple of two.[24] Further, income levels of Negroes are only slightly more than half those of whites and actually showed a relative

---

[20] Such policies by business enterprises are not arbitrary and capricious. Given a choice between workers with specific credentials and workers with none, on balance, it is probably safer to employ those with the credentials.

[21] The matter of the empirical evaluation of these propositions will be undertaken in a latter portion of this volume.

[22] See Becker (10) and Krueger (107).

[23] An excellent analysis of the causes and significance of the economic status of the Negro in contemporary America may be found in Tobin (190).

[24] See U.S. Department of Labor (208), Table A-11.

decline over the decade of the 1950's, although there are signs of improvement in more recent years.[25]

The apparent weakness of the Negro in the labor market can be explained in a variety of ways: (1) discrimination against the Negro due to his race; (2) lack of educational opportunity for Negroes which operates to deprive them of necessary labor market skills; (3) the differential impact of variations in levels of economic activity upon the economic position of Negroes and whites; or (4) factors associated with the Negro culture in the United States which make it difficult for him to partipicate fully in the American economic system.[26] The impact of this complex of factors in producing such a markedly lower economic status for the American Negro makes a great contribution toward generating many of the tensions and difficulties that have marked the racial scene in recent years. That these factors exert their impact through the labor market mechanism almost goes without saying. Discrimination against Negroes in employment opportunities because of employer attitudes regarding the desirability of hiring them,[27] inability of Negroes to compete effectively for jobs either due to prior educational discrimination or problems arising out of the existence of a Negro subculture in the United States, and the differential impact of cyclical swings in economic activity are all labor market manifestations of basic characteristics of the contemporary American society.

In many respects the remarks concerning the relationship between poverty and the labor market are applicable to the economic problems of Negroes. Discrimination, lack of education, and the like operate to make many Negroes "marginal" participants in the labor market. And,

---

[25] For discussions of the behavior of relative incomes of Negroes, see Batchelder (**6**); Becker (**10**); Fein (**51**); and Rayack (**157**). Becker and Rayack find that during the relatively prosperous 1940's Negro relative income improved. However, Batchelder shows that in the 1950's with a somewhat more sluggish economy, the relative income of Negro males declined. Recent evidence presented by Fein indicates that the prosperity of the 1960's has reestablished the trends observed by Becker and Rayack.

[26] In an as yet unpublished paper, Katzner (**97**) estimates that the total cost of economic discrimination in 1959 was 4.36 percent of national income. He divides the cost into two categories: (1) that accruing from a failure to provide equal educational opportunities for Negroes (1.23 percent of national income) and (2) that arising out of a nonoptimal utilization of existing skills of Negroes (3.13 percent of national income). His concept of nonoptimal utilization of skills is really a residual cost which includes everything but the educational factor. Some additional work along these lines has been done by Michelson (**134**). He tends to accord less importance to education as a source of racial income differentials than Katzner. For a discussion of Negro unemployment levels, see Gilman (**78**) and (**77**). A treatment of the impact of variations in general levels of economic activity may be found in Anderson (**125**).

[27] It should be kept in mind that employer prejudices in hiring may be derived from either the prejudices of other workers against working with Negroes or consumer prejudices against being served by Negroes.

with marginal participation in the labor market go the possibilities of progressive isolation from the mainstream of economic life and poverty levels of income. Consequently, it is no surprise to find that, relatively, Negroes account for about two and one-half times as much poverty as whites.[28] While one cannot say exactly what the contribution of this relative lack of success of the Negro in the labor market is toward generating the current racial unrest in the United States, it is fairly clear that it is a significant factor. Certainly, elimination of the differential results of Negro and white labor market participation would be helpful in easing the bitterness that presently characterizes interracial relations.

VI. CONCLUDING REMARKS

With almost monotonous regularity the importance and significance of labor market mechanisms in the American economy have been reiterated. This is not to say that labor markets are the device with the greatest influence on contemporary economic life. However, some poetic license must be granted the researcher whose primary interest is labor markets if he seemingly exaggerates the importance of his subject. But, even discounting the previous discussion to take account of such exaggeration it seems clear that labor market mechanisms are a significant factor in today's economy. The reason for that significance is the potential that labor markets have for dealing with the variety of problems we have discussed. Two basic issues arise in connection with those problems: (1) the ability of labor markets to promote a more efficient use of manpower resources and (2) the extent to which labor markets are capable of producing an equitable distribution of the gains from economic activity within-the society. Examples of these aspects of the functioning of labor markets are easy to find. Reductions in unemployment and higher growth rates clearly suggest a more efficient use of resources while the ease with which a system of labor markets shifts people from poverty to nonpoverty levels of income has definite implications for the very important question of economic equity. Consequently, the manner in which labor markets operate has some significance for the formulation of public policy with respect to such issues. With this in mind, the remainder of this volume will be devoted to a discussion of various aspects of American labor markets in action.

A variety of issues will be treated commencing with a consideration of the factors influencing the quantity of human resources which are supplied to various portions of the economy. Following this will be sections dealing with the relationship of the labor market to the problems

---

[28] For specific data on Negro income levels in the post-World War II period, see U.S. Department of Commerce, Bureau of the Census (203).

of unemployment, inflation, and economic opportunity. And, finally, an attempt will be made to formulate policy suggestions which might contribute to the development of an optimal labor market policy. The last section is really the focal point of the entire discussion, for this is essentially a public policy-oriented volume which is designed to provide some insights into possible solutions to the variety of economic problems that are reflected in labor market phenomena.

chapter TWO

The Aggregate Labor Force

ANY labor market is merely an institution where a supply of labor is confronted with a demand for labor and it is the end result of such a confrontation, viz, the interaction between the supply and demand factors, which determines how a given labor market will perform. The demand for labor in any market is derived from the demand for consumer goods and is the direct result of an attempt by a business enterprise to satisfy such a demand.[1] However, in this chapter we are not concerned with the demand for labor. Rather, the focus will be upon the conditions determining the supply of labor in American labor markets. Specifically, the factors affecting what may be called the aggregate supply of workers or the size of the aggregate labor force will be treated.

First, the meaning of the concept "aggregate labor force" needs to be defined. In essence, it is the total number of laborers who offer their services to employers in all labor markets in the economy, but, more precisely, the term aggregate labor force is considered to be synonymous with the statistical measure called the "civilian labor force participation rate for the population 14 and over."[2] When defined in this fashion

---

[1] For a discussion of the conventional theory of the demand for labor, see Cartter (26), Chapters 1 through 4. For an extensive discussion of the pros and cons of applying the conventional theory to labor market problems, see Lester (120, 118), and Machlup (130, 131).

[2] Recent changes in labor force definitions have raised the lower age level to 16 in the conventional measures of labor force participation. However, since the data which will be used throughout this chapter antedate this change, the age

the size of the aggregate labor force is an approximate measure of the total stock of human resources available to be employed in the society's business of producing goods and services. More important, the magnitude of that stock is a vital determinant of the level of real output of the economy and, as outlined earlier, it is important to know whether variations in it are sensitive to changing labor market conditions. If they are, this would imply that existing labor market mechanisms are capable of responding to variations in the aggregate demand for labor.

I. LONG-RUN VARIATIONS IN THE AGGREGATE SUPPLY OF LABOR

Variations in the aggregate labor force can occur in two major forms: (1) long-run or secular changes, or (2) cyclical shifts. Both of these are significant and in recent years there has been some concern with respect to the extent of these movements.[3] Turning first to the matter of long-run trends in labor force participation rates in the United States, some consideration must be given to Clarence Long's (128) interesting thesis, remarkable in both its simplicity and complexity, concerning the nature of the intertemporal behavior of the aggregate labor force participation rate. Briefly stated, the thesis maintains that there is an unusual stability in the aggregate labor force participation rate through time. Long notes (in a chapter appropriately titled "The Stable Labor Force under Rising Income and Employment") that: "Labor force participation in relation to population as a whole did not change materially

---

14 and over distinction will be maintained. For a brief description of current labor force definitions, see Rowan and Northrup (167).

The general framework of these definitions is that of the market economy. Very simply, the definitions of labor force status try to make operational the idea that individuals in the society exercise a free choice of whether to work. Consequently, the emphasis in the definitions (particularly in the case of the unemployed) is on the individual's perception of his status in the labor market. This emphasis on individual choice explains why most people refer to the civilian labor force since the military does rely in part on conscription to obtain manpower. Also, it should be kept in mind that certain arbitrary definitions are invoked. In particular, this is the case with the minimum age requirement for inclusion in the labor force. This merely reflects the society's attitudes toward child labor and the age at which individuals are capable of exercising choice in labor markets. In another time (say 1820) the 14 or 16 year old cutoff would certainly have been inappropriate.

[3] The concern has focused largely on the implications of such changes for forecasting the size of the labor force in the United States. See Bowen and Finegan (15); Dernburg and Strand (37); Strand and Dernburg (181); and Tella (185, 186). A slightly earlier study is that of Hansen (82). These all deal with the cyclical behavior of labor force participation and focus on the post-World War II period. Mincer (137) evaluates several of these studies. For longer term studies of labor force levels, see Bancroft (3); Durand (42); Kuznets, Miller, and Easterlin (109); Lebergott (115); and Long (128).

during peacetime periods of rising income and high employment in the five countries studied."[4]

In addition to Long's evidence, the stable labor force thesis has also received support from the econometric investigations of Klein and Kosobud, Denison, and the labor force projections of the Bureau of Labor Statistics and the Census.[5] Perhaps the best comment with respect to the holding power of the stable labor force thesis is Denison's remark that, "Whether or not Long's explanation is accepted, the historical record itself appears impressive" (36, p. 54).

To be more specific, the Long thesis is something more than a mere empirical observation that the aggregate labor force participation rate is remarkably stable through time. This, in itself, would be interesting but Long pushes beyond that to suggest that this stability is not a mere whim of chance. Quite the contrary: according to Long the observed stability in the labor force is the result of a systematic tendency for changes in the labor force participation rate in one sector of the economy to be offset by changes in the other direction in other sectors. The classic example of this which is suggested is the behavior of labor force participation rates among men and women in the United States. It is well known that through time the labor force participation rate of both elderly and very young men has fallen while the participation rate for women has been on the increase.[6] Long (128, p. 23) explains this phenomenon by noting "that women may have both pushed and pulled young and elderly males from the labor force, to some extent seeking jobs that had been or were being sought by males, and to some extent being drawn into the labor force by the vacuum left by the exodus of males for other reasons."

This is a very intriguing contention. For one thing, it is not in conflict with some of our accepted theoretical constructs relating to the labor market. After all, an increase in the supply of female labor should, *ceteris paribus*, lower the overall wage rate and drive some males out of the labor force. Similarly, a decrease in the supply of male labor should, *ceteris paribus*, increase the overall wage rate and attract females into the labor force. Further, within the confines of a particular family unit it is not unreasonable to hypothesize shifts in labor force participa-

---

[4] The five countries studied were the United States, Great Britain, New Zealand, Canada, and Germany.

[5] See Klein and Kosobud (103) and Denison (36). Klein and Kosobud suggest that perhaps the aggregate labor force participation rate should take its place alongside the other "great" constants in economics, e.g., the relative share of wages, the capital-output ratio, and the stability of consumption expenditures out of disposable income. Denison does not pass judgment on the stable labor force thesis but admits he feels more comfortable with it (p. 54). The Census A and B projections as well as those of the Bureau of Labor Statistics show little change in the aggregate labor force participation rate through 1980.

[6] For details of these changes see Table 2–1 of this chapter.

tion of the type envisaged by Long.[7] Thus, the shifts in labor force participation rates suggested by ordinary economic theory are in the appropriate directions. As a consequence, it would not be surprising to find that there is some tendency toward systematic stability in the aggregate labor force participation rate.[8] However, granted this, some disturbing questions remain, namely: How stable does the aggregate labor force participation rate have to be in order to be regarded as unusually stable? How do we test to determine whether stability exists? These are difficult, although not unique, questions; the economic literature is replete with discussions of the alleged constancy of certain statistical values and with the difficulties of testing to determine whether they are truly stable.[9] The answers in this particular case are important since unusual stability in the aggregate labor force participation rate implies that it will not be especially responsive to variations in the aggregate demand for labor and that our labor market institutions are not performing one of the functions that is characteristic of an efficient system of labor markets.

Fortunately, some extremely helpful pathbreaking has been done along the lines of providing answers to such questions by R. M. Solow (177) in his discussion of the stability of the wage share of national income. In his paper Solow develops a method for evaluating the frequently made contention that the wage share of national income is unusually stable. Solow's technique consists of comparing the variance through time of the aggregate wage share with an expected variance computed on the basis of an assumption that the behavior of the wage share in the individual sectors of the economy is such that the average correlation coefficient between the wage shares for pairs of sectors is zero. This amounts to an assumption that the individual sectors vary in a chance fashion and are completely independent of one another. Such an assumption implies an absence of any systematic stability in the aggregate wage share and, consequently, provides a basis for evaluating its stability. If the wage share is systematically stable, negative correlations between the sectoral wage shares will predominate and the observed

---

[7] Within a family unit, income of a primary earner provides what amounts to intrafamily transfer payment income for other family members. Thus, if a male primary earner withdraws from the labor force a wife might enter. Similarly, if a young male attends school and receives such intrafamily transfers this may induce a mother to enter the labor force. A fuller discussion of the economic theory of how intrafamily transfers operate to affect labor market behavior will be found in Chapter Nine.

[8] There will be some changes, for it is clear, barring chance compensatory shifts, that the normal adjustment in the labor market will result in an altered aggregate labor force participation rate. Given the change in the overall wage rate which follows a supply shift in one sector, ceteris paribus, there must be a change in the quantity of labor employed which, assuming full employment, means a change in the labor force participation rate.

[9] See Klein and Kosobud (103), for example.

variance of the aggregate wage share will be significantly less than the zero-correlation predicted variance.

Clearly, the Solow technique for evaluating stability in the aggregate wage share is applicable to the problem of measuring the stability of the aggregate labor force participation rate. By comparing the observed variance of the aggregate labor force participation rate with a calculated variance assuming zero intersectoral correlations it should be possible to determine whether the stable labor force thesis is valid. If the thesis holds, the observed variance of the aggregate labor force participation rate through time will be significantly less than the zero-correlation variance. If it is not valid, the observed variance will be approximately equal to the predicted variance (or perhaps greater).

The Solow statistic is given by the expression:

$$\hat{\sigma}_0^2 = \sum_{i=1}^{n} \alpha_i^2 \sigma_i^2$$

where $\hat{\sigma}_0^2$ denotes a predicted zero-correlation variance, α_i represents the relative weight of the ith sector, and σ_i^2 is the variance in the ith sector.

This statistic was calculated for several sets of data. Initially, Long's data for the period 1890–1950 (at 10-year intervals) were employed with age and sex sectors and with age, sex, and rural-urban sectors. These data as well as the values used in computing the Solow statistic are shown in Tables 2–1 and 2–2. In both cases the aggregate labor force participation rate time series employed was Long's series standardized for changes in the composition of the population according to the sectoral classification used (i.e., when only age and sex sectors are used, the aggregate series is standardized only for changes in the age-sex composition of the population).[10] Since Long uses 1940 weights for standardizing purposes, the 1940 distribution of the population by sector was employed to estimate the α_i values required for the analysis.

The first statistic computed is for an age-sex classification (Table 2–1). The results are as follows: the actual variance of the standardized time series for the aggregate labor force participation rate is 0.000047 while the predicted zero-correlation variance is 0.000329. Thus, the actual variance is only one seventh of the predicted variance assuming zero correlations among the sectors of the labor force. This is impressive evidence in support of the stable labor force thesis since the actual variance is clearly significantly less than the predicted variance at the 0.05 level of significance.[11] A clear idea of the impact of the compensating adjustments in labor force participation rates can be obtained by com-

---

[10] Long's standardizing technique is identical with Solow's use of fixed weights in (177).

[11] The test used is described in Gallaway (62).

TABLE 2–1

Labor Force Participation Rates, by Age and Sex, United States, April, 1890–1950

Sex and Age Group	Participation Rate							Weight in Aggregate Series (α_i)*	Variance
	1890	1900	1910	1920	1930	1940	1950		
Male									
14–19	0.571	0.611	0.562	0.526	0.411	0.344	0.399	0.0732	0.010586
20–24	0.920	0.917	0.911	0.909	0.899	0.880	0.828	0.0564	0.001048
25–44	0.976	0.963	0.966	0.971	0.975	0.950	0.928	0.1939	0.000293
45–64	0.952	0.933	0.936	0.938	0.941	0.887	0.879	0.1325	0.000814
65 and older	0.739	0.683	0.581	0.601	0.583	0.415	0.416	0.0435	0.015035
Female									
14–19	0.244	0.268	0.281	0.284	0.228	0.188	0.225	0.0722	0.001214
20–24	0.308	0.321	0.355	0.381	0.425	0.451	0.425	0.0584	0.003060
25–44	0.156	0.180	0.210	0.225	0.254	0.302	0.330	0.1978	0.003974
45–64	0.126	0.141	0.171	0.171	0.187	0.198	0.286	0.1266	0.002692
65 and older	0.083	0.091	0.086	0.080	0.080	0.059	0.076	0.0455	0.000103
Both sexes									
14 and older†	0.528	0.533	0.538	0.541	0.539	0.522	0.537	1.0000	0.000047

* Based on population of the United States in 1940.
† Standardized for age-sex composition on the basis of the population of the United States in 1940.
Source: Long (128), Table A-2, pp. 287–88.

paring the actual range of variation in the aggregate labor force participation rate to an estimated range which would occur under conditions of chance relationships between the sectors. The actual range is 1.9 percentage points with a standard deviation of 0.7 percentage points. Now, the standard deviation of the aggregate labor force participation rate under chance conditions is 1.8 percentage points, which would indicate a range of about 4.9 percentage points. Thus, the systematic offsets in sector labor force participation rates operated to reduce the range of the overall participation rate to about 40 percent of what it would have been simply as the result of chance.

The second test conducted employs data classified by the urban-rural character of the population as well as by age and sex (see Table 2-2). The results are somewhat different: the actual variance of the aggregate labor force participation rate through time is 0.000064 while the predicted zero-correlation variance is 0.000146. The actual variance is still significantly less than the predicted variance but the impact of the systematic offsets on the range of variation of the aggregate participation rate is much less marked. The actual range of the aggregate rate is 2.2 percentage points with a standard deviation of 0.8 percentage points. Based on an estimated standard deviation of 1.2 percentage points under chance conditions, the range of the aggregate rate would have been 3.3 percentage points in the absence of systematic offsets. Thus, the reduction in the range of variation brought about by systematic offsets is about 33 percent whereas it is about 60 percent with only an age-sex classification.

The sizable differences in the results obtained suggest quite clearly that the systematic stability which is observed in the aggregate labor force participation rate may be highly dependent upon the way in which the data are classified. In order to explore this possibility further, several additional tests were performed. The results of these tests are summarized in Table 2-3. As can be seen from this table, the Solow statistic is computed on the basis of different combinations of sectoral divisions of the labor force. Four criteria for classifying the labor force are used: age, sex, urban-rural status, and nativity (native white, foreign-born white, and nonwhite). The data used are Long's for the population aged 14 and over. The results of these tests are extremely enlightening; quite obviously, the most significant factor in producing systematic offsets in labor force participation rates is the sex classification. When sex alone is used as the basis for delineating sectors of the labor force, the actual variance in the aggregate labor force participation rate is only 13.6 percent of that which would be expected if the correlation coefficient between the two sectors were zero. The next most important source of systematic offsets appears to be the age classification: using only age as a basis for delineating sectors, the actual variance is 51 percent of

TABLE 2-2
Labor Force Participation Rates, by Age, Sex, and Urban-Rural Attachment, United States, April, 1890–1950

Type of Group	Participation Rate							Weight in Aggregate Series (α_i)*	Variance
	1890	1900	1910	1920	1930	1940	1950		
Urban Male by Age:									
14–19	0.600	0.626	0.590	0.565	0.367	0.298	0.355	0.0366	0.019386
20–24	0.940	0.930	0.924	0.924	0.895	0.874	0.796	0.0317	0.002521
25–44	0.967	0.971	0.974	0.979	0.975	0.955	0.928	0.1167	0.000313
45–64	0.938	0.936	0.941	0.941	0.937	0.887	0.884	0.0781	0.000676
65 and older	0.666	0.631	0.540	0.581	0.542	0.370	0.400	0.0227	0.012331
Urban Female by Age:									
14–19	0.362	0.398	0.400	0.403	0.294	0.233	0.265	0.0386	0.005086
20–24	0.479	0.477	0.481	0.490	0.523	0.555	0.482	0.0356	0.000895
25–44	0.248	0.243	0.276	0.289	0.312	0.370	0.371	0.1246	0.002549
45–64	0.158	0.157	0.197	0.202	0.216	0.237	0.325	0.0781	0.003278
65 and older	0.084	0.076	0.077	0.079	0.079	0.064	0.085	0.0277	0.000047
Rural Male by Age:									
14–19	0.557	0.603	0.542	0.494	0.455	0.392	0.451	0.0366	0.005290
20–24	0.907	0.909	0.898	0.893	0.905	0.888	0.885	0.0247	0.000091
25–44	0.981	0.955	0.951	0.961	0.974	0.942	0.930	0.0772	0.000306
45–64	0.959	0.931	0.931	0.934	0.946	0.888	0.867	0.0781	0.003278
65 and older	0.765	0.704	0.609	0.616	0.622	0.464	0.441	0.0208	0.013763
Rural Female by Age:									
14–19	0.179	0.190	0.181	0.172	0.152	0.135	0.165	0.0336	0.000357
20–24	0.180	0.202	0.220	0.240	0.269	0.290	0.296	0.0227	0.001980
25–44	0.807	0.121	0.133	0.135	0.154	0.186	0.240	0.0732	0.002455
45–64	0.105	0.130	0.145	0.131	0.143	0.133	0.201	0.0485	0.000867
65 and older	0.082	0.099	0.094	0.082	0.082	0.050	0.056	0.0178	0.000335
Urban–Rural—Both sexes, age 14 and older†	0.540	0.542	0.544	0.545	0.538	0.522	0.533	1.0000	0.000064

* Based on population of the United States in 1940.
† Standardized for age-sex and urban-rural composition on the basis of the population of the United States in 1940.

Source: Long, (138), Table A-4, pp. 292–93.

TABLE 2–3

Actual and Zero-Correlation Variances and Actual and Predicted Range of
Values, Labor Force Participation Rates, Various Sectoral
Classifications, United States, Selected Years, 1890–1950

Basis of Classification	Variance		Range	
	Actual	Zero-Correlation	Actual	Predicted*
Age-sex-urban-rural.....	0.000064	0.000146	0.022	0.033
Age-urban-rural.........	0.000138	0.000131	0.031	0.029
Sex-urban-rural.........	0.000142	0.000320	0.031	0.047
Age-sex...............	0.000047	0.000329	0.019	0.049
Age..................	0.000106	0.000208	0.029	0.041
Sex..................	0.000084	0.000616	0.027	0.073
Urban-rural............	0.000243	0.000154	0.042	0.033
Age, sex-nativity........	0.000083	0.000264	0.019	0.034
Sex-nativity...........	0.000107	0.000553	0.025	0.057
Nativity..............	0.000115	0.000145	0.030	0.034

* Estimated by assuming that the range is proportional to the expected standard deviation under conditions of zero average correlation among the sectors.
SOURCE: Long (128), Tables A-2, A-4, pp. 285–96 and calculations.

the zero-correlation variance. As to the other bases of classifications, nativity and urban-rural status, the impact of these as sources of systematic stability in the aggregate labor force participation rate is highly questionable. In the case of classifying sectors solely by nativity, the actual variance is 79.3 percent of the zero-correlation variance while with an urban-rural classification the actual variance in fact exceeds the zero-correlation variance.

One additional test was performed, this with respect to the impact of different time periods on the stable labor force thesis. According to Long (128, p. 19), time should have little impact. He maintains that, "In time of peace the total labor force in the United States has been a relatively stable proportion of the total population 14 and older in the short run (1947–1956)." For testing purposes, Long's data for 1947–56 (annual average participation rates by age and sex) were used (see Table 2–4). The results confirm the long-run findings: the predicted zero-correlation aggregate participation rate variance is 0.000079 while the actual variance is 0.000038. This suggests that on an age-sex basis there are systematic offsets in labor force participation rates in the short run. However, it should be noted that Long's short-run data are classified by extremely broad age groups: 14–24, 25–64 by sex, and over 65. Since these classifications are not the same as those used in the long-run analysis, the same test was conducted using the age classifications employed by Long in presenting the 1890–1950 decennial census data (see Table

TABLE 2-4
Labor Force Participation Rates, by Age and Sex, United States, Annual Averages, 1947–56

Age Group	Participation Rate										Weight in Aggregate Series (α)	Variance
	1947	1948	1949	1950	1951	1952	1953	1954	1955	1956		
14 to 24 (both sexes)	0.528	0.537	0.537	0.539	0.541	0.527	0.512	0.503	0.506	0.521	0.2179	0.000198
25 to 64 (male)	0.939	0.940	0.936	0.931	0.939	0.940	0.943	0.946	0.942	0.940	0.3347	0.000016
25 to 64 (female)	0.318	0.330	0.337	0.347	0.359	0.364	0.364	0.369	0.382	0.394	0.3448	0.000554
65 and over (both sexes)	0.265	0.265	0.267	0.261	0.252	0.240	0.243	0.232	0.236	0.239	0.1026	0.000184
Male												
14 to 19	0.542	0.543	0.536	0.532	0.537	0.519	0.509	0.493	0.495	0.514	0.0580	0.000353
20 to 24	0.848	0.856	0.877	0.890	0.910	0.920	0.922	0.915	0.908	0.908	0.0524	0.000710
25 to 44	0.968	0.969	0.969	0.968	0.973	0.978	0.979	0.978	0.979	0.977	0.1952	0.000024
45 to 64	0.929	0.930	0.920	0.919	0.921	0.924	0.928	0.931	0.928	0.931	0.1369	0.000021
65 and over	0.478	0.468	0.469	0.458	0.449	0.426	0.416	0.405	0.396	0.400	0.0484	0.000987
Female												
14 to 19	0.316	0.325	0.325	0.315	0.321	0.315	0.305	0.298	0.299	0.319	0.0568	0.000098
20 to 24	0.449	0.453	0.450	0.461	0.466	0.448	0.445	0.453	0.460	0.464	0.0525	0.000053
25 to 44	0.340	0.349	0.356	0.364	0.375	0.379	0.376	0.378	0.382	0.392	0.2050	0.000265
45 to 64	0.291	0.304	0.313	0.332	0.344	0.351	0.355	0.364	0.389	0.409	0.1404	0.001369
65 and over	0.081	0.091	0.096	0.097	0.089	0.091	0.100	0.093	0.106	0.109	0.0543	0.000068
Both Sexes												
14 and older*	0.566	0.573	0.574	0.575	0.582	0.580	0.578	0.577	0.581	0.589	1.0000	0.000038
14 and older†	0.572	0.577	0.579	0.583	0.589	0.590	0.589	0.589	0.593	0.601	1.0000	0.000072

* Standardized for changes in broad classification age-sex composition on basis of population in United States in 1950.
† Standardized for changes in narrow classification age-sex composition on basis of population in United States in 1950.
SOURCE: Long (**128**), Table B–2, pp. 323–28 and (**208**), Statistical Appendix.

2–4). The result is surprising, if not shocking. In this case, the actual variance in the aggregate labor force participation rate was almost twice the zero-correlation predicted variance, absolutely the reverse of the result obtained with Long's original data.

This strange and unexpected development is at first somewhat perplexing. However, a second thought on this matter suggests a reasonable explanation for the results obtained. Apparently, the broad short-run classifications employed by Long combine age-groups which have labor force participation rates which are highly correlated with one another through time. The effect of this is to greatly increase the value of the α^2 term (e.g., the α^2 for a sector formed by combining two sectors of equal weight is twice the sum of the α^2 of the original sectors) without a proportionate decrease in the variance of the combined sector (due to the high intersectoral correlations). Consequently, the zero-correlation predicted variance is increased by such combinations and the aggregate labor force participation rate is made to appear more systematically stable. This being the case, a strong argument can be made that in the short run there is no systematic offsetting of changes in labor force participation rates between age-groups. Also, it suggests that perhaps a narrower age classification in the long-run data would eliminate any tendency for systematic offsetting among age-groups over long periods of time. At any rate, the idea that there are systematic offsets in labor force participation rates among age-groups is decidedly weakened by these findings.

At this point we can ask, "What import do these empirical findings have for the stable labor force thesis?" If offsets by age-group are eliminated, all that remains of the thesis are the systematic offsets based on the sex classification. These are still present in the short run: the zero-correlation variance is 0.000055 while the actual variance is 0.000033 if only a sex differentiation is employed. However, since there are only two possibilities in the sex classification, this merely amounts to a negative correlation between male and female labor force participation rates. Thus, shorn of its elaborate trappings the stable labor force thesis possesses a surprisingly emaciated body. Out of all the possible sectoral classifications the division by sex is the only one which definitely produces compensatory offsets in both the short and long run.

Now, on this basis, it is possible to argue that the stable labor force thesis is a meaningful and rich contribution to our knowledge of labor market mechanisms. However, in order to do this it is necessary to impute some type of causality to the relationship between male and female labor force participation rates, such as the theoretical interrelationship suggested earlier. Such a relationship must imply substitutability between men and women in the labor market, i.e., that women either push men out of the labor market when they enter it or are pulled into the market by the vacuum created when men withdraw from the labor force. Apparently, this substitution (if it exists) occurs only at the extremes of the age distribution of males: as Long notes, the declines in male labor force participation occur among the very young and the elderly, while the increase in women's participation is fairly general. Thus, by arguing that a widespread increase in female labor force participation has either led to or resulted from decreases in male labor force participation among the very young and the elderly, some meaningful content can be given to the stable labor force thesis.

In all fairness, though, it should be noted that the very real possibility exists of an alternative explanation of the observed negative correlation between male and female labor force participation rates. On the one hand, the works of Jacob Mincer (136) and Glen Cain (24) suggest that in general the labor force participation rates of women are markedly influenced by the market alternatives they face, e.g., wage rates, unemployment rates, and the like. Further, in a recent study Richard Easterlin (44) concludes that Long's belief that women pushed men out of the labor force is unsubstantiated and that women were pulled into the labor force to only a limited extent by the withdrawal of men from the labor force. He concludes that the primary factor (particularly in the last two decades) operating to increase female labor force participation has been the general aggregate demand-supply situation in labor markets, only a portion of which reflects a lack of labor supply induced by labor force withdrawal among men.

Consequently, the relationship between female labor force participation and the labor force activity of elderly and young males would seem to be somewhat weak. Rather, what seems to have been happening is that labor force participation rates among men have been declining because of increasing school enrollment among younger males and the growth of the importance of the Old Age Survivors Disability and Health Insurance (OASDHI) system among elderly workers[12] while the labor force activity of women has been increasing in response to market factors in the economy. This conclusion is not a categorical denial of the existence of some substitutive relationship between male and female labor force participation rates. However, it is one thing to admit the existence of some degree of substitution between male and female members of the labor force and quite something else to construct an elaborate theory of compensatory offsets in labor force participation upon the basis of a single observed negative correlation. If a skeptical view may be pardoned, a much more satisfactory explanation of the apparently narrow range of variation in the aggregate labor force participation rate would seem to be one which relies upon the premise that there are some

---

[12] For a discussion of the impact of OASDHI on labor force participation of the elderly, see Gallaway (71).

positive and some negative correlations among sectors and that, consequently, when these sectors are combined to form an aggregate, the laws of chance operate to reduce the variation in the aggregate labor force participation rate to the levels which have been observed.

II. CYCLICAL VARIATION IN AGGREGATE LABOR SUPPLY

The second aspect of variation in the aggregate labor force—cyclical movements in labor force participation—has recently become the focus of a good deal of analysis.[13] Actually, the question of cyclical swings in labor force participation has a hoary history tracing back to W. S. Woytinsky's (214, 215) hypothesis that, "During the depression the number of persons seeking jobs tends to outrun the number of persons who have lost jobs. On the other hand, with progressive recovery the re-employment of usual gainful workers is likely to bring about the gradual withdrawal of additional job seekers" (215, chap. 24). Woytinsky's conclusion has come to be known as the "added worker" thesis and, if true, suggests that in the aggregate the responses of individuals on the supply side of labor markets tend to be disequilibrating. Obviously, this reflects adversely upon the ability of labor markets in general to respond to the problems created by a decline in aggregate demand in the economy.

Needless to say, the "added worker" thesis has been challenged.[14] In fact, Woytinsky (215, p. 321) himself argued that there are forces at work which will lead workers to withdraw from the labor market in response to declines in the general level of economic activity, although he obviously felt that this "discouragement" effect is dominated by the "added worker" phenomenon. From a theoretical standpoint there is a good reason to expect both of these effects to be present in a labor market. The elimination of a primary earner's job through unemployment obviously reduces the amount of income available to a family. In a very real sense this income is the source of transfer payment income for members of the family who are not labor force participants. Consequently, when it disappears as the result of unemployment, individuals in the family other than the primary earner experience an "income effect" which will operate to shift some individuals into the labor force.[15] This is the added worker effect.

---

[13] See Bowen and Finegan (15); Barth (5); Dernburg and Strand (37); Strand and Dernburg (181); and Tella (185, 186).

[14] See, e.g., Long (127).

[15] If workers are considered to choose between income and leisure in making their labor market decisions, the disappearance of the primary earner's income results in a negative income effect. Such a reduction in income causes individuals to reduce the quantity of leisure they demand, i.e., increase their labor force activity.

At the same time, the presence of a substantial amount of unemployment in the economy may operate to alter negatively individuals' perceptions of the wage alternatives available to them in the labor market. For example, as an individual is frustrated in attempts to find employment he may decide that the effective wage rate he can command in the labor market is substantially below what he normally receives.[16] As this perceived wage rate drifts lower, beyond some point an individual will simply elect to withdraw from the labor force rather than continuing to seek employment. The point at which this withdrawal occurs will depend in part on the availability of alternative sources of income, e.g., personal savings or public and private charity.[17]

Since both added worker and discouragement effects are consistent with the economic theory of individual behavior in the labor market, the matter of which is the more important becomes essentially an empirical matter. Consequently, it is surprising that a reasonably clear-cut answer to the empirical question of which effect is dominant has only been developed recently. However, the studies of the past few years relating to this question quite clearly demonstrate that the "discouragement" effect dominates the "added worker" effect. For example, Dernburg and Strand (37, p. 74) estimate that the net effect of these factors is that "over the decade covered by the data 1953–62, one person appears to have left the labor force for every two who lost jobs." This is in general agreement with several other studies of this relationship although Mincer (137) and Easterlin (45) feel that the actual net impact of unemployment on labor force participation is something less than one half of that reported by Dernburg and Strand.

Even though there may still be some dispute over the exact magnitude of the impact of unemployment on labor force participation the evidence now overwhelmingly indicates the dominance of the "discouragement" effect. Equally important is the information which has been developed with respect to the differential impact of the discouragement and added worker effects among different age and sex groups. These findings indicate that the discouragement effect is quite strong among the young, the old, and women. For example, the Dernburg-Strand analysis indicates that a change in total employment of 1,000 workers will produce a change in the same direction in the female labor force of 306 compared to a change in the male labor force of 148 (37, p. 80). Further, the change in the male labor force is almost exclusively in the age-groups 14–19 and 65 and over (these age groups account for a change in the labor force of 127 workers) while the change in the female labor force is

---

[16] It is even possible for an individual to perceive a zero wage rate being available to him in the labor market.

[17] An excellent analysis of the impact of public charity (in the form of general assistance payments) on work activity may be found in Brehm and Saving (18).

more evenly distributed across all age-groups (the youngest and oldest age-groups account for only 113 of the total of 306 female additions to the labor force). Actually, these results are not surprising, for the brief theoretical observations made earlier would suggest that the discouragement and added worker effects would be much stronger in those groups who are marginal participants in the labor force, viz, the young, the old, and women.

Given the evidence showing relatively strong discouragement effects among those individuals who are marginally attached to the labor force, it might also be hypothesized that this effect would be relatively strong among low-income groups in the society—in particular among Negroes. Some data on the matter of the impact of the discouragement effect among different racial groups is available and its details will be presented later in this volume. This material shows that hidden unemployment of the type produced by the discouragement effect is about 55 percent more prevalent among Negro males than among white males and 35 percent more prevalent among Negro females.[18]

III. THE AGGREGATE LABOR FORCE: AN OVERVIEW

The discussion to this point argues strongly that variations in the size of the aggregate labor force in the United States are responsive to changes in general levels of economic activity. The responsiveness which has been shown in the variety of evidence that has been presented is quite clearly in directions that are consistent with an efficiently operating labor market. For example, whether in the short or long run or over the course of the business cycle, "tighter" labor markets (i.e., an increasing demand for labor) evoke an increase in the number of people willing to work while "looser" labor markets (a decreasing demand for labor) are characterized by a reduction in the aggregate labor force. Since "tighter" labor markets are generally associated with relatively higher wages (as well as greater job opportunities), this, in turn, suggests that individuals are more willing to participate in labor markets when wages are relatively high. In short, the behavior of variations in the size of the aggregate labor force is quite consistent with the supply curve for labor which emerges from the conventional economic theory of labor supply; i.e., a positive relationship between the quantity of labor supplied to the market and wage levels.

The positive relationship between wage levels and the willingness of individuals to participate in the labor market is confirmed by data available from the Social Security Administration records accumulated in the course of administering the OASDHI system. These data show average earnings covered by the social security system per year employed

---

[18] See Gallaway (61), Chap. 6.

TABLE 2–5
Percent of Workers Employed in 1960, by Age and Mean Earnings per Year Employed, 1951–59

Age Group	*Percent Employed*				
	$1 − 1,199	*$1,200 − 2,399*	*$2,400 − 3,599*	*$3,600 − 4,199*	*$4,200 and over*
Less than 25.....	88.1	98.0	99.0	99.0	100.0
25–49...........	53.0	83.9	91.3	98.3	97.7
50–59...........	46.2	72.0	78.5	95.7	96.0
60–64...........	40.6	63.7	67.4	90.2	94.3
65 and over......	17.8	29.6	28.6	56.8	67.6

SOURCE: Social Security Administration, One Percent Continuous Work History Sample.

over the period 1951–59 as well as employment status in 1960 for male workers (see Table 2–5).[19] Crudely, the average earnings per year employed may be interpreted as a measure of the wage rate available to individuals in the labor market.[20] If this is done, the percentage of individuals employed in 1960 can be viewed as a measure of the responsiveness of individuals to differing wage alternatives. In general, these data show a marked positive relationship in all age groups between earnings per year employed and the percentage employed in 1960. This is quite consistent with the relationships suggested by the previous discussion of the behavior of the aggregate labor force.[21] Thus, the broad, general conclusion that American labor market mechanisms are capable of responding in the appropriate directions to changes in the aggregate demand for labor is reinforced.

[19] These data were made available to the author while a member of the staff of the Social Security Administration. They were first presented in Gallaway (64).

[20] This assumes that previous earnings patterns are highly correlated with present earning capacity.

[21] It should be clearly kept in mind that this is crude evidence of the positive relationship between wages and the quantity of labor supplied. It does not constitute an empirical estimate of a labor supply curve in that the income-leisure preferences of various income groups may be quite different. For a fuller discussion of some of the difficulties implicit in these data, see Taussig (184), and Gallaway (65).

chapter THREE

Mobility in the
Labor Market:
The Interindustry Case

THE conclusion that the size of the aggregate labor force is positively responsive to changes in the general level of economic activity argues that the labor market decisions of individual workers are in reasonable agreement with the behavior patterns which are postulated for workers by the conventional economic theory of the labor market. However, this is only a part of the problem of how labor supply behaves in the United States. The second, and perhaps most important, aspect of labor supply is how workers are distributed among the various sectoral labor markets in the economy. This is merely a matter of the composition of the aggregate labor supply and an effectively functioning set of labor markets will allocate labor toward those areas where it is most in demand. In fact, under certain assumptions, this allocation is entirely demand determined. If workers are homogeneous in all respects, are strict maximizers, and there are (1) no differences in the cost of employment in various markets (either objective or subjective), and (2) no movement costs or barriers to mobility between markets, a single aggregate wage will prevail in all labor markets and the supply of labor to each market will be perfectly elastic.[1] For a variety of

---

[1] This assumes that all labor markets are so small relative to the economy as a whole that the impact of changes in employment in a single labor market on aggregate demand levels and the position of the demand curves for labor in all other labor markets can be ignored.

31

reasons, though, these assumptions are not realized. First, workers are not homogeneous in all respects. Differences in natural ability and levels of acquired ability differentiate one worker from another. Admittedly, it is possible to abstract from differences of this sort by expressing all labor inputs in terms of some "numeraire" which measures a "normal" unit of labor input or by considering the wage rate to be a combination of a pure return to a labor input and returns to acquired or inherited abilities (rents or returns to investment in human capital).[2] However, these do not disguise the fact that because of differences in workers wage rates vary between markets.

In a very real sense some of the variation in wage rates across markets reflects a deviation from the assumption of no movement costs, for in many cases the differentiation between workers is the result of their having undergone training of some type. This training has some cost associated with it and, consequently, is merely a cost of moving between markets for those who have the ability to receive the training.[3] In addition to costs of this sort there are any number of other movement costs between markets as well as unique costs of employment associated with various markets.[4] Consequently, the assumptions detailed earlier are, in reality, violated substantially. In fact, even the maximizing assumption has been seriously questioned in some cases.[5]

The fact that the premises underlying the simple model of how the aggregate supply of labor is distributed are not met raises some questions with respect to how well labor market mechanisms work in our economy. One of the beauties of the simple model is that it produces a Pareto optimal allocation of labor as long as employers are maximizers in both their labor and commodity markets and as long as these markets are free of imperfections. However, the severe departures from the assumptions of the model open up the very real possibility that labor market

---

[2] For the better treatments of the concept of human capital, see T. W. Schultz (169) and Gary S. Becker, (9).

[3] Differences in the ability to absorb training lead to individuals' being able to command economic rents in labor markets. For example, a laborer might aspire to be a physician but due to limited capabilities he might find that he was unable to undergo successfully the training required to become a physician. To the extent that individuals are barred from pursuing the practice of medicine by limitations of this type, practicing physicians receive income which is properly construed to be a rent which accrues to them due to their possessing certain unique gifts.

[4] Examples of such costs might be the climate associated with a particular geographic area (which might be favorable or unfavorable) or aspects of certain occupations which discourage entry into them such as the risk to health incurred by coal miners due to their inhaling particles of coal dust.

[5] The classic instance of maximizing behavior in the marketplace being called into question is the famous Lester and Machlup dispute cited in footnote 1 of Chapter Two. A latter-day version of that controversy centers about a 1965 article by Rottenberg (164). This piece provoked comments by Lampman (110); Lester (119); and Dow (39), followed by Rottenberg's replies (165, 166).

mechanisms in the United States do not tend to allocate the aggregate supply of labor resources in an efficient fashion. An examination of the literature describing the way in which workers move between labor markets (i.e., labor mobility) generates the distinct impression that labor markets do not perform very well in allocating labor resources between markets. With rare exceptions the emphasis in such literature is not upon workers responding appropriately to differential economic advantages (the maximizing hypothesis) but upon workers simply taking whatever jobs are available (the job vacancy thesis).[6] Unfortunately, if the latter thesis is valid, the resulting allocation of labor may be far from optimal in that workers may be retained in relatively inefficient positions at relatively low wage rates. This can be contrasted with a market mechanism in which workers are responsive to different wage rates. In such a market labor resources would be progressively shifted toward the relatively efficient markets which could afford to pay higher wages and would wish to in order to attract workers. Conversely, resources would be shifted out of the low wage, relatively inefficient markets. From this, it is obvious that the question of whether worker movements between labor markets are responsive to differential economic advantages is an important one from the standpoint of assessing the effectiveness of labor markets in distributing the aggregate supply of labor.

I.   THE ECONOMIC THEORY OF LABOR MOBILITY

In order to explore the question of how responsive patterns of human resource movement between markets are to varying wage rates, it is necessary to spell out more precisely the formal economic theory underlying such movement.[7] That theory is merely a special case of the theory of consumer demand and, thus, let us consider first the behavior of an individual in a single labor market where it is well known that a maximizing worker will adjust his offerings of labor so that his marginal rate of substitution of income for leisure is just equal to the real wage rate in that market. In this simple case, labor mobility on the part of an individual consists solely of his varying the quantity of labor he supplies to the market. More realism can be added by expanding

---

[6] Through the early 1950's the view was generally held that workers were not responsive to differential economic advantage but instead were influenced primarily by the availability of job opportunities. Perhaps the best summary of those views is contained in Parnes (148). However, in more recent years there has been a greater tendency for the differential economic advantage thesis to receive more support. Some of the more interesting studies have been: Batchelder (7); Bunting (22, 23); Gallaway (57–61, 63); Gallaway, Gilbert, and Smith (74); Greenwood (81); Kaun and Fechter (98); Lansing (111); Lansing and Morgan (112); Lansing and Mueller (114); Raimon (155, 156); Sjaastad (175); and Tarver (182, 183).

[7] A more complete discussion of the economic theory of labor mobility is presented in Gallaway (61), chap 2.

the scope of the treatment to include the possibility of an individual's participating in more than one labor market. To simplify matters, consider initially only two markets, each being associated with a different sector of the economy. The addition of another market means that an individual must now choose between alternative wage rates and alternative locations for offering his labor services in the marketplace. This presents no special complications if there are no unique costs (either objective or subjective) associated with employment in either of the two markets. Then, the choice becomes one between two "optimal" situations in both of which the rate of substitution of income for leisure is equated with a wage rate. Now, if there is any difference in the two wage rates, a maximizing individual will elect the higher one provided that other costs are absent.

However, if there exist unique costs associated with employment in either or both markets or costs of movement between these markets, the decision-making process is somewhat more complex. Fortunately, though, such costs can be incorporated in the analysis with only slight modifications. Their presence makes a market less attractive as an employment possibility, for when individuals evaluate various possible employment opportunities they discount offered wage rates by whatever amount is necessary to compensate for these costs. The discounted wage rates can be thought of as "shadow" wage rates and the choice situation facing an individual can now be described as consisting of comparing alternative "shadow" wage rates and selecting the one that is highest. Obviously, the key factors influencing this type of choice are the forces that determine the levels of the offered wage rate and the various costs associated with employment in and moving between markets. The higher the offered wage and the lower the costs, *ceteris paribus,* the higher the shadow wage rate and the more attractive an industry is to an individual.

The foregoing suggests that in actual labor markets there will be a tendency toward a movement of human resources toward high wage areas until the wage differentials between markets reflect any differences in the cost of employment in markets and the cost of movement between them. In this equilibrium position there will still be gross flows of labor between markets over time due to workers having different perceptions of the costs involved and due to shifts in workers' perceptions of such costs. However, the net flows of labor should approximate zero in equilibrium.

So much for the straightforward economic theory of labor mobility with its emphasis on workers consciously considering a number of labor market alternatives and then selecting the most attractive. While this is as it should be, given a free market economy, it tells only a portion of the story of labor mobility, for no provision has yet been made to take account of the possibility of job changing which is not voluntary in character. For example, there is the situation of the worker who is dismissed from or threatened with the loss of an existing job he holds by a reorganization of the productive process. Or, there is the possibility of physical injury or disability requiring some change of job. In instances such as these, there is one fundamental difference from the voluntary type mobility situation described earlier: the worker is deprived of a very significant degree of freedom in his choice in that his most recent job is not among the set of alternatives available to him. As a consequence, he may not have the same amount of time to discover and consider alternatives, which is simply another way of saying that in cases of involuntary mobility the worker is subjected to a much more restrictive time constraint than is present in the voluntary mobility situation.

The time constraint on the involuntarily mobile worker operates because (1) he typically has limited labor market information, and (2) he has limited resources with which to sustain himself while he seeks another job. The lack of complete labor market information possessed by a worker necessitates a "search" process on his part for such information. But, this search is not without cost, either in the form of money outlays or in the shape of the opportunity costs implicit in allocating time to the search process.[8] Given these search costs it is not surprising that a worker may forego a more costly search for a higher paying job in favor of a less costly search for a lower paying one.[9] Further, in the case of involuntary mobility there would appear to be a strong likelihood that the worker in question will not be particularly competitive in the labor market. After all, dismissal because of poor work performance, skills which are being rendered obsolete by changes in either technology or demand, or physical shortcomings are not exactly substantial credentials to present to a prospective employer.

As the result of this complex of factors the involuntarily mobile worker would seem to be under pressures which would push him toward the labor markets where job opportunity is most abundant. After all, more abundant job opportunity is likely to increase the probability of a worker being aware of the presence of jobs and those jobs may embrace a range of skills which is sufficiently wide to permit the relatively unskilled to be employed. This hypothesis concerning worker behavior when involuntarily displaced is simply the job vacancy thesis referred to

---

[8] For a discussion of the economic costs of "search," see Stigler (178, 179).

[9] However, this does not preclude him from continuing his search once reemployed and "correcting" his decision toward a more optimal position. In fact, it is entirely possible that with sufficient time for such corrections, the movement patterns of the involuntarily displaced would be the same as for those engaged in voluntary movement.

earlier. Consequently, in a set of labor markets in which both voluntary and involuntary mobility are present, mobile workers might be expected to respond both to differential economic advantages and job vacancies depending on whether they are voluntarily or involuntarily mobile.

II. INTERINDUSTRY MOBILITY: SOME EMPIRICAL OBSERVATIONS

The theoretical discussion of labor mobility provides a rich store of hypotheses which are potentially susceptible to empirical verification. We will now attempt to test some of these propositions using data obtained from the Social Security Administration's records of earnings and employment of individuals working in employment covered by the OASDHI system.[10] The data in question provide information relating to the industry of major job of workers in 1957 cross-classified by industry of major job in 1960.[11] Fortunately, there is sufficient detail in the data to permit breakdowns by sex and five-year age-groups. In this discussion, age-group data for all male workers will be employed. In addition to the data describing the industry of major employment of workers, information relating to the earnings of these workers is also available for the two years in question.[12]

1. The Behavior of "Stayers"

As a first step in analyzing the interindustry mobility of workers let us focus on those workers who can be thought of as "stayers," i.e., workers whose major industry of employment was the same in both 1957 and 1960. From the theoretical discussion we might expect that there would be some significant relationship between the earnings of workers, unemployment rates in various industries, and the proportion of workers who remain employed in a given industry. Worker behavior that is responsive to differential economic advantage implies that the greater the earnings of workers in an industry the stronger the attraction of that industry as a source of employment and the fewer the workers

---

[10] These data are taken from the *One Percent Continuous Work History Sample* maintained by the Social Security Administration. This is a sample of all workers who have been in employment covered by the OASDHI system since its inception. Workers are selected for inclusion in the sample according to terminal digits of their social security account number. Once included in the sample, a worker remains there permanently.

[11] Industry of major job is determined by the industry in which a worker receives the major part of his earnings in a given year.

[12] The level-of-earnings data are mean estimated wages of workers. Wages must be estimated in some cases because of the presence of a maximum limit on earnings which are taxable under social security. Wages in excess of this limit are not recorded by the Social Security Administration in most cases. The estimating technique employed is described in Appendix B of Gallaway (**61**).

who will desire to leave it. All that is necessary to ensure that this occurs is that (1) the bundle of objective and subjective costs of movement between two sectors exceeds the costs associated with remaining employed in the same sector and (2) the distribution of money wage rates and costs of movement about their respective mean values is roughly similar in all sectors. If these conditions are satisfied, workers who leave high wage industries will be more likely to suffer losses of income than workers who leave low wage industries. Consequently, if workers are purposive in their behavior and attempt to maximize the net advantages associated with their employment, we would expect fewer of them to leave employment in high wage industries and, therefore, a strong positive relationship between earnings in an industry and the percentage of workers who "stay" in the industry would be expected.

In addition, unemployment in an industry should be a significant factor affecting an individual's willingness to remain employed in that industry. On two counts such a relationship would be expected. First, unemployment in an industry will tend to create uncertainty in individuals' minds concerning future employment opportunities in that line of work. Assuming that workers are risk averters, this would serve to make the industry less attractive to them, i.e., it increases the subjective costs of employment in the industry. Second, a high incidence of unemployment in an industry will tend to force some movement of individuals between industries simply because of the workers in that industry being displaced from their jobs at a greater rate than in other industries.

Since the data at our disposal differentiate between workers by age, some specific consideration of the effect of age on mobility patterns is necessary. Obviously, age enters into the theoretical framework we have described by imposing costs of movement upon individuals. These costs may take several forms. First, there is the very real consideration that workers may not be able to fully transfer pension rights accumulated in retirement programs associated with their job situation. Or, there is the strong possibility that individual movement will be deterred by the fact that older workers will have a much greater tendency toward high levels of physical investment in a given location and there might well be costs associated with liquidating certain forms of such investment—such as real estate, for example. Further, there are various subjective costs associated with worker movement between labor markets—costs such as the psychic difficulties implicit in uprooting one's self from a particular job. The significance of this is that as workers age this type of cost may greatly increase.

Beyond these considerations, as workers age their income levels tend to rise up to certain age levels.[13] As this occurs, certain barriers to

---

[13] This is a very broad generalization. Clearly, there will be substantial variation in the nature of the earnings life cycle for individuals with different occupational and industrial attachments to the labor force.

the free flow of labor between markets begin to assert themselves. In particular, an older worker who contemplates movement to another market is likely to run afoul of the seniority system which, very simply, functions to differentiate workers from one another, i.e., it renders them less than perfect substitutes for each other. A worker with 5 to 10 years' seniority employed in market A is clearly not the same as one working in market B who might decide that wage levels have become sufficiently attractive in A to induce him to leave his present employment in order to work in the high wage market. If he did this, he would be required, in effect, to start at the very bottom of the employment hierarchy in his new job. Consequently, the difference in the shadow wage rates between markets which a worker perceives is affected by an amount that takes into consideration the income reduction implicit in his loss of seniority as well as any additional insecurity involved in commencing at the bottom of the ladder in the new employment.

The preceding discussion argues that the proportion of workers in an industry who do not change jobs will be positively associated with both industry earnings levels and age and negatively associated with unemployment. This suggests a relationship of the following type:

$$S_{kj} = a + b(E_I)_j + cA_{kj} + e(U_I)_j \tag{1}$$

where S_{kj} denotes the percentage of workers in the kth age-group with the same industry of major job in both 1957 and 1960 (that is, those who stayed in the jth industry), E_I denotes 1960 industry earnings levels for all male workers, A is a variable measuring the age of workers, and U_I is the 1960 industry unemployment rate.[14] Such a relationship can be estimated in least squares regression form from the data at our disposal but, before this is done, some other factors must be considered. For example, what about the possible impact of age group earnings levels on the mobility patterns of workers? Earlier, it was noted that workers' earnings vary across their lifetime and that this may be a factor which influences their mobility patterns. At that time it was implied that this would have a negative impact on mobility. However, it might also be maintained that the higher earnings levels associated with increasing age are also indicative of a better asset position among workers and that this would encourage mobility. The exact effect of differences in age-group earnings on observed labor mobility patterns would seem to depend on whether the movement of workers was primarily of the voluntary or involuntary character. If it is essentially voluntary, then the asset effect of age earnings levels will probably dominate and a negative relationship would be expected between the proportion of

---

[14] The age variable takes the value 1 for the youngest age-group, 2 for the next youngest, and so on with a maximum value of 11 for the oldest age-group.

stayers and age-group earnings. On the other hand, if involuntary mobility is the rule, age-group earnings levels will probably measure the degree of insulation from the forces that produce such movement and a positive relationship between the proportion of stayers and age earnings would be anticipated. With these considerations in mind, it seems appropriate to include a specific age-group earnings variable in expression (1). This variable (denoted by the symbol E_a) is the 1957 earnings level of workers in a particular age group in the jth industry.

Using the data of Table 3–1 as the dependent variable a least squares regression equation embodying the relationships already discussed produces the following results:[15]

$$S_{kj} = 21.9168 + 0.0022 \ (E_I)_j - 0.4975 \ (U_I)_j$$
$$\qquad\qquad (4.88) \qquad\qquad (2.83)$$
$$\qquad\qquad + 2.2955 \ A_{kj} + 0.0070 \ (E_a)_{kj}, \ R^2 = 0.91 \qquad (2)$$
$$\qquad\qquad (10.06) \qquad\quad (14.57)$$

These results are extremely interesting. For one thing, the regression equation explains over 90 percent of the variance in the dependent variable. Second, they are in substantial agreement with what the economic theory of individual behavior in the labor market suggests. Thus, with regard to the tendency of workers to remain employed in the same industry through time, there is every indication that workers are responsive to differential economic advantages. In addition, the regression coefficients associated with the independent variables indicate that they have substantial quantitative effects on S_{kj}. The range of the $(E_I)_j$ variable is about \$3,700 which would account for about an 8 percentage point variation in S_{kj}. Similarly, the range of $(U_I)_j$ is somewhat less than 10 percentage points which produces about a 5 percentage point variation in S_{kj}. Thus, none of these variables can be ignored if one wishes to explain the magnitude of the percentage of workers who remain employed in an industry through time. As to age, an additional five years of age increases S_{kj} by about 2.3 percentage points.

Certain qualifications should be added to the interpretation of these regression results. First, the age-group earnings variable is highly significant with a positive sign which, in line with the earlier discussion, suggests that there is a sizable element of involuntariness involved in interindustry movement of workers. Second, with respect to the coefficient associated with the unemployment variable, it must be kept in mind that its significance may result from either a calculation of the additional uncertainty generated by unemployment or as a result of an involuntary displacement of workers from an industry as the result of unemployment.

---

[15] The values in parentheses beneath the regression coefficients are their respective t-values.

TABLE 3-1
Percent of Male Stayers, by Age and Industry

Industry	Age in 1960										
	Under 20	20–24	25–29	30–34	35–39	40–44	45–49	50–54	55–59	60–64	65 & over
Agriculture	35.5	34.7	51.6	61.7	63.2	69.0	72.3	76.4	76.2	78.1	81.1
Mining	29.4	42.6	49.9	61.2	68.8	72.8	75.6	72.3	77.1	80.0	75.4
Construction	38.4	43.6	59.2	69.4	72.7	75.1	75.1	76.2	76.7	77.3	79.4
Manufacturing											
Durable goods	52.9	58.4	68.8	78.2	81.5	85.2	86.5	88.8	89.0	90.5	85.3
Nondurable goods	34.3	47.3	62.7	74.2	78.0	81.3	83.7	85.1	86.3	87.1	84.6
Transportation, communication and public utilities	23.6	43.7	67.6	78.0	81.2	82.7	85.1	86.9	88.1	88.5	80.2
Wholesale and retail trade	49.8	46.2	59.2	68.5	72.7	74.7	77.5	77.8	79.3	80.8	83.1
Finance, insurance, and real estate	22.5	41.9	61.6	75.6	77.1	80.0	82.9	86.6	86.5	87.2	89.2
Services	26.4	37.4	56.0	67.7	71.4	72.3	76.1	79.7	82.1	84.5	85.9
Government	28.2	33.2	52.7	68.8	76.8	80.4	83.0	86.9	88.3	90.4	89.9

SOURCE: Social Security Administration, One Percent Continuous Work History Sample.

To the extent that the latter is the case the observed behavior of S_{kj} reflects more than just maximizing activity by workers. Unfortunately, the data which are available do not lend themselves to estimating the relative importance of the two aspects of the effect of unemployment on S_{kj}. However, the behavior of the age-group earnings variable would seem to indicate the presence of substantial amounts of involuntary movement.

2. The Behavior of "Movers"

The analysis of the behavior of workers who stay in a particular industry is suggestive but it is only a part of the phenomenon of inter-industry labor mobility. A complete picture of such mobility must also include some consideration of the industrial destination of workers who leave a particular industry. Again, a conceptual framework for evaluating these patterns of movement is suggested by the theoretical discussion as well as by the previous findings with respect to the behavior of stayers in an industry.

The economic theory of labor mobility contains a very obvious explanation for gross flows of labor between industries, viz, that workers will flow in greater numbers toward the industries with the higher wage rates. Further, given the findings with respect to stayers it would seem that unemployment rates by industry might also explain the pattern of gross flows of workers over time. Add to this the age and age-group earnings variables and it would seem that the analysis employed in the case of stayers can be repeated by fitting a least squares regression equation of the form

$$M_{kij} = a + b\ (E_I)_{kj} + d\ (U_I)_j + d\ (A_{ki}) + c\ (E_a)_{ki} + u \qquad (3)$$

where M_{kij} denotes the gross flow of labor into industry j from industry i within the kth age group, u is a random error term, and the other symbols retain their previous meanings. However, there is one complication. In order to estimate expression (3) in a meaningful fashion it is necessary to standardize the gross flow data to take account of differences in the number of workers in each age-group in the various industries. One method of doing this would be to express the data in percentage form as was done in the "stayer" analysis. However, an alternative is to include in the regression equation a "scale" variable which takes this into account.[16] When such a variable is included, the results of the estimation process are:

---

[16] Either approach will work satisfactorily. However, the "scale" variable technique has the pragmatic advantage that it seems to allow the impact of the other independent variables to come through more clearly in the regression equations.

$$M_{kij} = 64.7086 + 0.0107 \ (E_I)_{kj} + 0.1896 \ (U_I)_j$$
$$\qquad\qquad\quad (4.21) \qquad\qquad (0.17)$$
$$- 3.5335 \ (A_{ki}) - 0.0183 \ (E_a)_{ki} + 0.0254 \ S_{ki}, \ R^2 = 0.37 \qquad (4)$$
$$(2.59) \qquad\quad (5.97) \qquad\qquad (18.91)$$

Since the unemployment variable was not significant, the regression was reestimated excluding this variable with the following results:

$$M_{kij} = 65.9247 + 0.0106 \ (E_I)_{kj} - 3.5388 \ (A_{ki})$$
$$\qquad\quad (4.21) \qquad\qquad (2.60)$$
$$-0.0183 \ (E_a)_{ki} + 0.0254 \ S_{ki}, \ R^2 = 0.37 \qquad (5)$$
$$(5.97) \qquad\qquad (18.92)$$

Interestingly, all the independent variables are significant at, at least, the 5 percent level with age-group earnings, industry earnings, and the scaling variable being significant beyond the 0.1 percent level. As to signs, the industry earnings variable has the expected positive sign, age has the anticipated negative sign, and the age-group earnings variable has a negative sign which is consistent with the analysis of stayers' behavior which was presented earlier.

There is a disturbing element in expression (5), though. Only a little over one third of the variance in the dependent variable is explained by (5). This raises the possibility that omission of unspecified independent variables that are correlated with the existing independent variables is producing spurious results. This cannot be ignored, but the general consistency of the stayer and mover analysis would seem to suggest that the results of the gross flow analysis are valid.

III.   CONCLUSIONS

The general pattern of interindustry mobility suggested by the data is quite consistent with the formal economic theory of why people move between jobs. Clearly, differences in income levels among industries are a strong factor in explaining why people change their industry of major job—a finding which would indicate that patterns of interindustry labor mobility tend to promote a more optimal allocation of labor resources in the United States. It will be interesting to see whether these same relationships exist when geographic and occupational mobility flows are examined. Admittedly, the apparent presence of a substantial element of involuntary mobility in the interindustry case does provide grounds for feeling less than certain that the end product of the process of interindustry mobility is the absolutely most efficient allocation of labor resources.

chapter FOUR

Geographic Labor Mobility in the United States

T_{HE} literature dealing with the movement of individuals between differing geographic locations is more substantial than that for interindustry movement of workers. However, the same basic question is raised in that literature, namely, "Do workers respond to differential economic advantages when they are geographically mobile?"[1] The theoretical framework for explaining such mobility is identical to that employed in the discussion of interindustry movement. Also, the basic data source used in the previous chapter provides information on geographic movement of workers as well as for interindustry movement. The sample of data taken from the records of the Social Security Administration describes the regional location of a worker's major job in both 1957 and 1960. Nine regions are employed—the basic Census Bureau's classifications of New England, Middle Atlantic, South Atlantic, East North Central, East South Central, West North Central, West South Central, Mountain, and Pacific States. The data are available on exactly the same basis as the interindustry information except for the age detail. Only three age categories are used, less than 25, 25–39, and 40 and over. The restriction on the age detail was necessitated

---

[1] The bulk of the literature cited in footnote 6 in Chapter Three deals with geographic labor mobility flows. For an excellent summary of the controversy surrounding the "differential economic advantage" concept, see Raimon (155, 156).

by the fact that the amount of geographic job changing observed in the sample of workers was less than one third of that found in the interindustry case (about 7 percent compared to 25 percent movement between industries).

I. THE BEHAVIOR OF STAYERS

Following the procedure of the discussion of interindustry movement, the behavior of those workers whose major job was in the same region in both 1957 and 1960 is examined first. Three of the same variables are hypothesized to affect the proportion of the workers in a region who can be regarded as stayers (S), viz, income levels in that region (E_r), the age of workers (A), and the level of earnings in the worker's age-group (E_a). No unemployment variable is included since it was found to be an insignificant influence on worker behavior. In addition, one other explanatory variable has been incorporated into our conceptual framework. This variable is designed to measure the relative attractiveness of a region from the climatic standpoint. The rationale for including it is straightforward: obviously, it can be reasonably hypothesized that one of the subjective factors which would affect a worker's decision to move between regions would be the desirability of the climate in the various areas which are alternative living locations. The variable we have designed to measure this is an index of the severity of a region's climate and is simply an estimate of the number of severe weather days which are typical of a region. Severe weather days are defined as winter days with a temperature of 32° F. or below and summer days with a temperature of 90° F. or above.[2] The variable is denoted by the symbol C and it is hypothesized that workers would prefer a mild climate to a severe one. Consequently, a negative relationship between the proportion of workers who are stayers and the climate variable is anticipated.

The data describing the proportion of stayers by age and region are presented in Table 4–1. Using these as the dependent variable, the following regression was estimated:

$$S_{kj} = 72.8973 + 0.0035\ (E_r)_j - 0.0019\ (E_a)_{kj}$$
$$\phantom{S_{kj} = 72.8973 +}\ (3.29)\ (2.02)$$
$$+\ 6.0138\ A_{kj} - 0.0579\ C_j,\ R^2 = 0.65 \quad (1)$$
$$(3.51)\phantom{\ 6.0138\ A_{kj}\ }\ (2.44)$$

where the symbols are the same as those used previously and the age variable is a dummy which takes the value one for the age less than 25 group, two for the 25–39 group, and three for the 40 and over group. The values in parentheses beneath the individual coefficients, again, are

---

[2] The source of these estimates is a *Rand McNally Road Atlas*.

TABLE 4–1
Percent of Stayers, 1957–60, by Region and
Age-Group, Males

Region	Percent Stayers		
	Age under 25	Age 25–39	Age 40 and over
New England	93.07	90.81	95.15
Middle Atlantic	91.19	92.22	96.25
South Atlantic	87.49	90.26	93.96
East North Central	90.15	90.48	94.66
East South Central	81.53	86.10	92.75
West North Central	87.36	87.16	93.31
West South Central	89.33	89.04	93.60
Mountain	79.48	83.32	89.14
Pacific	91.00	90.56	94.71

SOURCE: Social Security Administration, One Percent Continuous Work History Sample.

the t-values associated with them and from these it can be seen that all four of the independent variables are significant at the 5 percent level or beyond and, overall, the percentage of the variance explained by the regression is significant at the 0.1 percent level. Also, the signs of the age and regional earnings level variables are in the expected direction. Interestingly, the age-group earnings variable has a negative sign indicating that its cumulative impact is to encourage mobility between geographic regions. This can be interpreted as suggesting that the age-group earnings variable functions as a proxy for differences in the asset position of workers. As noted earlier, the rationale of such an interpretation is the possible impact of a superior asset position on the part of a worker in facilitating his bearing the monetary costs of movement between geographic regions.[3] Finally, as expected, the climate variable has a negative sign. In general, then, the empirical results reported in expression (1) are quite consistent with the formal economic theory of workers responding to differential economic advantage when moving geographically. In fact, the pattern of geographic movement is more consistent with the theory than interindustry movement in that the direction of the impact of the age-group earnings variable suggests that voluntary movement dominates geographic mobility.

II. THE BEHAVIOR OF MOVERS

We now turn to the behavior of movers between broad geographic regions. Specifically, patterns of gross labor flows between regions within

[3] Some modest support for the premise that asset position is a significant influence on geographic mobility may be found in Lansing and Mueller (114), pp. 190–94.

and across age-groups will be examined. Some additional complications arise in the conduct of such an analysis. First, when dealing with movement between regions some explicit account must be taken of differences in the distance between regions. There are several alternatives here but the distance variable which will be used in the analysis which follows is an ordinal rather than a cardinal one. More precisely, distance is measured roughly in terms of the number of regional boundaries which must be crossed by a worker in order to reach another region. Thus, the distance variable ranges from one to six with the maximum value representing the distance between New England and the Pacific region.

TABLE 4–2

Distance Variables Used in Regression Analysis of Gross Flows of Labor

Region of Origin	Region of Destination								
	A	B	C	D	E	F	G	H	I
New England (A)............	–	1	2	2	3	3	4	5	6
Middle Atlantic (B)..........	1	–	1	1	2	2	3	4	5
South Atlantic (C)...........	2	1	–	1	1	2	2	3	4
East North Central (D).......	2	1	1	–	1	1	2	2	3
East South Central (E).......	3	2	1	1	–	2	1	2	3
West North Central (F)......	3	2	2	1	2	–	1	1	2
West South Central (G)......	4	3	2	2	1	1	–	1	2
Mountain (H)..............	5	4	3	2	2	1	1	–	1
Pacific (I).................	6	5	4	3	3	2	2	1	–

The full set of distance variables used in the analysis is shown in Table 4–2.[4] A second complication has already been dealt with in interindustry mobility (Chapter Three), i.e., the problem of standardizing the gross flow data to control for variations in the number of workers in each age group in the various regions. Again, the "scale" variable technique will be used.

---

[4] It could be argued that the distance variable is something of an oversimplification in that the regions in the far west are larger and thus the distance variable used here is not strictly proportional to the actual distance between regions. However, there is probably not much distortion from this. Several forms of the distance variable were tried in various regressions. In particular, when the square of the distance variable was used the results were poorer. Further, when a quadratic form including both the present distance variable and its square was estimated, in those cases where the square of the distance variable was significant, it had a negative sign suggesting, if anything, that the distance variable used here overstates the impact of distance when the distance variable is relatively large. However, the quadratic term generally was not particularly significant, either statistically or quantitatively.

When the appropriate regression equation is estimated using the data of all nine regions simultaneously, the results are:[5]

$$M_{kij} = 53.4819 + 0.0482(E_r)_j + 0.0581(E_a)_{ki} - 86.4522A_{ki}$$
$$\phantom{M_{kij} = 53.4819 +} (6.01) (6.77) \phantom{+ 0.0581(E_a)_{ki}} (6.41)$$
$$- 48.2610D_{ij} + 0.0039S_{ki} - 1.4493C_j, \; R^2 = 0.65 \quad (2)$$
$$ (12.64) \phantom{D_{ij} +} (5.64) \phantom{S_{ki} -} (6.39)$$

where M_{kij} denotes the number of workers in the kth age-group moving between the ith and jth regions, D_{ij} represents the distance between the ith and jth regions, S_{ki} is the "scale" variable (the number of workers in the kth age group and ith region), and the other symbols retain their previous meaning.

Clearly, all six of the independent variables have regression coefficients which are significantly different from zero at the 0.1 percent level or beyond.[6] In addition, the signs associated with the independent variables are all in the appropriate direction. Naturally, the distance variable has a negative sign while the regional earnings variable is strongly positive. The age variable has the anticipated negative sign which is consistent with the previous analysis which showed a positive relationship between this variable and the proportion of stayers (the inverse of mobility). As to age-group earnings, its sign is positive which is again consistent with the previous analysis in that a positive sign is indicative of greater mobility with higher age-group earnings levels. Of course, the same interpretation, a predominance of voluntary movement in the geographic case, should be applied to this result as was in the discussion of stayer's behavior. Finally, the climate variable has the expected negative sign.

One aspect of the behavior of the distance variable should be noted. The quantitative size of its coefficient suggests that it is measuring more than just the monetary costs of movement. Roughly, the distance

---

[5] Initially, regressions of this type were estimated for each of the nine regions. However, there are massive multicolinearity problems inherent in this approach due to interdependence among the age, age earnings, and scale variables. When the data for all nine regions are pooled, enough of this colinearity disappears to permit the independent variables to show a significant relationship with the dependent variable. The colinearity problem limited the use of other variables which are known to influence geographic mobility. Among these, for example, are educational levels of workers (see Lansing and Mueller [114], pp. 43–44 and 51–53) which are highly correlated with age.

[6] The elasticities at the mean of gross labor flows with respect to the independent variables (other than scale) are: regional earnings $((E_r)_j)$, 2.02; age (A_{ki}), 1.55; climate (C_j), −1.09; age-group earnings $((E_a)_{ki})$, 1.71; and distance (D_{ij}), −0.98. Similar estimates for the stayers regression are: regional earnings $((E_r)_j)$, 0.18; age (A_{kj}), 0.13; climate (C_j), −0.05; and age-group earnings $((E_a)_{kj})$, 0.07.

coefficient in (2) says that it would require an income differential of about $1,000 to just offset the impact of having to cross one additional regional boundary.[7] With any reasonable assumption about the time horizon workers employ in decision making, the discounted present value of a permanent income differential of this magnitude is far in excess of what the monetary costs of movement would be. But, what else might this variable be measuring? One possibility is that it also reflects the subjective costs of moving between regions. This it certainly does, but another very real, and in many respects more appealing, explanation for the high value of the distance coefficient is that the distance variable is capturing the impact of barriers to the flow of labor market information between areas. In effect, distance may be thought of as a filter through which labor market information must flow and the greater the distance between regions, the greater the filtering effect.[8] This is a hypothesis which is deserving of consideration.

III. SOME ADDITIONAL TESTS[9]

The results of analyzing the mobility data derived from the Social Security Administration records are quite consistent with the orthodox economic theory of why workers would move between regions. This is encouraging from the standpoint of how well American labor markets operate to efficiently allocate labor resources on an interregional basis. However, this is only one sample, albeit a very large one, at one point in time. What about the functioning of labor markets in this respect over protracted periods of time? Fortunately, information is available in the various decennial censuses since 1850 which provide some extremely interesting insights into this question. This material is in the form of data describing the state of residence of individuals according to their state of birth. Such data provide a capsule summary of long-term or "life-time" mobility of the population as contrasted to the shorter term view given by the Social Security Administration data. There are objections to the data which should be noted. First, they are much more prone to exclude short-distance migration or not measure multiple moves than is the case with the social security data because of the much longer time horizon encompassed by the data. Second, they do not measure

---

[7] The "tradeoff" between distance and earnings is calculated by dividing the distance coefficient (−48.2610) by the earnings coefficient (.0482). Since the signs of the two coefficients are opposite, the result is an estimate of how much of an increase in earnings would be required to just offset an increase of one (or one more regional boundary to cross) in the distance variable.

[8] This argument is made more fully in Gallaway (**60**).

[9] The empirical results reported in this section are the product of an investigation of internal migration patterns by Gallaway and Vedder. The author is indebted to Professor Vedder for his permission to use these results here. A more detailed discussion of them is contained in Gallaway and Vedder (**210**).

mobility over a clearly defined span of time as does the social security information. The 1960 Census, for example, records not only moves made during the 1950's, but even some movement made before 1900. While the time horizon is admittedly somewhat vague, an examination of these data over an extended period of time should permit an evaluation of the changing relative importance of the various factors which influence migration.

Before proceeding to utilize those data it is necessary to make certain revisions in the conceptual framework that has been used to this point. Two of the variables employed previously are retained in approximately the same form: regional income levels and distance. The income measure which will be used is per capita income by state when available. Easterlin, *et al.*, have developed individual state estimates of per capita income for the years 1880, 1900, and 1920.[10] No estimates are available for 1850—the first year for which the state of birth data are present—but Easterlin (**43**, pp. 73–140) has made estimates for 1840. There is no obvious reason to assume that relative state per capita income levels shifted violently between 1840 and 1850. Consequently, the 1840 estimates will be used with the 1850 state of birth mobility data. One post-1920 Census is selected for analysis, 1960, and standard U.S. Department of Commerce per capita income estimates will be used with these data.[11] Distance will be measured by estimating the distance in statute miles between the population centers of the various states. This is somewhat crude as no attempt is made to adjust the estimates for differences in the availability of transportation facilities in the various states. However, there is no obvious way in which such adjustments can be made without resorting to a number of value judgments.

One variable is included in the analysis which is somewhat similar to the climate variable used in the previous discussion. This variable may be thought of as a regional affinity measure and it encompasses climatic differences but, additionally, also measures a number of other factors which may be hypothesized as being influential in causing people to wish to settle in a state which is similar to their state of birth, such as social and cultural institutions. The regional affinity variable is constructed by defining regions which can be considered to be homogeneous with respect to these factors. This is, admittedly, a somewhat arbitrary process, but the United States has been divided into four broad areas: northern, temperate, southern humid, and southern arid.[12] On the basis of these divisions, it is possible to create a quantita-

---

[10] Lee, Miller, Brainard, and Easterlin (**116**, p. 753).

[11] As reported in U.S. Department of Commerce (**201**).

[12] The northern states are Maine, New Hampshire, Vermont, New York (because of the upstate part), Michigan, Wisconsin, Minnesota, North Dakota, South Dakota, Montana, Idaho, and Washington. The temperate are Massachusetts, Rhode Island, Connecticut, New York, Pennsylvania, New Jersey, Delaware, Maryland, West

tive variable which measures the impact on mobility of affinity for one's own region by assigning a state outside the region in which a person's state of birth is located one value and a state within that region a higher value.

Two other variables are also included in the analysis. One is a specific measure of the availability of job opportunities within a state. The job opportunity (or job vacancy) thesis has already been discussed but in the analysis to this point there did not seem to be a practical method of introducing a job opportunity variable (other than unemployment) without coming dangerously close to defining a tautological relationship. In the analysis of the state of birth data, it is possible to introduce as a measure of job opportunity the total number of jobs in a state at various points in time without in effect saying that "people move where people move." However, even here, though, caution is warranted, for the number of jobs in a state is closely correlated with the population size of a state and, consequently, this type of job opportunity measure may be nothing more than a proxy for population size.[13] Nevertheless, it is desirable to introduce such a measure, if possible, given the attention it receives in certain circles.[14] Job opportunity data of the type described are available for 1880, 1900, and 1920 from Easterlin, et al.[15] For 1850, Census data describing the total number of workers in each of the states may be used while for 1960 total employment is a suitable measure.[16]

The last variable to be considered is mandatory given the historical scope of this phase of the discussion. Any view of geographic mobility commencing with 1850 must take account in some fashion of the impact of the availability of land upon the movement patterns of individuals. There are abundant references in the historical literature to the importance of the availability of land as a factor in inducing people to migrate to the American West.[17] For the purpose of measuring the

---

Virginia, Ohio, Indiana, Illinois, Michigan. Wisconsin, Iowa, Missouri, Nebraska, Kansas, Oklahoma, Wyoming, Colorado, Utah, Nevada, Oregon, and California. The southern humid are Virginia, North Carolina, South Carolina, Georgia, Florida, Kentucky, Tennessee, Alabama, Mississippi, Arkansas, Louisiana, and Texas. The southern arid are Texas, New Mexico, Arizona, and California. Note that some states appear in more than one category. This is because it is felt that parts of them possess characteristics which would place them in more than one classification.

[13] In the extreme case, 1900, the zero-order correlation coefficient between population size and the number of jobs is 0.995.

[14] One of the best examples of a work emphasizing the job opportunity framework is Lowry (129).

[15] Lee, Miller, Brainard, and Easterlin (116), p. 753.

[16] *The Seventh Census of the United States* (Washington, D.C.: Robert Armstrong, Public Printer, 1853) and U.S. Department of Commerce, Bureau of the Census, *United States Decennial Census* (Washington, D.C.: U.S.G.P.O., 1961).

[17] The availability of relatively free land is at the heart and core of Frederick Jackson Turner's "frontier thesis" (191).

availability of land, a very straightforward variable is employed—the population density of a state.[18] The reasoning is that land would be expected to be more readily available where population density is low and vice versa. Clearly, objections similar to those which can be voiced with respect to the distance data are appropriate here. In no way is there an attempt made to control for the quality of the land in question, just as no attempt is made to adjust for qualitative differences in transportation systems with the distance data. This makes the measure of land availability somewhat crude. However, the proof of the pudding will be whether it contributes anything to explaining long-term movement patterns among the American population.

The preceding discussion suggests that the movement of population between the ith state and all other states can be explained by interstate

TABLE 4–3
Number of Significant* Regression Coefficients Obtained in Analysis
of Census Long-Term Migration Patterns

	Census Year					
Variable	1850	1880	1900	1920	1960	Total
Per capita income.........	9	32	39	38	48	166
Distance.................	20	37	41	47	47	192
Job opportunity..........	28	45	48	48	48	217
Population density........	22	31	37	36	26	152
Regional affinity..........	13	30	34	24	14	115

* At 5 percent level or beyond.

differences in income levels, the distance from state i to the various other states, differences in the number of jobs in the states to which natives of i move, interstate variations in the availability of land, and the desire of natives of i to settle in states which they consider to be similar to i. In order to test these hypotheses, multiple regression equations embodying these relationships have been estimated for each of 29 states in 1850, 45 states in 1880, and 48 states in 1900, 1920, and 1960. The significance of the results is summarized in Tables 4–3 and 4–4. Table 4–3 indicates the number of regression coefficients which are statistically significant at the 5 percent level or beyond for each of the five independent variables and Table 4–4 indicates the mean elasticity of migration with respect to income, distance, job opportunity,

---

[18] This variable is simply the population of a state at a particular point in time divided by its area. An alternative specification might be rural population divided by land area. However, these are for the most part highly correlated with one another.

TABLE 4–4
Mean Values of Estimated Relationships* Between Migration and Various
Independent Variables Obtained in Analysis of Census Long-Term
Migration Patterns

	Census Year				
Variable	1850	1880	1900	1920	1960
Per capita income.......	0.89	0.91	1.42	1.71	2.35
Distance..............	−1.84	−1.34	−1.43	−1.35	−1.03
Job opportunity........	1.18	1.14	1.14	1.16	1.08
Population density	−0.85	−0.58	−0.56	−0.62	−0.34
Regional affinity........	2.9	3.0	2.4	1.8	1.3
R^2....................	0.71	0.74	0.79	0.80	0.80

* Values are elasticities for Income, Distance, Job Opportunity, and Population Density variables,
the factor by which migration is multiplied when it is between two states within the same broad region
for the Regional Affinity variable, and the coefficient of determination for R^2.

and population density and the average factor by which migration is
multiplied if it is between states within the same broad region.

Turning first to Table 4–3, the results fairly clearly indicate that
the purely economic variables dominate in terms of their significance.
Of the 218 coefficients which are estimated for each variable, 217 of
the job opportunity coefficients, 192 of the distance coefficients, and 166
of the income coefficients are significant at the 5 percent level or beyond.
Not that the other variables involved in the analysis perform that badly;
152 of the population density and 115 of the regional affinity coefficients
are significant at the 5 percent level. Some interesting changes occur
in the patterns of significance over time. In 1850 per capita income
levels perform the poorest of all the variables in terms of the number
of significant coefficients. However, it becomes increasingly more significant with the passage of time so that by 1960 the per capita income
variable coefficient is significant for every state. There is little variation
in the significance of the job opportunity measure over time but the
distance variable tends to increase in importance in terms of the number
of significant coefficients which are found. On the other hand, both the
population density and regional affinity factors are most significant in
1900 and decline in importance thereafter. This suggests that the lure of
land was strongest in the post-Civil War period and that the tendency to
be somewhat provincial in one's moving patterns was also strongest in
this interval. The latter may well reflect nothing more than the impact
of the Reconstruction Era on cultural and social attitudes within the
United States.

The mean values for the various coefficients presented in Table 4–4
confirm the patterns shown in Table 4–3. The mean elasticity of internal
migration with respect to per capita income rises consistently over time

reaching a value of 2.35 by 1960.[19] In the meantime, the quantitative impact of every other variable on migration decreases—even that of distance which showed some tendency toward an increase in the number of significant coefficients over time. The decrease in the importance of the job opportunity variable is so slight that it is probably safest to regard it as not having changed in importance between 1850 and 1960. However, the trends in the coefficients of all the other variables are unmistakably clear. Interstate variations in per capita income levels become more and more important as an explainer of long-term migration patterns of native-born Americans.[20] Collectively, the five variables employed here to explain migration patterns do an excellent job of accounting for the variation in the flows of people between states over this extended time period. At the least, these variables will explain over half of the variation in migration patterns and after 1850 over 60 percent. On the average, they explain between 70 and 80 percent of the variance in long-term gross population flows with the maximum being 80 percent in both 1920 and 1960.

IV. CONCLUSIONS AND SUMMARY

The empirical evidence with respect to geographic mobility of workers and people seems to quite strongly argue that their behavior is reasonably consistent with the premises of conventional economic theory. This is not to say that the only factor which influences the mobility decisions of people is "differential economic advantage." It is only one among several factors which may shape and structure geographic movement. However, it is clearly an important one. Whether the data under consideration are the social security records of short-term movement or the Census descriptions of long-term migration patterns, income differences are a powerful force in determining where people choose to go. Add to this the fact that there is nothing in the action of the other explanatory variables included in the analysis which is inconsistent with the economist's concept of maximizing behavior and you have a strong argument that geographic mobility decisions can be rather neatly described by economic theory. After all, individuals should respond negatively to the distance between regions when contemplating moving and

---

[19] It is interesting to note the consistency of the elasticity estimates derived from the social security short-term data and the Census long-term records. The social security data show an elasticity of migration with respect to regional earnings levels of 2.02 compared to the Census data's 2.35. Similarly, the respective distance elasticities are —0.98 and —1.03. Such consistency is reassuring.

[20] These findings refer only to native-born Americans. However, there is also evidence that immigrants to the United States respond in a similar fashion to interstate income differences. This evidence is summarized in Vedder and Gallaway (211).

they should respond positively to the presence of jobs in other areas, for those jobs lessen the uncertainty associated with changing geographic location. All in all, then, the picture created by the evidence which has been marshalled is one of individuals moving between geographic areas in a highly purposive and intelligent fashion in quest of better economic opportunities.[21]

---

[21] This broad conclusion is consistent with much of the more recent work being done in the mobility area. See, particularly, Greenwood (81), Kaun and Fechter (98), Raimon (155, 156), and Sjaastad (175).

chapter FIVE

Occupational Mobility of Labor

ONE additional facet of labor mobility remains to be explored—movements of workers between occupational classes. In some respects this may be the most important aspect of mobility in that it has very substantial implications for both the allocation of human resources among different kinds of work activity and the degree of economic opportunity available to individuals. Consequently, the policy implications of occupational mobility of labor are quite broad and, therefore, our picture of overall patterns of movement of labor resources would be incomplete if it were ignored.

Conceptually, occupational labor mobility may be viewed as either (1) movement between occupations during a given worker's lifetime or (2) intergenerational changes in occupation, i.e., the movement of the offspring of individuals into occupations other than those of their parent(s). Both of these are highly significant, whether one is interested in the impact of occupational mobility upon overall patterns of resource allocation or upon the amount of economic opportunity available to individuals. Clearly, the crucial matters here are whether workers move toward the higher income occupations and the degree to which movement between occupations takes place.

I. OCCUPATIONAL MOBILITY WITHIN WORKERS' LIFETIME

Turning first to occupational movement within the lifetime of workers, two major studies provide a wealth of data through which patterns of

55

occupational movement can be discerned. These are Jaffe and Carleton's (91) analysis of flows of workers between occupations for the period 1930 to 1950 and Aronson's (2) updating and extension of the Jaffe and Carleton study to cover the period 1950 to 1960. The primary problem encountered by these researchers was the lack of information describing gross flows of workers between occupations such as that employed in the previous two chapters to discuss interindustry and geographic labor mobility. Rather, they have had to rely on point-in-time observations taken from the decennial censuses of the years 1930, 1940, 1950, and 1960. Consequently, no gross flow data are available and all the analysis must be couched in terms of net flows of workers. An additional complication implicit in using this type of data is the problem of distinguishing between net changes in the number of individuals in an occupation which result from new entries into the labor force and those that stem from workers already in the labor force actually changing occupations. However, this has been overcome through the use of an ingenious model devised by Jaffe and Carleton (91, chaps. 8–13), which divides the net change in the number of workers in an occupation into four components: (1) new entries into the labor force, (2) worker deaths, (3) withdrawal of workers from the labor force due to retirement, and (4) net movements of workers between occupations. Using this model, Aronson (2) updated Jaffe and Carleton's 1930–50 analysis to 1960.

TABLE 5–1
Components of Occupational Change, Experienced Male Labor Force (in thousands), 1950–60, and 1960 Median Income, by Occupation

Occupation	Beginning of Decade	New Entries	Net Mobility	1960 Median Income
All occupations................	42,265.6	9,567.5	...*	$4,907
Professional, technical and kindred workers..............	3,076.0	790.3	1,184.0	6,619
Farmers and farm managers.....	4,222.2	203.7	−861.9	2,169
Managers, officials, and proprietors.................	4,373.1	327.2	1,077.3	6,664
Clerical and kindred workers....	2,749.7	859.1	−48.5	4,785
Sales workers.................	2,673.4	991.6	−220.1	4,987
Craftsmen, foremen, and kindred workers..............	8,074.3	1,278.0	1,364.1	5,240
Operatives and kindred workers....................	8,737.1	2,231.2	−322.3	4,299
Service workers...............	2,614.6	726.2	147.9	3,310
Farm laborers and foremen......	2,063.8	985.1	−1,532.5	1,066
Laborers, except farm and mine..................	3,681.4	1,175.1	−788.0	2,948

* Total may not add to zero because of rounding errors.
SOURCE: Aronson (2).

His data describing the new entries and net mobility components of change between 1950 and 1960 are shown in Table 5–1 for 10 broad occupational classes: professional, technical, and kindred workers; farmers and farm managers; managers, officials, and proprietors; clerical and kindred workers; sales workers; craftsmen, foremen, and kindred workers; operatives and kindred workers; service workers; farm laborers and foremen; and laborers except farm and mine.

These data permit the testing of some of the same hypotheses which have been explored earlier—particularly the maximizing one that is the cornerstone of the conventional economic theory of the labor market. For example, the maximizing hypothesis argues that the net flow of workers into the high earnings level occupations will be greater than that into the low earnings level types of work. Using the data of Table 5–1 and median income levels by occupation taken from the 1960 decennial census the existence or nonexistence of such a relationship can be determined. Figure 5–1 is a scatter diagram which depicts the relationship between income levels and net occupational mobility. Obviously, there is a very strong relationship between these variables. Its precise nature is indicated by the following least squares regression equation:

$$N_j = -1,961.3643 + 0.4660 \ w_j, \ R^2 = 0.79 \tag{1}$$
$$(5.51)$$

where N_j denotes the net flow of workers into the jth occupation between 1950 and 1960 and w_j represents the 1960 median income level in the jth occupation. The results are clearly significant at the 5 percent level which is strikingly consistent with the maximizing hypothesis. It appears obvious that when workers move between occupations they are quite responsive to differential economic advantages. This bodes well for the ability of the labor market to efficiently allocate human resources among different occupational groupings.[1]

The pattern shown by the net flows of workers between occupations is quite different from that exhibited by new entries into occupations. Figure 5–2 shows the relationship between new entries and 1960 median

---

[1] Inclusion of an unemployment rate variable in the analysis did not produce any significant increase in the explanatory power of the regression. In his analysis, Aronson (2) found a similar result using more detailed occupational classifications. Across 119 occupations the rank order correlation between earnings and net mobility (expressed as a percentage of those in the occupation in 1950) is +0.598. Note that regression (1) is couched in terms of absolute net flows into various occupations. This is in some respects a strong test of the maximizing hypothesis in that it maintains that it operates independent of job opportunity considerations. However, it runs the risk of providing spurious results in that earnings and job opportunity may be highly correlated, producing the results shown in (1). This is not the case, though, for when a job opportunity variable (the number of workers in an occupation in 1950) is included in the regression, it is not significant and does not alter the significance of the earnings variable.

FIGURE 5–1

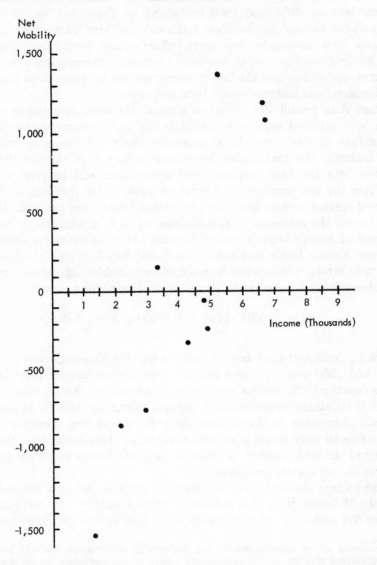

income levels and it appears from this diagram that there is virtually no relationship between these two magnitudes. This is confirmed by the following regression:

$$E_j = 977.7168 - 0.0050 \ w_j, \ R^2 = 0.00 \qquad (2)$$
$$(0.05)$$

where E_j denotes new entries into an occupation.

The lack of any relationship between new entries into occupations

FIGURE 5–2

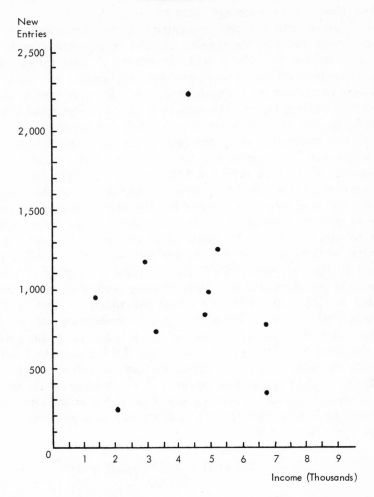

and their income levels argues that there are certain traditional entry occupations that are not particularly high income. For example, the laboring occupations have very substantial amounts of entry into them despite their being very low paid. Also, the operatives category appears to be a very significant entry path into the labor force as well as the sales and craftsmen occupations. On the other hand, the relatively high-paid managers, officials and proprietors group have relatively few new entries. This is not surprising in that some substantial degree of labor force experience may be required for movement into this occupation. This rather diverse and mixed pattern of occupational entry suggests that new entrants to the labor force select occupations on the basis of factors other than the earnings levels found in those occupations.

One such factor might well be the availability of job opportunities. At first glance, there does not seem to be much relationship between potential job opportunities and new entries. A simple rank order correlation coefficient between the number of jobs in an occupation in 1960 and new entries is only +0.27. However, if two rather special cases—managers, officials, and proprietors, and farmers and farm managers—are eliminated from consideration, the rank order correlation rises to +0.71. Omitting the two occupations from the analysis has a certain rationale to it in that these are areas of endeavor which would require very special circumstances to function as an entry occupation. In the case of farmers, for example, the death of an existing farmholder might be required in order to permit a farmstead to pass into the hands of a younger member of the labor force. Or, in the case of the managers, officials, and proprietors category either the same thing might have to occur or a very substantial capital investment might be required in order to facilitate entry. In short, there are very substantial barriers to entry in these areas which are not related to the actual numbers already in the occupation. With this in mind, a very good case can be made to the effect that the choice of entry occupation is significantly affected by job opportunity considerations which, in turn, are only mildly related to earnings levels (rank order correlation equal to +0.37).

This raises the possibility that the entry patterns of those moving into the labor force are such as to vitiate the impact of net mobility flows on the allocation of resources. To test the extent to which this is true the total impact of new entries and net mobility on the distribution of workers among occupations can be analyzed in the same fashion as was done earlier with the net mobility and new entry data. When this is done the result is:

$$M_j = -\ 983.6506 + 0.4610\ w_j,\ R^2 = 0.63 \tag{3}$$
$$(3.68)$$

where M_j denotes the number of new entrants plus net mobility into the jth occupation. The results are significant at the 5 percent level and rather clearly indicate that even though new entrants are strongly influenced by job opportunity considerations, this does not materially distort the overall impact of workers' choice of occupation on the allocation of human resources.

One further point needs to be explored, namely, the extent of occupational movement within the labor force. A summary glance at the data of Table 5–1 suggests that it is substantial. For example, net mobility plus new entrants into the professional, technical, and kindred workers occupational groups over the period 1950–60 amount to about 65 percent of the total number of individuals in those occupations in 1950. An approximate measure of the frequency of movement between occupations can be obtained by estimating the minimum number of job changes which would be required between 1950 and 1960 to accomplish the net changes observed in Table 5–1.[2] In the case of male occupational mobility this amounts to 3,723,000 job changes or 8.8 percent of all jobs at the beginning of the decade. The minimum percentage of job changes required to accomplish the net changes in interindustry and geographic distributions of workers in the previous two chapters are 2.1 and 0.8 percent, respectively. Put on an average annual change basis this indicates that the extent of occupational movement in the United States requires at least 0.9 percent of the labor force to change jobs each year as compared to 0.7 percent for interindustry movement and 0.3 percent for geographic. Thus, the frequency of occupational movement would seem to be comparable with that of interindustry movement which suggests a substantial amount of opportunity for workers to alter their occupation.[3]

II. INTERGENERATIONAL MOVEMENT OF WORKERS AMONG OCCUPATIONS

Occupational movement within a worker's lifetime is only one aspect of the total picture of occupational mobility. In addition, it is necessary to consider the extent of movement among occupations between successive generations. This has become particularly important in recent years since, in the context of the "War on Poverty," a widespread conviction that poverty is inheritable has developed in the United States.[4] This implies that to a very sizable extent workers inherit occupational status from their parents. In order to determine whether this is true and to test the maximizing hypothesis with respect to intergenerational occupational mobility the data shown in Table 5–2 will be utilized. These

---

[2] The required minimum number of job changes is estimated by summing the net flows irrespective of sign and dividing by two.

[3] There are some problems in comparing annual average rates of change computed on the basis of time periods of different length. It is well known that those who change jobs in one time period are more likely to change again in some future time period than those who do not shift in the original period. For example, see Blumen, Kogan, and McCarthy (12). Thus, the longer the time period under consideration the more likely it is that there will be repeat movement which is masked by the use of net flow data and, consequently, the measure of the extent of job changing used here is biased downwards in the case of occupational mobility.

[4] For example, see Harrington (83) p. 21; Sargent Shriver's statement to Congress in reference to the Economic Opportunity Act of 1964 (172, p. 35); President Johnson's message to the Congress (93, p. 2); and Economic Report of the President (49), 1964: pp. 69–78, 1965: p. 170, 1966: p. 96, 1967: p. 142.

TABLE 5-2
One-Generation Occupation Transition Matrix, Noninstitutional Male Population, 25–64 Years of Age, March, 1962

Father's Occupation	a,*	Son's Occupation									
		Managers, Officials, and Proprietors	Professional, Technical, and Kindred	Craftsmen, Foremen, and Kindred	Sales	Clerical and Kindred	Operatives and Kindred	Service, including Private Household	Laborers, except Farm and Mine	Farmers and Farm Managers	Farm Laborers and Foremen
Managers, officials, and proprietors	0.116	0.341	0.216	0.139	0.090	0.070	0.085	0.026	0.019	0.010	0.003
Professional, technical, and kindred	0.047	0.175	0.408	0.087	0.090	0.069	0.103	0.030	0.020	0.013	0.004
Craftsmen, foremen, and kindred	0.185	0.165	0.130	0.294	0.047	0.078	0.175	0.052	0.048	0.008	0.003
Sales	0.040	0.301	0.194	0.119	0.150	0.062	0.104	0.032	0.020	0.017	0.001
Clerical and kindred	0.034	0.178	0.281	0.169	0.079	0.096	0.092	0.061	0.031	0.014	0.000
Operatives and kindred	0.155	0.122	0.117	0.238	0.044	0.066	0.258	0.060	0.076	0.010	0.010
Service, including private household	0.047	0.142	0.101	0.210	0.057	0.095	0.210	0.111	0.062	0.011	0.002
Laborers, except farm and mine	0.065	0.080	0.059	0.226	0.037	0.080	0.265	0.091	0.142	0.012	0.012
Farmers and farm managers	0.282	0.115	0.053	0.197	0.025	0.047	0.205	0.052	0.085	0.178	0.042
Farm laborers and foremen	0.029	0.073	0.023	0.204	0.020	0.038	0.261	0.082	0.134	0.062	0.102

* Relative importance of occupation among fathers.
SOURCE: U.S. Department of Commerce, Bureau of the Census (198), Table 1.

were assembled by Duncan and Blau[5] in the course of their conducting an investigation of patterns of occupational movement between generations. As shown here these data describe the occupation of adult males (as of March 1962) aged 25 to 64 in the noninstitutional population classified by their father's occupation. The data have been modified from their original form in that only 10 occupational groupings are employed whereas 11 were used in the original data. However, the 11th among the fathers' occupations was entitled "occupation not reported" and the 11th among the younger generation was "not in the experienced civilian labor force." Since these are not identical concepts, these cate-

TABLE 5–3
Occupational Distribution of Fathers and Sons and 1960 Median Income, by Occupation

Occupation	Fathers	Sons	Difference	1960 Median Income
Managers, officials, and proprietors	0.116	0.161	+0.045	$6,664
Professional, technical, and kindred	0.047	0.125	+0.078	6,619
Craftsmen, foremen, and kindred	0.185	0.207	+0.022	5,240
Sales	0.040	0.051	+0.011	4,987
Clerical and kindred	0.034	0.066	+0.032	4,785
Operatives and kindred	0.155	0.189	+0.034	4,299
Service	0.047	0.059	+0.012	3,310
Laborers, except farm and mine	0.065	0.069	+0.004	2,948
Farmers and farm managers	0.282	0.056	−0.226	2,169
Farm laborers and foremen	0.029	0.018	−0.011	1,066

SOURCE: U.S. Department of Commerce, Bureau of the Census (**198**), Table 1.

gories were omitted from the data and the remainder were adjusted to produce the information shown in Table 5–2.

Using these data the maximizing hypothesis as applied to occupational changes across generations can be treated by comparing the differences in the occupational distributions of fathers and sons with 1960 median earnings by occupation. The necessary information is presented in Table 5–3 and when it is used to estimate a least squares regression equation the results are:[6]

---

[5] The data are contained in U.S. Department of Commerce, Bureau of the Census (**198**). They were obtained on behalf of a research project which was supported by a grant from the National Science Foundation to the University of Chicago with Peter M. Blau and Otis Dudley Duncan as investigators.

[6] Inclusion of a 1960 unemployment rate variable in the regression does not produce any significant difference in the results.

$$D_j = -0.1154 + 0.00003 \ w_j, \ R^2 = 0.37 \tag{4}$$
$$(3.02)$$

where D_j denotes the difference between the proportion of fathers and the proportion of sons employed in the jth occupation. The results in this case are significant at the 10 percent level. This is a somewhat weaker relationship than that found in the discussion of occupational change within a worker's lifetime but this is due almost exclusively to the tremendous decline in the proportion of farmers and farm managers between the two generations. If this observation is omitted, the resulting regression is:

$$D_j = -0.0298 + 0.000012 \ w_j, \ R^2 = 0.73 \tag{5}$$
$$(4.05)$$

which is clearly significant at the 5 percent level. Such results are again quite consistent with the premise that workers are highly responsive to economic advantages when changing occupations.

The foregoing suggests that workers evidently have a substantial amount of freedom to move between occupations across generations. However, the intensity and fervor with which pronouncements on this subject are made necessitates a more detailed inquiry. Perhaps the best summary statement of the bulk of current opinion[7] on the matter of intergenerational economic opportunity is the statement which may be found in Chapter 2 of the *Economic Report of the President, 1964* (**49**, pp. 69–70), which reads as follows:

Poverty breeds poverty. A poor individual or family has a high probability of staying poor. Low incomes carry with them high rates of illness; limitations on mobility; limited access to education, information, and training. Poor parents cannot give their children the opportunities for better health and education needed to improve their lot. Lack of motivation, hope, and incentive is a more subtle but no less powerful barrier than lack of financial means. Thus, the cruel legacy of poverty is passed from parents to children.

Taken literally, this strongly asserts that economic status tends to be inheritable, a proposition that is extremely significant in a society which prides itself on the great amount of economic opportunity that it presents to its citizens. Whether this is actually the case is what we wish to determine and in order to facilitate this the remaining discussion will be divided into two parts: (1) a treatment of what is meant by economic opportunity and the inheritability of economic status, and (2) an empirical evaluation (using the data of Tables 5–2 and 5–3) of the extent to which economic opportunity is present in the United States.

---

[7] See the following references: Harrington (**83**, page 21); Shriver (**172**, p. 35); Johnson (**93**, p. 2); and *Economic Report of the President* (**49**).

The meaning of the term "economic opportunity" is somewhat vague, particularly when value laden qualifiers such as "lack of" or "equality of" are appended to it. However, what is usually implicit in the use of the term is some notion of the ability of individuals to move from one economic group to another. Conceptually, such movement may be expressed in the form of a transition matrix of the following type:

Economic Group	a	Economic Group b	c	d
a	P_{aa}	P_{ab}	P_{ac}	P_{ad}
b	...	...	...	...
c	...	...	...	...
d	P_{da}	...	...	P_{dd}

The entry in the ath row and ath column (P_{aa}) represents the probability of an individual's remaining in the ath economic group through time. By definition, the economic groups a, b, c, and d include all possible states of economic achievement; consequently, the sum of the elements of any row of the matrix will be equal to unity.

A matrix such as this can be used to illustrate the relationship between the economic status of parents and that of their children by letting the vertical economic group designations represent the economic accomplishment of parents and the horizontal designations represent the economic status of offspring. For example, let us assume that all children inherit the economic position of their parents. Under such an assumption the transition matrix assumes the following form:

Economic Group (parents)	a	Economic Group (children) b	c	d
a	1	0	0	0
b	0	1	0	0
c	0	0	1	0
d	0	0	0	1

All the diagonal values equal unity, indicating that each child retains the economic status of his parents—a situation which amounts to a complete lack of opportunity for economic advancement from generation to generation. In short, this matrix depicts a perfect economic caste system. On the other hand, we might move to the opposite extreme and assume a situation in which the economic achievement of the parent has absolutely no impact on the economic prospects of the children. In this situation all the elements in a particular column of the matrix are equal to one another, i.e., each child has the same probability of being in a particular economic class irrespective of the economic status of his parents. Obviously, these probabilities correspond to the aggregate distribution of the younger generation among the various economic groups.

The two extreme cases presented here provide a foundation for evaluating the actual movement between economic groups on an intergenerational basis. For example, by utilizing these extreme cases an aggregative economic opportunity index can be formulated. It takes the form

$$0 = \frac{\sum_{i=1}^{n} \sum_{j=1}^{n} (P_{ij} - P_j^*)}{2(n-1)} \tag{6}$$

where 0 represents a measure of economic opportunity, P_{ij} the probability that the child of a parent in the ith economic group will move to the jth group, P_j^* the proportion of the younger generation in the jth economic class, and n the number of classes. The statistic 0 has a range from zero to one, for in the case of no relationship between parental status and a child's position, the numerator of (6) equals zero, whereas in the instance of a child's economic position being completely determined by the parent's status, this numerator degenerates to $2(n-1)$. Consequently, the closer to zero the value of 0, the greater the amount of opportunity to move between economic groups from generation to generation.

Expression (6) is simply an unweighted index of economic opportunity, unweighted in the sense that no account is taken of the differential impact of various barriers to economic opportunity upon the income opportunities of the younger generation. This shortcoming can be eliminated by assigning income weights to the various components of the unweighted index. By doing this, we are simply saying that certain movements between occupational classes are more important than others in terms of their impact on the income of the movers. The weighted opportunity index is defined as follows:

$$0_w = \frac{\sum_{i=1}^{n} a_i \left| \sum_{i=1}^{n} B_j P_{ij} - \sum_{i=1}^{n} B_j P_i^* \right|}{\sum_{i=1}^{n} a_i \left| \sum_{j=1}^{n} B_j - \sum_{j=1}^{n} B_j P_i^* \right|} \tag{7}$$

where a_i denotes the relative importance of the ith sector in the older generation and B_j the level of income in the jth sector. Like the unweighted opportunity index, 0_w varies from zero to one with the same interpretation being placed on the limiting values.

The economic opportunity indexes which have been described can be calculated from the data of Tables 5–2 and 5–3. From these the opportunity statistic described in expression (6) was computed to be 0.24. Similar results are obtained when the weighted opportunity statistic is computed—a value of 0.31, somewhat larger than that for the unweighted index but still substantially less than unity. Unfortunately, there is no simple way to interpret these statistics. For one thing, the boundary values used to define the indexes have certain shortcomings. The basis of the denominator used in expressions (6) and (7) is the simple assumption that the occupational status of sons is completely determined by the fathers' occupations. Such an assumption implies that the percentage distribution of individuals into occupational groups remains the same with succeeding generations; this we know is not true. Consequently, there is an irreducible minimum of intergenerational occupational mobility which is required to accommodate a changing occupational mix. This causes our computed opportunity indexes to be biased toward showing more mobility than actually exists.

Any correction for this bias necessarily involves some assumption as to how the changes in occupational mix take place. One possibility is to establish an occupational hierarchy and then assume that any changes in occupational distribution are accomplished by shifts between adjacent occupations in the hierarchy. For example, the younger generation in the sample has 16.1 percent of its members in the highest income group (managers, officials, and proprietors), whereas only 11.6 percent of their fathers were in this occupation. Under the assumption stated here, the difference of 4.5 percentage points would be drawn from the next adjacent group in the hierarchy. Thus, movement into occupational groups remains strictly a function of the fathers' occupational classes. If this type of adjustment is carried out throughout the entire transition matrix, a new matrix, which will generate the necessary occupational distribution while retaining the strict relationship between the fathers' and sons' occupations, can be estimated and used to calculate appropriate denominators for expressions (6) and (7). In the case of expression (6) the denominator becomes

$$\sum_{i=1}^{n} \sum_{j=1}^{n} |\hat{P}_{ij} - P_i^*|$$

where $\hat{P}_{ij}$ denotes the intergenerational transition rates between occupational groupings, which are calculated on the basis of the previously stated assumption. For expression (7) the change in the denominator is somewhat minor—the subscript j is substituted for i in the term a_i (the relative importance factor).

These operations were carried out with the data of Table 5–2 and the result is a modest increase in the opportunity statistics. The unweighted statistic rises to 0.29 (an increase of 0.05) and the weighted index increases to 0.40 (a change of 0.09). This eliminates one type of bias in the opportunity index, but there is another type which is somewhat more intractable. This bias arises as a result of the fact that the other boundary value used in calculating the income opportunity statistic is based on a rather stringent concept of equality of economic opportunity. In essence, it implies an absence of inherited factors which might affect occupational achievement, including any genetically transferable characteristics. Now, if there is some relationship between native ability and occupational success, and if some of this native ability (abstracting from cultural differences) is transferable through the biological mechanism, the assertion that equal economic opportunity for the younger generation requires an economic opportunity index of zero is a bald overstatement. In fact, if the observed economic opportunity index were actually zero, one might suspect that occupational selection is really not based on native ability. After all, a zero index is also compatible with a purely random process of selection for various occupations. Consequently, the failure to allow for the biological transmission of ability (and I know of no way to incorporate it here) tends to bias the economic opportunity statistics upwards.

Given this bias, the task of assigning meaning to these statistics still remains. There is no statistical test of significance which will indicate whether these values are significantly different from zero or unity. They may be significantly different from both, but the important question is by how much? To some, a value for the opportunity statistic varying between 0.30 and 0.40 may be unsatisfactorily high. My own view (considering the upward bias in the indexes) is that it is indicative of a fairly high degree of occupational mobility between generations. To illustrate this more dramatically, let us abandon for the moment the highly aggregative opportunity indexes, statistics which are somewhat antiseptic in character. In Table 5–4 data are presented which graphically illustrate the extent of economic opportunity for the sons of fathers with differing occupational backgrounds. These permit comparing 1960 census median income by occupation with a weighted average of the median incomes of sons who had fathers in particular occupations. The latter is merely the

$$\sum_{j=1}^{n} B_j P_{ij}$$ term of expression (7). These data show, for example, that

whereas the median income of farm laborers and foremen in 1960 was $1,066, the weighted average of the 1960 incomes of the sons of farm laborers and foremen is $4,021.[8] This may be compared with a weighted

---

[8] The weighted average of medians can be interpreted as a weighted average of probabilities. In this case the probability is 0.50. Therefore, what the weighted average of medians says is that there is a probability of 0.50 that an individual will have at least this high an income.

average median income of $4,907, which would have resulted if the sons of farm laborers and foremen were distributed by occupation in the same fashion as the entire sample. Thus, for the sons of those at the very bottom of the economic hierarchy, levels of income have been achieved which have greatly lessened the gap which would have existed between their income and a typical level of income if they had inherited their fathers' occupational status. In fact, 77 percent of that gap has been eliminated. In all fairness, however, it should be kept in mind that the declining importance of the farm laborer-foremen occupational group in itself would force some improvement in the economic status of the

TABLE 5-4

Median Income, 1960, and Weighted Average Median Income, Noninstitutional Male Population, 25–64 Years of Age, March, 1962, by Occupation

Father's occupation	a_j*	Median income 1960	Weighted average medan income†
Managers, officials, and proprietors..................	0.161	$6,664	$5,747
Professional, technical, and kindred.....................	0.125	6,619	5,735
Craftsmen, foremen, and kindred.....................	0.207	5,240	5,195
Sales.........................	0.051	4,987	5,608
Clerical and kindred............	0.066	4,785	5,504
Operatives and kindred..........	0.189	4,299	4,834
Service, including private household..................	0.059	3,310	4,833
Laborers, except farm and mine......................	0.069	2,948	4,686
Farmers and farm managers......	0.056	2,169	4,234
Farm laborers and foremen.......	0.018	1,066	4,021

* Relative importance of occupation among sons.
† Computed using weights for various occupations given in rows of matrix of Table 1.
SOURCE: *U.S. Census, 1960*; Table 5–2, and computations.

offspring of this group. However, on the basis of the same assumption that was used in correcting the aggregative indexes for this factor, the record is still impressive, with about 74 percent of the potential income gap being eliminated.

A broad overview of the evidence presented to this point generates the distinct impression that there is a substantial amount of occupational mobility from generation to generation. The apparent existence of such mobility in turn generates an interest in what its effect might be on generations more than once removed from the father—for example, upon the economic status of grandchildren of men in particular occupations. A simple estimate of the impact of occupational mobility on grandchildren may be had by assuming that the process of intergenerational movement from occupation to occupation is Markovian in character, i.e., that the integration transition rates from occupation to occupation depend only on the occupational status of the father. Thus, the transition rates for the grandchildren of a given individual depend upon the occupational status of his son. On the basis of this assumption, a two-generation transition matrix can be estimated by squaring the matrix shown in Table 5–2. This produces Table 5–5, from which economic opportunity statistics of the type previously calculated may be derived. The unweighted statistic is 0.09 and the weighted statistic is 0.11. Neither of these, however, makes allowance for the minimal amount of mobility which is necessary to accommodate the changed occupational mix implicit in the matrix of Table 5–5. Allowance for this increases the unweighted statistic to 0.12 and the weighted one to 0.14.

III. CONCLUSIONS

Two rather obvious conclusions would seem to emerge from the evidence presented here. First, workers do seem to be responsive to differential economic advantages when moving between occupations—whether it be movement within their lifetime or movement between generations. In combination with our previous conclusions with respect to patterns of interindustry and geographic mobility this lends strong support to the premise that existing labor market mechanisms have the capacity to allocate human resources efficiently. At least, from the labor supply side of the market, there appears to be little in the way of workers' reactions to economic differentials which would inhibit an efficient pattern of resource allocation. This does not rule out the existence of artificial barriers to the free flow of human resources between sectors of the labor market, imperfections which could distort the allocative pattern away from the optimal.

The second major conclusion which emerges is that there appears to be a substantial amount of opportunity for individuals to move between different occupations. This is particularly evidenced by the analysis of intergenerational occupational movements which seems to provide a strong argument against the idea that the economic status of parents is a major determinant of the economic success of offspring. Keeping in mind the fact that there is an upward bias in the calculation of the intergeneration opportunity indexes (due to no allowance for inherited differences in native ability), the low values of these indexes indicate a substantial amount of mobility between generations.

Further, one cannot avoid being impressed by data which show that in one generation 74 percent of the potential gap in income between the lowest paid occupation and all occupations is eliminated through the movement of male progeny into other occupations. Data such as

TABLE 5-5
Estimated Two-Generation Occupation Transition Matrix

Grandfather's Occupation	Grandson's Occupation									
	Managers, Officials, and Proprietors	Professional, Technical, and Kindred	Craftsmen, Foremen, and Kindred	Sales	Clerical and Kindred	Operatives and Kindred	Service, including Private Household	Laborers, except Farm and Mine	Farmers and Farm Managers	Farm Laborers and Foremen
Managers, officials, and proprietors	0.234	0.231	0.162	0.082	0.072	0.127	0.040	0.033	0.013	0.004
Professional, technical, and kindred	0.205	0.269	0.146	0.083	0.071	0.130	0.041	0.034	0.014	0.005
Craftsmen, foremen, and kindred	0.189	0.187	0.205	0.066	0.075	0.162	0.051	0.048	0.012	0.005
Sales	0.233	0.224	0.162	0.085	0.071	0.130	0.041	0.035	0.015	0.004
Clerical and kindred	0.203	0.236	0.169	0.078	0.074	0.138	0.046	0.038	0.014	0.004
Operatives and kindred	0.174	0.174	0.209	0.063	0.074	0.179	0.055	0.055	0.013	0.007
Service, including private household	0.183	0.177	0.203	0.066	0.076	0.171	0.057	0.052	0.013	0.005
Laborers, except farm and mine	0.159	0.150	0.220	0.058	0.076	0.194	0.062	0.065	0.013	0.007
Farmers and farm managers	0.160	0.135	0.212	0.052	0.068	0.190	0.057	0.066	0.042	0.016
Farm laborers and foremen	0.144	0.119	0.224	0.049	0.070	0.209	0.065	0.076	0.026	0.018

SOURCE: U.S. Department of Commerce (198), Table 5-2, and computations.

these certainly weaken the case for those who argue that there is a "vicious cycle of poverty." Apparently, the inheritability of poverty is not nearly so great as is implied by some, and apparently, there exists in the current American economy a substantial amount of occupational mobility between succeeding generations. Such a conclusion receives support from a more detailed analysis of the data source from which the information in Tables 5–2 and 5–3 were derived.[9] Overall, this presents a rather optimistic view of the capacity of the American labor market to perform the functions envisaged for it by formal economic theory.

[9] Duncan (40) argues that much of what many interpret as inheritance of poverty is in reality attributable to the race of the individuals rather than to the economic status of their parents.

chapter SIX

Unemployment and
Inflation: An Overview

IN the introductory chapter reference was made to the
existence of a "tradeoff" between price inflation and unemployment in
the American economy. At that point, it was rather confidently asserted
that such a relationship, known as a Phillips' curve, did exist. I suspect
this raised some eyebrows as the presence of something called a Phillips'
curve for the American economy has been the subject of extensive controversy among economists. The basis for this controversy is the difficulty
of developing a solid theoretical explanation for there being some sort
of reasonably stable relationship between the rate of price inflation and
unemployment levels.[1] As originally postulated by Phillips (**152**) the
relationship in question is that between the rate of change in money
wage rates and the rate of unemployment. The line of reasoning is that
as the unemployment rate falls the level of money wage rates in the
economy will rise more rapidly due to the "tightening" of the labor
market. Conversely, as the unemployment rate in the economy rises,
it will be easier for employers to hire labor, and money wage rates
will rise more slowly, or even fall. Lipsey has rather aptly described
the unemployment rate as being a measure of "negative excess demand"
for labor.[2] The chain of causation is completed by reasoning further
that the rate of increase in money wage levels will be the prime determinant of the rate of price inflation in the economy. Thus, it would

---

[1] A rather extensive exploration of the theoretical aspects of the Phillips' curve
is contained in Phelps *et al.* (**151**).

[2] Lipsey (**124**).

73

be argued that as unemployment falls, money wage rates and prices will rise more rapidly and vice versa.

The difficulty with this whole concept is that it must in some fashion assume imperfections in the labor market mechanism. If money wages and prices were perfectly flexible, the only unemployment which would exist would be of the "frictional" type envisaged by Pigou (153). In fact, under these ideal conditions, all that would happen as levels of aggregate demand in the economy changed would be an inflation or deflation of price levels and little change in the unemployment rate. This suggests a very weak relationship between changes in aggregate demand and unemployment levels.[3] However, this is not what happens in the American economy. This is rather aptly indicated by Figure 6–1 which depicts graphically the relationship between percentage changes in money levels of gross national product and changes in the aggregate unemployment rate. No precise statistical evaluation of the degree of relationship between these magnitudes is required. Clearly, they move very closely together in an inverse fashion. The greater the percentage increase in gross national product, the greater the decrease (or the smaller the increase) in unemployment levels.

Figure 6–1 suggests the presence of imperfections in the labor markets of the American economy. Apparently, there are sufficient wage and price rigidities in the system to produce increases in unemployment as the rate of increase in aggregate demand falls. Actually, the relationship shown in Figure 6–1 indicates that a zero rate of increase in aggregate demand would be associated with about a 2 percentage point increase in the unemployment rate. It is reasonable to expect this to happen if prices are assumed to remain unchanged, for improvements in technology would enable the economy to produce the same quantity of goods and services with fewer workers. Add to this some normal increase in population and labor force and it is easy to see why unemployment might rise if there were no change in aggregate demand. But, and this is most important, this whole line of argument is dependent upon wage and price rigidities in the economy. And, it is these rigidities which underly the concept of a Phillips' curve. What apparently happens as aggregate demand changes is this: part of the impact of the change is reflected in shifts in levels of unemployment and part is translated into price changes instead of all of the impact being felt in the price sector. Therefore, when aggregate demand falls, unemployment increases and prices and wages do not fall as much as they would if the rigidities did not exist. Similarly, as aggregate demand rises, unemployment falls and prices and wages do not rise as much as they would in the absence

---

[3] Some of the contributions to Phelps et al. (151) attempt to develop theoretical explanations for the existence of the Phillips' curve which rely on models of labor market search. These do not require the presence of wage rigidities. See, in particular, Holt (90) and Mortensen (140).

FIGURE 6-1

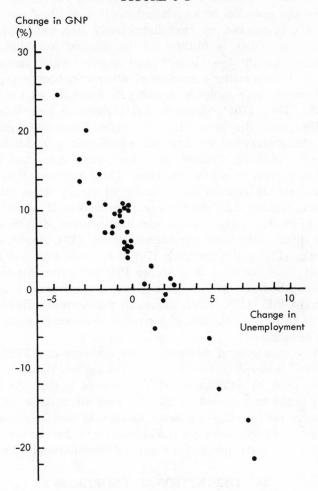

of the rigidities because of the existence of an unemployed pool of labor. In the process, the phenomenon of the tradeoff between unemployment levels and price levels is established.

I.   ATTEMPTS TO MEASURE THE PHILLIPS' CURVE
FOR THE UNITED STATES[4]

Given the foregoing discussion, the existence of the Phillips' curve relationship would seem to be self-evident. Yet, serious questions have

[4] The remainder of this chapter draws almost exclusively on an investigation of the Phillips' curve relationship for the United States conducted by Gallaway and Koshal. I am greatly indebted to Professor Koshal for giving his permission for use of this material in this volume.

been raised with respect to this issue. The rather voluminous literature inspired by the question of whether there is a Phillips' curve for the United States is marked by two distinctively different approaches to the matter; one which is faithful to the original formulation of the Phillips' curve by Phillips himself[5] and another which deviates from this path by incorporating a number of other variables in the Phillips' curve relationship or completely revising it. Examples of the latter are Perry (149), Kuh (108), Eckstein (47), Eckstein and Wilson (48), Phelps (150), and Brechling (17). Basically, these investigators have found the straightforward Phillips' curve relationship unsatisfactory for purposes of explaining changes in money wage rates and have felt compelled to expand it in new directions. Their judgment that the Phillips' curve does not explain the behavior of money wage rates in the United States (particularly in the post-World War II period) appears confirmed when the efforts of those who have attempted to fit a Phillips' curve in a direct fashion are considered. Bowen (13), Bowen and Berry (14), Bhatia (11), and Gilpatrick (79) have done this and have concluded that it is doubtful if a stable Phillips' curve for the United States exists. About the only dissenting note in this respect is a study by Liebling and Cluff (122), which argues to the contrary. However, their results seem to turn on the use of a particular unemployment rate and, thus, must be qualified.[6]

In the face of a general rejection of the existence of a Phillips' curve for the United States, how can the earlier claims that such a relationship does indeed exist be substantiated? The answer is that there seem to be certain problems inherent in the previous attempts to identify the Phillips' curve relationship—problems which may well be responsible for the inability to clearly delineate a Phillips' curve for the United States which is faithful to the spirit of the original formulation by Phillips.[7]

II. DEFINITIONAL PROBLEMS

Initially, it should be noted that the results achieved by various investigators of the Phillips' curve phenomenon seem to be extremely sensitive

---

[5] Lipsey's (124) formulation of the Phillips' curve relationship in a certain sense is an extension and modification of Phillips' original work. However, he does include variables other than unemployment rates or changes in unemployment rates in his version of the Phillips' curve.

[6] Liebling and Cluff use quarterly data in their study and, in addition, use the unemployment rate for males aged 20 and over.

[7] Lerner makes a straightforward argument for focusing solely on unemployment levels to explain changes in money wage rates in (117, p. 217): "the other elements that affect the movement of the money wage level must all be so closely related with the level of employment; so that bringing them in could only result in minor refinements." Liebling and Cluff (122) go even farther by arguing that the inclusion of these other variables quite frequently does nothing more than confuse the theoretical structure of the argument under consideration.

to the definitions they employ in assembling their data.[8] For example, in his evaluation of the post-World War II U.S. Phillips' curve, Bhatia (11) fits the following relationship:

$$\Delta E_t = a + bU_t + c\Delta U_t + e \tag{1}$$

where ΔE_t is the percentage change in money wage levels between the end of December in year $t - 1$ and the end of December in year t, U_t is the annual average unemployment rate in year t, ΔU_t is defined as $[(U_{t+1} - U_{t-1})/2U_t]$ 100, and e is a random error term. He finds that this relationship will only explain 28 percent of the variance in ΔE_t over the period 1948–58. But, Liebling and Cluff (122) point out that a different definition of ΔE_t (using annual average wages as the basis for calculating the percentage change in money wages) will yield results which are much better statistically. In fact, they claim that it will raise the proportion of explained variance to 0.55. These are substantial differences and would seem to merit some explanation. Fortunately, it is not difficult to find one. Specifically, Bhatia's formulation is as follows:

$$(E_t^* - E_{t-1}^*)/E_t^* = a + bU_t + c(U_{t+1} - U_{t-1})/2U_t + e \tag{2}$$

where the * associated with E means money wage levels at the *end* of the year which is subscripted. In effect, this procedure centers the change in money wages and the unemployment rate variables on July 1 of year t. Thus, there are no lags between the dependent and independent variables.

On the other hand, the Liebling-Cluff suggestion centers the change in money wage rates on January 1 of year t. Consequently, the unemployment variables are lagged in a crude fashion by about six months. If a simple change in the implicit lag relationship between the dependent and independent variables is capable of producing changes of this magnitude, it would seem that the definition of the variables themselves may be critical from the standpoint of the "goodness of statistical fit" when estimating relationships such as (2). Unfortunately, a number of different methods of defining variables have been suggested. Lipsey (124) uses the first central difference method, an example of which is Bhatia's change in unemployment rate variable. Bowen and Berry (14) have advocated the averaging method, i.e., defining the change in money wages as $(E_{t+1} - E_t)/E_t$ and the unemployment rate as $(U_t + U_{t+1})/2$. Other methods can also be derived but these samples should suffice to illustrate the basic difficulty inherent in the definition problem, namely,

---

[8] This sensitivity prompted Rees and Hamilton (158) to remark: "Our final caution is that we have been astounded by how many very different Phillips curves can be constructed on reasonable assumptions from the same body of data. The nature of the relationship between wage changes and unemployment is highly sensitive to the exact choice of other variables and to the regression and to the forms of all the variables."

the impact of different definitional schemes on the lag structure of the Phillips' curve relationship.

III. SPECIFICATION PROBLEMS

The act of defining the variables to be incorporated in a Phillips' curve also has implications from the standpoint of how the equation in question is specified. Take, for example, expression (2) which seems straightforward enough in that it incorporates both a level of unemployment and a change in unemployment variable in a linear equation. Actually, this expression is not truly linear with respect to all of its independent variables and has the additional undesirable property of assigning a priori weights to certain of the independent variables. When fully expanded (2) becomes:

$$\frac{E_t^* - E_{t-1}^*}{E_t^*} = a + \frac{2bU_t^2}{2U_t} + \frac{cU_{t+1}}{2U_t} - \frac{cU_{t-1}}{2U_t} + e \tag{3}$$

From this it is clear that there are actually three independent variables in (2): U_t, U_{t+1}, and U_{t-1}. Also, this relationship is obviously nonlinear in U_t and two of the independent variables are assigned the same weight in the final results by being combined into a single variable through the process of subtraction. The rationale for this functional form is not obvious. It is one thing to say that the rate of change in money wage rates is related to U_t, U_{t+1}, and U_{t-1} in some undetermined fashion, but it is quite something else to say that U_{t+1} and U_{t-1} have exactly the same effect in opposite directions and that U_t is related to changes in money wage rates in some particular nonlinear fashion.

As another case in point, take Bowen and Berry's (**14**) favored formulation of the Phillips' curve relationship:

$$\frac{E_{t+1} - E_t}{E_t} = a + b\frac{U_{t+1} + U_t}{2} + c(U_{t+1} - U_t) + e \tag{4}$$

where the data are all annual averages. It is interesting to note that both of the independent variables are combinations of U_t and U_{t+1}. The importance of this can be seen by expanding (4) as follows:

$$\frac{E_{t+1} - E_t}{E_t} = a + (b/2 + c)U_{t+1} + (b/2 - c)U_t + e \tag{5}$$

Again, it is clear that weights have been implicitly assigned to U_t and U_{t+1} by this equation specification. In fact, (4) constrains the variables in such a fashion as to make the quantitative importance of U_{t+1} relative to U_t equal to the ratio $[(b/2) + c]/[(b/2) - c]$. This may, or may not, be the appropriate set of weights to attach to the various measures of unemployment.

IV. DATA PROBLEMS

Certain questions have arisen in the literature with respect to the appropriate set of wage rate data which should be employed in estimating the Phillips' curve relationship. Ideally, labor would be considered a purely variable factor of production and straight-time hourly earnings would be the obvious choice as a measure of money wage rates. However, this ideal is not realized in practice for two reasons: (1) following Oi's analysis (144) labor may be a quasi-fixed factor of production and (2) straight-time hourly earnings data are not sufficiently available. Due to the second of these points, some substitute must be found for straight-time earnings. Two data sources can be used: average hourly earnings in manufacturing and compensation of full-time equivalent employees for the entire economy. The first of these is the most widely used and is subject to the criticism that (1) it includes premium payments for overtime and (2) its coverage is limited to the manufacturing sector of the economy. Given the possibility of labor being a quasi-fixed productive factor, the inclusion of overtime payments in the wage rate may not be a particular problem in that a reasonable adjustment response of employers to a tightening labor market would be to lengthen the workweek of their employees and to pay overtime premiums.[9]

The second possible data source, annual compensation of full-time equivalent employees, has been criticized for incorporating cyclical changes in the workweek in the data. However, this criticism may also be directed at hourly earnings in manufacturing data, as already noted. At least, the annual compensation data have the virtue of incorporating workweek changes in all directions whereas manufacturing hourly earnings only measure them when they involve payment of overtime premiums. Further, the coverage of the annual compensation data is for the entire economy and not just manufacturing employment. Given these considerations, it is not clear that one data source is eminently superior to the other. Consequently, at least initially, both will be used.

V. A SPECIFICATION OF THE PHILLIPS' CURVE

On the basis of the previous discussion of definitional and specification problems inherent in earlier formulations of the Phillips' curve for the United States, it was decided to estimate expressions of the following type for purposes of delineating a Phillips' curve:

---

[9] It is interesting to note that Phelps (150) employs a length of workweek variable in one of his formulations of a Phillips' curve.

$$\frac{E_{t+1} - E_t}{E_t} = a + bU_{t-1} + cU_t + dU_{t+1} + e \qquad (6)$$

and

$$\log \frac{(E_{t+1} - E_t)}{E_t} = \log a + b \log U_{t-1} + c \log U_t + d \log U_{t+1} + \log e \quad (7)$$

The rationale of these is very simple. On economic grounds it can be argued that employers' decisions with respect to changes in money wage rates are influenced by what unemployment rates have been, what they are, and what they are expected to be.[10] On statistical grounds, these expressions have the advantage of allowing the regression coefficients to determine the relative weights of the independent variables while offering a substantial range of lags between the independent and dependent variables. The lag structure is not predetermined but is set by the regression coefficients at somewhere between −18 months and +6 months. The −18-month lag is between U_{t-1} and ΔE_t since ΔE_t is centered on January 1 of year $t+1$ and U_{t-1} is centered on July 1 of year $t-1$. Similarly, U_t lags ΔE_t by 6 months and U_{t+1} leads by 6 months. Thus, U_{t+1} incorporates the expectational effects. Through these formulations, it is hoped that the problems discussed earlier can be overcome.

VI. SOME POST-WORLD WAR II RESULTS

Since the crux of most current discussions of the Phillips' curve in the United States is whether one has existed in the post-World War II period, that interval is examined first. As an initial step, the results of estimates for the period 1948–58, which is the one analyzed by Bhatia and Bowen and Berry, are reported. Using manufacturing hourly earnings as the data source for the dependent variable, the following results were obtained from estimating (6) and (7):[11]

$$\Delta E_t = 3.6371 + 0.6166\ U_{t-1} + 0.6008\ U_t - 0.8486\ U_{t+1},$$
$$(2.49) \qquad (2.54) \qquad (4.47) \qquad\qquad (8)$$
$$R^2 = 0.88,\ D\text{-}W = 2.6465$$

---

[10] In a discussion of data problems, Bowen and Berry (14) seem to say that use of U_{t+1} as a variable is inappropriate as "causation cannot run backwards." Of course, while this is so, expectations can run forward. Also, this statement is doubly puzzling in that U_{t+1} is a part of both their independent variables in their favored formulation of a Phillips' curve.

[11] D-W denotes the Durbin-Watson statistic for testing for the presence of serial correlation. Unless otherwise noted in the remainder of this chapter, it indicates either an absence of serial correlation or is indeterminant.

and

$$\log \Delta E_t = 0.6144 + 0.3656 \log U_{t-1} + 0.6289 \log U_t$$
$$\quad\quad\quad\quad (2.14) \quad\quad\quad\quad\quad (3.78)$$
$$\quad - 0.8786 \log U_{t+1}, \ R^2 = 0.92, \ D\text{-}W = 2.4051 \quad (9)$$
$$\quad (6.13)$$

Statistically, the results are quite impressive. The R^2 for the linear relationship is 0.88 compared to Bhatia's 0.28 (or 0.55 if you take the Liebling-Cluff modification of Bhatia) and 0.92 for the nonlinear.[12] All the independent variables are statistically significant and the nonlinear formulation appears to be the superior one although both perform quite well.

Economically, the results are also comforting in that they are logically what one would expect on the basis of the Phillips' curve type relationship. For example, the positive sign of the coefficients associated with U_{t-1} indicates that, *ceteris paribus*, an increase in U_{t-1} would mean a smaller rise (or greater decline) in unemployment and a greater increase in E. On the other hand, the negative sign of U_{t+1} means that, *ceteris paribus*, a greater value for U_{t+1} will produce a greater rise (or smaller decline) in unemployment and a smaller increase in E. The interpretation of U_t is somewhat more complex as variations in it will produce effects in both directions. Consequently, it is difficult to postulate a priori expectations with respect to its sign. This will depend on the particular lag structure that exists between ΔE_t and the various unemployment measures.

The results shown in expressions (8) and (9) are confirmed when the annual compensation of employees (C) data are used as the dependent variable:

$$\Delta C_t = 3.1504 + 0.3692 \ U_{t-1} + 0.9185 \ U_t - 0.8563 \ U_{t+1},$$
$$\quad\quad\quad\quad (1.75) \quad\quad\quad (4.55) \quad\quad (5.30) \quad\quad\quad\quad (10)$$
$$\quad\quad\quad\quad\quad\quad\quad\quad R^2 = 0.91, \ D\text{-}W = 1.3462$$

and

$$\log \Delta C_t = 0.5970 + 0.1451 \log U_{t-1} + 0.9596 \log U_t$$
$$\quad\quad\quad\quad (0.62) \quad\quad\quad\quad\quad (4.22)$$
$$\quad - 1.0002 \log U_{t+1}, \ R^2 = 0.88, \ D\text{-}W = 1.7942 \quad (11)$$
$$\quad (5.11)$$

Here, the R^2's are slightly higher in the linear case and lower in the nonlinear and all variables except U_{t-1} are significant. In general, there is little to choose among the two sets of results. Consequently, given the preponderance of attention in the literature to the hourly manufacturing wage data, it will be employed in the remainder of this chapter.

---

[12] Bowen and Berry (14) find an R^2 of 0.66 for 1948–58 in their preferred form of the Phillips' curve. This is still substantially less than the value reported here.

Some further insight into the nature of the relationship between the rate of change in money wage rates and unemployment levels can be obtained from Table 6–1 which contains some of the stepwise regression results obtained in estimating (8) and (9). Employing U_t alone as the independent variable yields poor results but U_{t+1} by itself produces very good results ($R^2 = 0.57$ in the linear form and 0.56 in the nonlinear).

TABLE 6–1
Stepwise Regression Results for Phillips' Curve for United States, 1948–58*

Regression Form	Constant	U_{t-1}	U_t	U_{t+1}	R^2
Logarithmic.....	0.1979	0.7951 (2.08)	...	...	0.3514
Logarithmic.....	0.3949	...	0.4445 (1.01)	...	0.1125
Logarithmic.....	1.1639	...	...	−0.8937 (3.26)	0.5706
Logarithmic.....	0.0537	0.7364 (1.85)	0.3070 (0.78)	...	0.4032
Logarithmic.....	0.7714	0.5461 (1.95)	...	−0.7077 (3.06)	0.7222
Logarithmic.....	0.8318	...	0.7284 (3.71)	−0.9871 (5.99)	0.8551
Linear..........	0.6043	1.0770 (2.52)	...	...	0.4427
Linear..........	2.8502	...	0.4849 (0.89)	...	0.0906
Linear..........	8.6674	...	...	−0.9194 (3.18)	0.5583
Linear..........	−0.5152	1.0276 (2.31)	0.3342 (0.76)	...	0.4848
Linear..........	4.9296	0.7586 (2.36)	...	−0.7275 (2.97)	0.7536
Linear..........	6.2346	...	0.7337 (2.41)	−1.0235 (4.40)	0.7586

* Values in parentheses beneath coefficients are t-values.

This would seem to suggest that expected levels of unemployment are more important in the eyes of employers than present levels. This interpretation assumes, of course, that the employers' expectations of what unemployment levels will be in the future are reasonably accurate. If this is the case, actual unemployment levels six months in the future (the lead implicit in U_{t+1}) will be a good proxy for anticipated unemployment levels.

Even more interesting in Table 6–1 is the result of employing both U_t and U_{t+1} as independent variables. In expression (8) the R^2 rises to 0.76 and in (9) to 0.86 and both variables are statistically significant with opposite signs. Following the earlier reasoning with respect to the anticipated signs for the regression coefficients, this would seem to argue that the rate of change in the unemployment level is a crucial determinant of the rate of change in money wage levels. This would be consistent with Bowen and Berry's findings (14) which improve markedly when a change in unemployment variable is added.

The results reported to this point indicate quite strongly that the rate of change in money wage levels in the immediate post-World War II period (1948–58) can be explained by variations in unemployment levels. Thus, they differ substantially from the generally accepted position on this matter. The reasons for this have already been noted. But, what about longer periods of time? Does the Phillips' curve relationship exist beyond the confines of the period 1948–58?[13]

As a first step in answering the question of whether the Phillips' curve is a long-run phenomenon, the post-World War II analysis is extended to include the period 1948–68. The results are:

$$\Delta E_t = 8.3332 - 0.0780 \ U_{t-1} + 0.2241 \ U_t - 1.0414 \ U_{t+1},$$
$$(0.36) \qquad\qquad (0.91) \qquad\qquad (4.78) \qquad\qquad\qquad (12)$$
$$R^2 = 0.62, D\text{-}W = 1.2624$$

in the linear form and

$$\log \Delta E_t = 1.1747 - 0.1549 \log U_{t-1} + 0.3285 \log U_t$$
$$(0.83) \qquad\qquad\qquad (1.77)$$
$$- 1.1155 \log U_{t+1}, R^2 = 0.70, D\text{-}W = 0.8448 \qquad (13)$$
$$(5.90)$$

in the nonlinear.

These results are markedly different from those reported earlier. Again, the nonlinear form is superior to the linear *but* there are substantial changes in the values of the coefficients and a marked worsening of the fit as compared to the 1948–58 findings. Rather than explaining about 90 percent of the variance in ΔE_t, these explain, at best, 70 percent. Such a difference implies some fundamental change in the nature of the relationship under consideration. To test for this two additional versions of the nonlinear form of a 1948–68 Phillips' curve have been estimated. The first incorporates a time drift variable (t) and yields the following results:[14]

$$\log \Delta E_t = 1.1714 - 0.0522 \log U_{t-1} + 0.4261 \log U_t$$
$$(0.29) \qquad\qquad\qquad (2.10)$$
$$- 1.1044 \log U_{t+1} - 0.1073 \log t, R^2 = 0.76, D\text{-}W = 0.9366 \qquad (14)$$
$$(6.27) \qquad\qquad\qquad (1.86)$$

---

[13] Friedman (54) has argued that the Phillips' curve is strictly a short-run phenomenon. Thus, this is an important question for consideration.

[14] The time drift variable is a conventional one with the earliest year under consideration being assigned the value one and the remaining years being indexed in an integer fashion in chronological order.

This regression indicates that whatever structural change there has been in the Phillips' curve in the post-World War II period has led to a lower rate of increase in money wage rates being associated with the same unemployment experience as time passes. However, this must be interpreted cautiously, for the time drift variable is significant only at the 10 percent level.

The second additional regression introduces a shift (or dummy) variable covering the period 1959–68.[15] The results of the estimation process are:

$$\log \Delta E_t = 1.0142 + 0.0185 \log U_{t-1} + 0.4882 \log U_t$$
$$ (0.09) \phantom{\log U_{t-1} + } (2.34)$$
$$- 1.0754 \log U_{t+1} - 0.3064 \, D, \, R^2 = 0.76, \, D\text{-}W = 0.8955 \tag{15}$$
$$ (6.08) \phantom{\log U_{t+1} --} (1.88)$$

where D denotes the shift variable.

Generally, expression (15) confirms the results reported in (14) which suggest a weak negative shift in the Phillips' curve relationship in the post-World War II period. This is a finding which is consistent with the results reported by Liebling and Cluff (122). One problem remains, though. Is the weak negative shift that is observed in the post-World War II Phillips' curve, a phenomenon that occurs throughout the entire period or is it one that is associated with only the latter half of that interval? To test for this, the nonlinear relationship for 1948–58 was reestimated with a time variable included. The results are:

$$\log \Delta E_t = 0.6705 + 0.3537 \log U_{t-1} + 0.6204 \log U_t$$
$$ (2.11) \phantom{\log U_{t-1} + } (3.81)$$
$$- 0.8824 \log U_{t+1} - 0.0640 \log t, \, R^2 = 0.93, \, D\text{-}W = 2.7943 \tag{16}$$
$$ (6.30) \phantom{\log U_{t+1} --} (1.13)$$

Clearly, the time drift variable is less significant in a statistical sense than it is in (14) and it is also quantitatively smaller. This suggests that the time drift is more pronounced in the latter part of the 1948–68 period.

In general, the regressions which have been reported thus far imply some instability in the post-World War II American Phillips' curve

---

[15] It should be noted that there was a change in the definition of unemployment from 1957 forward. Bowen and Berry (14) deal with this by subtracting 0.4 percentage points from the estimated unemployment rate beginning with 1957. As an alternative approach, a one-zero shift dummy was introduced to deal with this problem and it was found to be insignificant. However, it should be realized that the negative shift which will be found in regression (15) may be biased by this definitional change. Actually, if such a bias exists, it will operate in the direction of producing an understatement of the magnitude of a negative shift. The same will hold true in the case of the inclusion of a time drift variable in the 1948–68 estimates.

with a weak tendency toward its becoming more favorable from the standpoint of dealing with the inflation-unemployment tradeoff dilemma. The interesting question this raises is whether this is a long-run phenomenon.

VII. THE LONG-RUN PHILLIPS' CURVE

To investigate the long-run Phillips' curve for the United States the same basic model has been estimated in linear form for the period 1900–68 with the conventional exclusion of the years 1915–20, 1933–34, and 1942–47.[16] The results are:

$$\Delta E_t = 3.7157 + 0.8784\ U_{t-1} - 0.1053\ U_t - 0.9176\ U_{t+1},$$
$$(6.43) \qquad\quad (0.54) \qquad\quad (7.13) \qquad\qquad (17)$$
$$R^2 = 0.70,\ D\text{-}W = 1.2224$$

Seventy percent of the variance is explained by the regression with the U_{t+1} and U_{t-1} variables being the dominant ones. The Durbin-Watson statistic in this case does indicate some serial correlation. However, it can be reduced to acceptable levels by the inclusion of a time drift variable. This is desirable at any rate since the question of a long-term time drift in the relationship should be explored. Inclusion of the time drift variable yields:

$$\Delta E_t = 2.1612 + 0.8700\ U_{t-1} - 0.1299\ U_t - 0.8906\ U_{t+1}$$
$$(6.80) \qquad\quad (0.71) \qquad\quad (7.37)$$
$$+ 0.0454\ t,\ R^2 = 0.74,\ D\text{-}W = 1.4218 \qquad (18)$$
$$(2.81)$$

Interestingly, the time drift variable is quite significant with a *positive* sign instead of the *negative* sign observed in the post-World War II period. This is somewhat puzzling. Possibly, it suggests a strong positive time trend in the earlier part of the century which has not been overcome by the post-World War II time drift. To test for this the period was divided into two parts—one extending from 1900 through 1932 and the other from 1935 to the present (remember that 1933 and 1934 are omitted)—and regressions similar to (18) estimated for both periods. The results are:

$$\Delta E_t = 3.4732 + 0.8475\ U_{t-1} - 0.2467\ U_t - 0.7138\ U_{t+1}$$
$$(4.41) \qquad\quad (1.28) \qquad\quad (5.51)$$
$$- 0.0951\ t,\ R^2 = 0.85,\ D\text{-}W = 1.9334 \qquad (19)$$
$$(1.88)$$

---

[16] The other studies of the Phillips' curve all exclude these years. The linear form was chosen for this regression because it yielded much superior results when the long-run Phillips' curves were being estimated.

for 1900–1932, and

$$\Delta E_t = 10.7041 + 0.5534 \; U_{t-1} + 0.0779 \; U_t - 1.0896 \; U_{t+1}$$
$$\quad\quad (2.26) \quad\quad\quad (0.28) \quad\quad\quad (5.05)$$
$$- 0.1714 \; t, \; R^2 = 0.64, \; D\text{-}W = 2.2722 \quad\quad (20)$$
$$(2.92)$$

for 1935–68.

These regressions are reasonably similar in terms of the coefficients of the unemployment variables. However, there are at least two substantial differences and one curious anomaly in them. First, the explanatory power of the 1935–68 regression is substantially less than that for 1900–32. Second, the constant terms of the two regressions are markedly different with the 1935–68 one being over three times that for 1900–32. Finally, there is the aforementioned anomaly. Strangely, both of the regressions have negative time drift variables although that for the 1935–68 period is larger than that for 1900–32. This would seem to contradict the earlier finding of a positive time drift across the entire 1900–68 time period. However, the contradiction is only an apparent one. What seems to have happened is that the Phillips' curve relationship shifted at some point in the middle of the overall time period. Such a shift is suggested by the much larger constant term in the 1935–68 regression and would account for an observed positive time drift in the regression covering the entire time period. To test for this possibility, a one-zero dummy shift variable was included in (18) and it was re-estimated with two time drift variables (one for 1900–32 and another for 1935–68).[17] The results are:

$$\Delta E_t = 4.2753 + 0.6494 \; U_{t-1} - 0.1909 \; U_t - 0.8104 \; U_{t+1}$$
$$\quad\quad (5.48) \quad\quad\quad (1.24) \quad\quad\quad (7.63)$$
$$- 0.0689 \; t_{<33} - 0.1314 \; t_{>32} + 5.1787 \; D_{>32}, \quad\quad (21)$$
$$(1.56) \quad\quad\quad (2.24) \quad\quad\quad (2.87)$$
$$R^2 = 0.83, \; D\text{-}W = 2.0627$$

These confirm the post-1932 shift hypothesis and indicate the operation of a weak negative time drift in the pre-1933 period and a stronger negative time drift in the post-1933 era. Thus, there seems to be a consistent tendency for the Phillips' type relationship to shift in a negative fashion. This should not be particularly surprising for it can be argued that since the presence of a Phillips' curve is itself a reflection of imperfections in the labor market adjustment mechanism, over time the im-

---

[17] The dummy variable takes the value one for post-1932 years and zero for years prior to 1933. The time drift variable for the pre-1933 period has the value zero for all post-1932 observations while the variable for the post-1932 period assumes the value zero for all pre-1935 observations.

proving of transportation and communications facilities might well operate to make the adjustment process more efficient and shift the Phillips'
curve negatively. In fact, such a line of reasoning is quite consistent
with the conclusion reached in Chapter Four with respect to changes
in the relative importance of the factors affecting geographic mobility
patterns between 1850 and 1960. There, it was found that the degree
of sensitivity of individuals to interstate differences in per capita income increased markedly over time. This would be compatible with
a lessening of the extent of imperfections in the labor market.

The behavior of the shift variable included in (21) is extremely interesting. Apparently, a major change occurred at the bottom of the depression of the 1930's which made the labor market adjustment process
less efficient. The most likely source of such a change would be the
legislative actions of the 1930's which gave such great impetus to trade
unionism. These appear to have produced a dramatic positive shift in
the Phillips' curve which has then been slowly reversed by the time
drift factor. Keeping these considerations in mind, it seems that regression (21) does provide a good estimate of the long-run relationship between the rate of change in money wage rates and unemployment levels
in the United States. Certainly, the proportion of the total variance
which is explained is acceptable and there is no evidence of serial
correlation.

VIII. CONCLUSIONS

The basic conclusion suggested by the preceding discussion of the
Phillips' curve relationship is that there is a meaningful connection between the rate of change in money wage rates in the United States
and unemployment levels in both the short run and the long run. Admittedly, these relationships do appear to lack stability in the sense
that they shift from time to time. However, the shifts themselves are
not of a purely random character. Quite the contrary: there is clear
evidence of a persistent negative drift over time in the relationship plus
a substantial shift in the long-run Phillips' curve beginning in the 1930's.
It can be argued that the former is consistent with a movement toward
a more efficient labor market mechanism as both transportation and
communications facilities improve. The latter would seem to be the natural outgrowth of the public policy innovations of the 1930's which introduced additional rigidities into labor market adjustment mechanisms
in the form of an extension of trade union collective bargaining rights.

From the public policy standpoint, the evidence which has been presented would argue that there is a tradeoff between unemployment levels
and price inflation. The nature of this tradeoff is suggested by Table
6–2 which shows the rate of change in money wage rates associated

TABLE 6–2
Tradeoff between Unemployment and
Rate of Change in Money Wage
Rates, United States, 1968

Unemployment Rate	Rate of Change in Money Wage Rates
2%................	8.4%
3................	6.3
4................	5.1
6................	3.5
8................	3.1
10................	2.6

SOURCE: Equation (14) and computations.

with various levels of unemployment in the United States as of 1968.[18] From this table it appears that price stability in the United States is roughly compatible with a 6 percent unemployment rate and an annual increase in productivity of American labor of from 3 to 4 percent.[19] Anything less than such a productivity increment would necessitate a higher unemployment rate in order to achieve price stability. This is not a particularly favorable tradeoff. However, it appears that barring any major institutional readjustments (such as those that occurred in the 1930's) the price of a particular level of unemployment in terms of price inflation has been declining and will continue to do just that. At least, the rather persistent negative time drift in the Phillips' curve which has been observed for almost 70 years in the United States would suggest this.

[18] These tradeoffs are estimated from expression (14) assuming the same level of unemployment in years $t - 1$, t, and $t + 1$ and the value of the time drift variable which is appropriate for 1968. All that is required for a tradeoff to exist is that the sum of the coefficients of the unemployment variables be negative. This is true in every regression reported except some for the 1948–58 period where only those which include U_t and U_{t+1}, or U_{t+1} alone, meet this criterion. This may also explain some of the previously noted difficulties encountered in estimating Phillips' curves for the United States for 1948–58.

[19] The rate of increase in money wage rates minus the annual increase in productivity is a measure of the inflationary potential of changes in money wage rates.

chapter SEVEN

Trade Unions, Unemployment, and Inflation

THE Phillips' curve relationship which has been described in Chapter Six argues that a substantial impetus to the rate of increase in money wage rates developed in the United States as the result of the shifts in public policy toward trade unions that took place during the 1930's. This raises an issue which is quite familiar to labor economists; the question of the impact of unions on wage levels in the United States. A number of investigations of this issue have been conducted with the best known one probably being that of H. Gregg Lewis (121).[1] Lewis' work attempts to estimate the impact trade unions have had on the interindustry wage structure in the United States and he concludes that in general trade unions have been able to increase the wage levels of their members relative to the wages of all labor by perhaps as much as 15 percent in the post-1933 period. Of great interest given the nature of this discussion is the fact that Lewis' estimates indicate that the impact of trade unions on the relative wages of their members was even greater prior to the depths of the Great Depression.[2] Even

---

[1] Other studies worth noting are Sobotka (176), Maher (132), Throop (188), and Hildebrand (87). For surveys of this question, see Reynolds (159) and Ross (160).

[2] Lewis (121, p. 193) estimates that in the period 1927–29 the wages of union labor were 15 to 20 percent higher than those of nonunion labor. As of 1957–58 the effect is estimated to be 10 to 15 percent.

allowing for a smaller relative amount of unionism in the economy prior to 1933, this would seem to indicate that no great shift in the pattern of wage determination took place commencing in 1933. Thus, the Lewis findings do not offer an obvious explanation for the empirical findings of the preceding chapter. This apparent contradiction requires some further analysis of the impact of unions on the economy and the remainder of this chapter will be devoted to just that.

I. THE LABOR MARKET IN GENERAL

Any analysis of the economic impact of trade union activity should commence with a general examination of the functioning of labor markets with particular emphasis on the operation of the "union" and "nonunion" sectors of those markets. In this context "union" is defined broadly to encompass both those markets which have formal trade union organizations and those which are, in effect, "satellites" of markets which are formally unionized. The latter would include nonunionized markets in which wage levels are strongly tied to wages in markets with trade unions. Of course, the "nonunion" sector would include all markets not identified as "union." The simpler of these sectors to deal with theoretically is the nonunion one which for the time being will be treated as roughly approximating the competitive model of a labor market.[3] However, the behavior of labor markets in the union sector is not as easily described. In fact, this has been a bone of contention among academic economists for some time and, consequently, an extensive examination of the theory of how union markets function is necessary.

II. THE FUNCTIONING OF THE UNION SECTOR
OF THE LABOR MARKET

The complicating factor in describing in theoretical form the manner in which wages are determined in the union sector of the labor market is the question of how trade unions behave in such markets. The behavior of the demanders of labor (employers) may be adequately treated by means of the conventional profit maximization assumptions employed in microeconomic theory of the firm. Unfortunately, the behavior of trade unions as economic institutions is not as easily handled: there are at least a half-dozen different models of the economic behavior of unions. Probably the simplest is that which views a trade union as a monopoly seller of labor with a monopolist's motives. In this model

---

[3] This is only a first approximation. Obviously, there are deviations from the competitive model in the nonunion sector but one must admit that the probability of these imperfections is less in the nonunion sector. Consequently, the nonunion sector is closer to the competitive model than the union.

the supply curve of labor is interpreted as indicating the marginal cost of labor to the union and the equilibrium wage rate chosen by the union is that which equates the marginal increment of wage income with the marginal cost of labor.

An alternative to the labor monopoly model modifies the subject of maximization, changing it to the gross wage bill. In effect, this substitutes a zero marginal cost of labor throughout for the monotonically increasing marginal cost of labor presumed in the labor monopoly model. The maximization of the gross wage bill model in turn has three variants. In its simplest form the equilibrium wage rate is that at which the marginal increment of wage income is equal to zero. However, this solution is subject to the condition that the supply curve for labor intersect the demand curve for labor either at or to the right of the equilibrium point. Failure to satisfy this condition creates the second variant of the wage bill maximization model. In this version the wage bill is maximized at the point at which the supply curve of labor intersects the demand curve for labor, i.e., the second variant is simply the result one would find in a competitive labor market.

The third variant of the wage bill maximization model results from incorporating the presence of unemployment insurance systems (either public or private) into the analysis.[4] This has the effect of shifting the zero throughout marginal cost curve of labor upward by the amount of the unemployment insurance benefit. Consequently, in instances in which the supply curve of labor intersects the demand curve at or to the right of the intersection of this new marginal cost curve and the marginal revenue curve associated with the demand curve, the combination of wage bill and unemployment insurance is maximized by setting the wage to produce the level of employment that equates the marginal increment of wage income with the unemployment compensation benefit.

While these models of union economic behavior are interesting, there is an element of unreality embodied in the limited horizon of union objectives which is implied in the behavioral assumptions. In an effort to transcend these limitations John Dunlop (41) suggested a model of trade union economic behavior which incorporates an assumption that a trade union is interested in maximizing its membership. The analytical device which embodies this assumption is Dunlop's "membership" function which describes the relationship between wage rates and the number of workers that these wage rates will attract into the union. As postulated by Dunlop, the "membership" function will be either identical with or lie to the left of the labor supply curve in the market. In those instances in which it lies to the left of the labor supply curve its shape will

---

[4] There may be some differences in the effect of private and public unemployment compensation plans. For a discussion of these, see Cartter (26), pp. 82–83.

depend on the nature of the demand curve for labor, for at extremely high wage rates the relative lack of employment will cause the membership function to be backward sloping (see Figure 7–1).[5] Thus, maximization of membership would imply selecting the wage rate associated with the point on the membership function at which its slope changes from

FIGURE 7–1

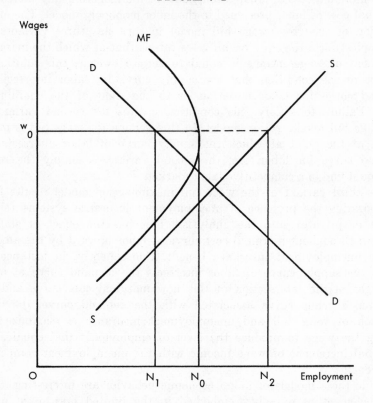

positive to negative.[6] In Figure 7–1 this is wage w_0 which would produce membership N_0, employment N_1, and unemployment $N_2 - N_1$. This is, of course, an illustrative solution and should not be interpreted as a typical one.

The models which have been discussed so far suffer from a complete reliance on maximization of objective factors such as wages or member-

---

[5] Dunlop (**41**) suggests a possible case in which the membership function might be to the right of the market supply curve. However, Cartter (**26**) argues rather convincingly that this suggested case in reality involves a rightward shift of both the supply curve and membership function with an end result that they are identical.

[6] The membership function as described here is modified from Dunlop's in that the monotonically increasing feature of his function is discarded. If this is not done, union membership is maximized at an infinite wage rate.

ship to the complete exclusion of a number of subjective factors which might influence trade union behavior.[7] Furthermore, the very existence of the objective functions involved in some of these models is a matter of debate. A most ingenious solution to this difficulty is suggested by Allan Cartter (**26**, pp. 86–94), who, taking a clue from William Fellner (**52**), incorporates subjective factors into a model of trade union behavior by applying the tools of indifference analysis to hypothetical

FIGURE 7–2

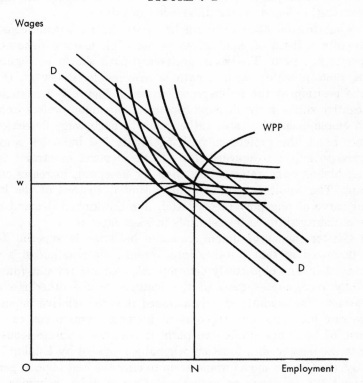

union preference functions. These preference functions express the union's attitudes toward different combinations of wage rates and employment. The type of preference function suggested by Cartter as typical of trade union attitudes is shown in Figure 7–2.

Obviously, the illustrated preference function treats wage rates and employment as substitutes for one another (hence, the convexity of the indifference curves). However, they are highly imperfect substitutes as depicted, for the indifference curves approach the shape of those associated with complementary products. The constraint necessary to derive

---

[7] For a discussion of these subjective factors, see Ross (**161**).

a unique solution is provided by a line DD which is nothing more than the demand curve for labor. This curve may be thought of as a wage-employment opportunity line and functions as the appropriate constraint only if we assume that the employer has the right to unilaterally determine the quantity of labor which will be employed at any given wage rate. Presumably, this would be done in accordance with normal profit maximization practices. Now, given the preference function and the demand constraint, a union would maximize its position by opting wage OW with its employment counterpart ON. This is merely the familiar tangency solution found in an indifference analysis.

Following this line of analysis further, shifts in the demand constraint will generate a locus of equilibrium points. This Cartter denotes as a wage preference path. The wage preference path shown in Figure 7–2 suggests that in reality such a path is irreversible. Below an existing wage the position of the indifference curves in Figure 7–2 is such that with negative shifts in the demand constraint the union prefers to adjust through employment decreases rather than through wage decreases. On the other hand, the preference path of Figure 7–2 indicates a greater willingness to adjust to upward shifts in the demand constraint by demanding higher wage rates rather than by accepting increases in employment. The result is a discontinuity similar to that of the kinked demand curve of oligopoly theory. And, like the kinked demand curve, the discontinuity shifts as adjustments in wage rates occur.

The Cartter model of union economic behavior is superior to the others discussed in that it takes into account the reaction of a union to factors other than objectively determinable cost and revenue functions. It actually incorporates most of the features of the other models in some fashion: for example, if it is assumed that the relative importance of wage rate increases and employment increases remain constant over the range of the wage preference path, it becomes a linear locus very similar to the membership function originally proposed by Dunlop.[8] Consequently, the Cartter model would seem to offer the best hope of generalizing about the economic consequences of trade union behavior.

III.   INTERRELATIONSHIPS BETWEEN UNION
AND NONUNION MARKETS

If we accept the Cartter model of union economic behavior, it is possible to describe analytically the responses of the labor market to

---

[8] It should be remembered that the membership function proposed by Dunlop differs somewhat from that employed in the earlier discussion in that it is a monotonically increasing one. This is plausible if the demand constraint is considered to shift appropriately (as it does in the Cartter model). However, if the demand constraint remains fixed, a simple linear membership function flies in the face of experience in that it assumes that the level of employment of workers has no bearing on their allegiance to the union.

changing demand conditions with some precision. For purposes of the discussion assume a two-sector market; one sector behaving along the lines of the Cartter model and the other in accordance with the economic theory of competitive markets. In addition, let us also assume an initial situation which corresponds to full employment. This is shown in Figure 7–3. Note that we only show the lower portion of the Cartter wage preference path. This is due to the full-employment assumption, for positive demand shifts when at full employment will not increase employment and, consequently, unions do not have to choose between employment and wage increases. This is the familiar situation of pure

FIGURE 7–3

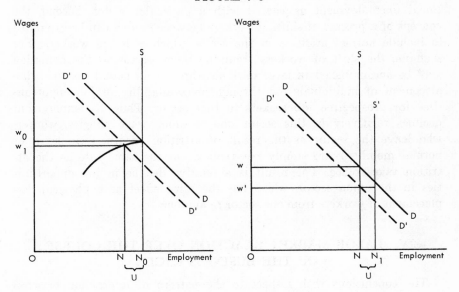

inflation. Now, introduce a similar negative shift in the demand curve for labor in each sector (the result of some change in the economy which is exogenous to the labor market itself). In the union sector (after allowing time for a full adjustment response) this has the effect of decreasing the wage rate from w_0 to w_1 and the employment level from N_0 to N, creating involuntary unemployment U. Meanwhile, if it is assumed that the nonunion sector is competitive, the wage rate in that sector moves from w to w' with no involuntary unemployment being generated. The critical question at this point is how the sector markets adapt to the involuntary unemployment U which exists in the union sector. There are two possibilities here: either the unemployment remains concentrated in the union sector or there is a movement of the unemployed from the union to the nonunion sector. If the latter occurs, the effect is to depress the wage rate in the nonunion sector to something less than w'. On the basis of other empirical studies, the shift of workers between the sectors appears to be the plausible explanation of how the markets adjust to the involuntary unemployment. This evidence indicates that changes in unemployment rates in various sectors (industrial, geographic, and occupational) are highly correlated with one another.[9] This is consistent with the shift explanation but not absolute proof as there is no certainty that disparate levels of unemployment ever existed in the various sectors.

Further realism can be added to this analysis by incorporating in it two modifications. First, the existence of a certain minimum level of unemployment of a frictional type can be handled by simply defining involuntary unemployment to mean unemployment in excess of the frictional unemployment associated with a particular sector. Second, the concept of a process of shifting workers between sectors can be expanded to include normal attrition in the sector which is losing workers. For example, the shift of workers from the union sector to the nonunion may be accomplished in large part not through an actual physical displacement of individuals but through nonavailability of job opportunities for prospective job seekers in that sector. Thus, as employment declines relatively in this sector due to union wage policies, workers who leave the sector as the result of attrition (death, retirement, or normal mobility) are simply not replaced at the same rate as the attrition takes place. The result is a relative decline in job opportunities in the union sector, which has the same effect as a physical displacement of workers from one sector to another.

IV. LABOR MARKET REACTION OVER THE COURSE OF THE BUSINESS CYCLE

The conclusions with respect to the pattern of interaction between the union and nonunion sectors of the economy have interesting implications for the behavior of unemployment over the course of the business cycle. These can be seen by abstracting from the labor demand shifts which occur as the result of economic growth and focusing strictly upon the shifts that take place during a typical business cycle. Assume initially that a full-employment situation exists in both sectors of the economy as shown in Figure 7–4. Now, introduce a similar negative shift in the demand for labor in both sectors, a shift presumably induced by an exogenous change in one of the parameters which de-

---

[9] Several tests of this proposition were made in the context of the "structural change" versus "deficiency of aggregate demand" controversy surrounding American unemployment experience in the post-World War II period (this will be discussed more fully in Chapter Eight). See Gallaway (**62**), Kalachek (**95**), and U.S. Congress (**193**). The tests conducted by Gallaway were subsequently updated and reconfirmed by Zaidi (**217**).

FIGURE 7–4

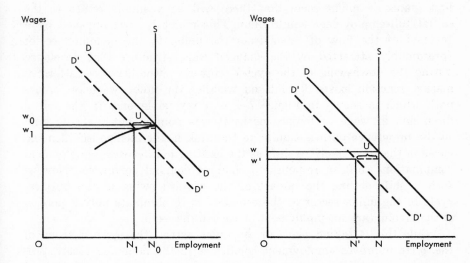

termines the aggregate level of demand in the economy as a whole. Further, assume that wage rates in the nonunion sector are insufficiently flexible to maintain full employment.[10] Thus, the downswing of the business cycle is triggered. In the union sector, trade unions prefer to adjust to the decrease in demand primarily through the medium of employment reductions rather than through wage rate decreases. The result is a decline in employment in this sector from N_0 to N_1 with a small reduction in wage rates. Obviously, this leads to involuntary unemployment U in this sector.

In the meantime, the negative demand shift will have produced a decline in both wage rates and employment in the nonunion sector. Also, in line with our assumption of insufficient wage rate flexibility in the nonunion sector, some degree of involuntary unemployment will result here. And, depending upon the speed with which intersector adjustments are consummated, there will be a certain amount of shifting of unemployment from the union to the nonunion sector. This will lead to further downward pressure on the wage rate in the nonunion sector due to the increased supply of labor that this produces. This leads to additional distortion of the wage structure away from that which would exist at full employment.

If we treat the negative demand shift as representing the full amount of downturn in the business cycle, then we can complete the analysis by reversing the shift. This is the equivalent of completing a full swing

[10] This is merely an assumption of "sticky" money wage rates which produce changes in real wage rates over the course of the cycle that generate involuntary unemployment in the downward phase of the cycle.

of the cycle. When this is done, the results are very interesting. At first glance it might seem that there will be a simple return to the initial full-employment equilibrium. This might be accomplished by a reversal of the flow of labor from the union to the nonunion sector (presumably attracted by the changed wage structure that developed during the downswing of the cycle). However, whether this pattern of market reaction exists depends on whether the union wage preference path which is shown in Figure 7–4 is a reversible one. In the initial discussion of wage preference paths it was pointed out that the kink in the preference path is similar to the kink in the oligopolist's demand curve in that it is likely to shift as the existing market wage-employment combinations shift in response to changed demand conditions. Now, if such a shift occurs, the impact of the upward swing of the business cycle in the union sector of the economy is to eliminate only a portion of the involuntary unemployment present in the sector.

While this is taking place in the union sector, the upward swing of the cycle improves employment conditions in the nonunion sector, presumably producing a return to a full-employment status although at a lower wage rate due to the shift in labor supply induced by the flow of labor from the union to the nonunion sector during the downswing of the cycle.

The net result of these changes (assuming a shifted wage preference path) is the existence of a changed wage structure (higher wage rates in the union sector compared to the nonunion) and some involuntary unemployment.[11] Now, to the extent that this unemployment is transferred to the nonunion sector there will be a further distortion of the wage structure in the direction of widening the gap between wage rates in the union and nonunion sectors.

V. LONG-RUN LABOR MARKET ADJUSTMENTS

The pattern of cyclical adjustments suggested in the preceding section generates an intriguing long-run pattern of labor market adjustment. Over the course of several business cycles the adjustment pattern just described would produce a consistent distortion of the wage structure in the direction of producing wage gains for the union sector at the expense of the nonunion. Further, the consistent downward pressure on the wage position of the nonunion sector could lead to substantial unemployment problems for the economy as a whole. This might result from the operation of statutory or "social" minimum wages, for given that the more unionized sectors of the economy are the high wage ones, the continued downward pressure on nonunion wage rates will act to in-

---

[11] The precise meaning of what is meant by a change in the wage structure will be discussed more fully later in this chapter.

crease the dispersion of sector wage rates about the average.[12] Such increased dispersion raises the probability of wage rates in the nonunion sector being "constrained" by some type of minimum wage.[13] If this happens, higher levels of unemployment would come about with the passage of time.

VI. SOME EMPIRICAL OBSERVATIONS

To this point the discussion has been couched in strictly theoretical terms. What has been developed is a model of the functioning of the labor market which generates wage gains for the unionized sector at the expense of the nonunionized. While this is all well and good, some empirical substantiation of the relationships postulated is desirable. However, before this can be done, one basic problem must be resolved. The previous studies of the impact of trade unions on wage rates have focused on the behavior of wage rates in unionized industries *relative* to wages in other parts of the economy (i.e., on the percentage wage differential). This is generally accepted but, strangely, it is not obviously apparent that it should be. In fact, it can be argued that relative wages are not the appropriate measure to consider but that absolute differences in real wages are. In the theoretical discussion the behavior of the union-nonunion wage differential was treated under somewhat artificial conditions. Specifically, no attempt was made to deal with the behavior of this differential in an environment characterized by economic growth. Rather, growth is ignored. However, the real world is marked by the presence of this phenomenon and its impact raises the following question: "What would be the behavior of the wage differential between two labor markets under conditions of rising levels of real wages if the standard competitive assumptions are satisfied in both of them?" The investigations of the impact of unions on the interindustry wage structure which concentrate on the relative wage structure implicitly assume that a constant percentage differential would be maintained. Perhaps this tendency to focus on relative wages is a product of economists' general concern with relative prices, to wit, the role that relative factor prices play in the theory of production. However, when the object of analysis is the behavior of wage differentials through time, it is by no means clear that relative wages are the appropriate magnitude to consider.

---

[12] Clarence Long (126) has argued that as educational and skill requirements are increased there is a widening productivity spread among workers in the labor force and that given some type of either a "social" or statutory minimum wage, low-productivity workers would find it increasingly difficult to find employment.

[13] There is a striking similarity between the working of Long's widening productivity spread and the functioning of the widening wage spread of this analysis. The fundamental difference is that Long's productivity phenomenon results from changes exogenous to the labor market which are simply measured by the market while the widening wage spread is the result of market imperfection.

Starting with the formal theory of consumer demand and applying it to worker behavior in labor markets, it can be argued that in a competitive labor market there will be a tendency toward an equilibrium wage structure which reflects two types of opportunity costs of mobility between markets: objective ones involving explicit money costs and subjective ones reflecting a variety of psychological considerations. Now, the contention that in the face of economic growth the whole wage structure shifts upward by the same percentage rate implies that these opportunity costs of movement also shift upward by that same percentage. Thus, if the general level of money wages rose by, say, 10 percent, this argument would seem to hold that the costs of movement between sectors would also rise by 10 percent. To the extent that increases in the general wage level reflect pure price inflation this would seem to be defensible. However, if the increase in the general wage level represents an increase in real wages, there is no compelling reason to expect the wage structure to respond in the fashion suggested by the advocates of relative wages as a criterion for evaluating the impact of trade unions in the market. Rather, certain of the objective costs of movement, such as relocation costs and out-of-pocket retraining costs, might be expected to remain fairly constant in real terms. Admittedly, it may be argued that some of the objective costs should properly be expressed in terms of "work time" lost in making the transition between jobs. This would be the case with respect to time spent in retraining or time spent in relocating the worker and his family. To the extent that this is the case and to the extent that these time intervals are intertemporally invariant, the real costs of these factors will increase in proportion to increases in the general level of real wages. However, it is by no means clear that the amount of "downtime" between jobs is invariant through time. As the real cost of such time increases, it is not unreasonable to anticipate that workers might make attempts to reduce the amount of it.

Turning now to the subjective costs of mobility, there is really no obvious reason for expecting anything other than constancy on the part of the real wage equivalent of such costs. To argue otherwise, and in particular to argue that such costs would change in direct proportion to changes in the general level of real wages, would seem to involve some very special assumptions regarding either the nature of workers' "leisure-income" preferences or the character of the subjective factors which gave rise to those costs in the first place.

To sum up, it has been suggested that there are good reasons to expect substantial portions of the real wage equivalent of the costs of labor mobility between sectors of the economy to remain fairly constant over time. If this line of argument is accepted, then it is not clear that it is appropriate to expect to find a constant relative wage structure

over time in a competitive labor market. At the same time, the discussion
to this point does not conclusively demonstrate that a wage structure
which exhibits constant real wage differentials is the appropriate norm
to employ in evaluating the impact of trade unions in the marketplace.
Thus, we face a dilemma. In order to provide some assistance in resolving
this difficulty, a modest empirical test may be helpful. Essentially, the
test consists of selecting a time period prior to the granting of exclusive
bargaining rights to trade unions (that is, prior to the mid-1930's) and
observing the behavior of the wage structure in this interval. If the
wage structure in such a period exhibits fairly constant real wage differentials, this would seem to argue against the relative wage structure
criterion. This test is probably a strong one in that trade union activity
was sizable in the period prior to unions receiving the grant of exclusive
bargaining rights. Thus, if the test is biased in any one direction, it
is toward refuting the argument that has been advanced.

If the date of unions' receiving their grant of bargaining rights is
arbitrarily set at 1935 (passage of the Wagner Act), we can observe
the behavior of the wage structure over a 17-year period (1919–35)
prior to the receipt of that grant. In Table 7–1 data are presented which
show compensation of full-time equivalent employees for union and nonunion sectors of the economy for such a period.[14] From these data the
wage differential (in real terms) between the union and nonunion sectors
can be estimated and then regressed against the level of real wages
for the economy as a whole. If the position taken by the advocates
of the relative wage criterion is borne out, the real wage differential
should be significantly related in a positive fashion to the overall level
of real wages. On the other hand, if no significant relationship exists
between these variables, support is accorded to the belief that absolute
differentials, rather than relative ones, are the appropriate criterion to
employ in evaluating the impact of trade union behavior in the marketplace. The results of the regression analysis are:

$$D = 569.38 - 0.2069 \ W, \ R^2 = 0.13$$
$$(1.47)$$
(1)

where D denotes the wage differential and W the general level of wages.
Clearly, the regression coefficient associated with W is not significantly
different from zero at the 5 percent level. Further, the negative sign
of the coefficient suggests a tendency toward a reversal of the differential.
However, the latter phenomenon is apparently a result of the behavior
of the wage differential during the deep depression years of 1931–33.

---

[14] The union sector is defined as including the mining, construction, manufacturing, and transportation, communications, and public utilities industries. The nonunion sector consists of the wholesale and retail trade, services, and finance, insurance, and real estate industries.

TABLE 7–1
Compensation per Full-Time Equivalent
Employee* (Column A), and Difference in
Compensation per Full-Time Equivalent
Employee between Union and Nonunion
Sector (Column B), United States, 1919–35
(1957–59 prices)

Year	Column A	Column B
1919	$2,037	$147
1921	2,098	121
1922	2,306	− 44
1923	2,319	131
1924	2,318	150
1925	2,319	92
1926	2,383	76
1927	2,386	158
1928	2,446	175
1929	2,624	147
1930	2,479	96
1931	2,586	− 6
1932	2,560	−151
1933	2,466	− 18
1934	2,455	26
1935	2,467	90

* In order to take account of changes in industrial mix through time, 1954 weights were used throughout to standardize the estimates of compensation per full-time equivalent employee. Thus, these estimates abstract from shifts in industrial structure.
Source: U.S. Department of Commerce, Bureau of the Census, *Historical Statistics, of the United States, Colonial Times to 1957*, Series D-685–D-719 (Washington, D.C.: U.S.G.P.O., 1960).

In these years, the differential reversed itself so that it was in favor of the nonunion sector. By 1935, though, this differential is again in favor of the union sector. If the observations from the deep depression years are eliminated from consideration, any semblance of a relationship between D and W disappears, as is shown by the following regression:

$$D = 143.2609 - 0.0162 \ W, R^2 = 0.00$$
$$(0.14)$$

(2)

What this suggests is that if we abstract from cyclical impacts on the union-nonunion wage differential, there is no relationship at all between the level of the wage differential and the level of wages in this period. Also, the distribution of the union-nonunion wage differential (excluding the 1931–33 period) shows a mean of $105 and a standard deviation of $55. Thus, the variable D seems to fluctuate within a fairly narrow range irrespective of the level of overall real wages in the period under consideration. This is certainly consistent with the proposition that the appropriate criterion to use in evaluating the impact of trade unions in the marketplace is that of constancy of absolute differentials in real wages.

With this in mind, we can now proceed to an examination of the empirical evidence relating to the hypotheses generated by the theoretical model already described. The portrayal of the adjustment process that characterizes union-nonunion market relationships implies that there will be an increase in the dispersion of sectoral wage rates about the average wage rate through time. Evidence relating to this dispersion shows that there has been a marked tendency toward an increasing dispersion when wages are considered on the basis of industrial sectors.[15] Further, the change in the dispersion of wage rates exhibits a pattern that is quite consistent with that suggested by the theory, viz, that wages in unionized sectors should exhibit gains at the expense of wages in the nonunion sectors. The data show that the highly unionized industrial sectors, such as contract construction, transportation, mining, and durable manufactures, have been large gainers in a wage sense in the post-World War II period while the services and trade sectors (with little union activity) have been substantial losers.[16]

In addition, the pattern of shifts in relative sectoral employment (on an industry basis) in the post-World War II period has been consistent with the model. It implies an increasing emphasis on employment in the nonunion sectors and relative declines in union sector employment. As a measure of the extent of this shift, consider that in 1950, 49.8 percent of nonagricultural wage and salary workers were employed in the highly unionized industrial sectors (manufacturing, construction, mining, and transportation) while in 1968 only 40.9 percent were employed in these sectors.[17] A word of caution is in order here, though, for these shifts are also consistent with some well-established long-run trends in the economy. But, at least, they are in the direction suggested by the theoretical discussion.

The consistency of certain secular trends with the suggested theory is certainly encouraging. However, the theory has more than secular

---

[15] The standard deviation is employed as a measure of the dispersion of the distribution of wage rates. In 1948 the standard deviation of the distribution of sector wage rates was $469 compared to a 1968 value of $962. Prior to calculating the standard deviation the 1968 wage data were expressed in terms of 1948 prices.

[16] Evidence dealing with the period 1948–60 is presented in Gallaway (62). When updated through 1968 this evidence indicates that in an absolute sense compensation of full-time equivalent employees increased between 1948 and 1968 by $5,216 in mining, $5,444 in construction, $5,677 in durable manufacturing, $5,986 in transportation, and only $3,754 in trade and $3,225 in services. In a relative sense, mining has gained 14.13 percent; construction, 19.07 percent; durable manufacturing, 24.41 percent; transportation, 30.93 percent; trade, 17.89 percent; and services, 29.46 percent.

[17] These data are taken from the U.S. Department of Commerce (194).

implications. To be precise, it suggests some very definite relationships over the course of a given business cycle, e.g., the pattern of trade union behavior which has been postulated should produce a distortion of the wage structure in the direction of increasing wages in the union sector at the expense of the nonunion sector. This tendency should be more pronounced on the upward swing of the cycle (due to the presence of downward wage inflexibility in both the union and nonunion sectors) and implies that the absolute wage differential (in real terms) between the union and nonunion sectors will widen progressively under the impact of the positive demand shifts which mark this phase of the cycle. Figure 7–5 shows graphically the extent to which this has actually happened in the post-World War II period in the United States. Commencing with the peak in unemployment in 1946 it can be seen that in every cycle since then the pattern has been for the real wage differential between the union and nonunion sectors to widen rapidly on the upswing of the cycle and then either level off or decline on the downswing.[18] The result is a "lace-edge" pattern along a trend line. This is precisely what would be expected if the theoretical model which has been postulated is a valid one.

The wage structure evidence is reassuring but there is always the haunting possibility that these results are not unique to the period shown here but are simply the rule in any cycle. In order to explore this possibility, similar data have been developed for the period 1919 through 1941. These are also shown in Figure 7–5 and, as noted earlier, they indicate that from 1919 to 1933 the absolute wage differential between the union and nonunion sectors fluctuated within a rather narrow range with, if anything, a negative trend. However, beginning in 1934 the post-World War II upward trend in the dispersion of wage rates begins to assert itself. By 1941, the wage differential between the two sectors has widened to approximately the same level as that existing in 1946.

Further, when the detailed pattern of wage movements over the course of the pre-World War II cycles is examined, it becomes apparent that the "lace-edge" effect is present as early as 1933. However, prior to 1933 the pattern of movements in wages over the course of the cycle is just the reverse: the difference between wages in the union sector and wages in the nonunion sector of the economy tends to fall during the upswing of the business cycle rather than rise. Thus, there is a "lace-edge" effect in the pre-1933 cycles but it is in the opposite direction. These data suggest that a marked change took place in the structure of the American labor market about 1933. Prior to then, the differential between wages in the union and nonunion sectors fluctuates within a

---

[18] The last full peak to peak unemployment cycle for which data are available is 1958–61. In all probability 1970 will be a peak unemployment year. However, the necessary data are not yet available.

FIGURE 7–5

Difference between Annual Compensation per Full-Time Equivalent Employee*
in Union Sector of Economy† and Nonunion Sector of Economy,‡
United States, 1919–61

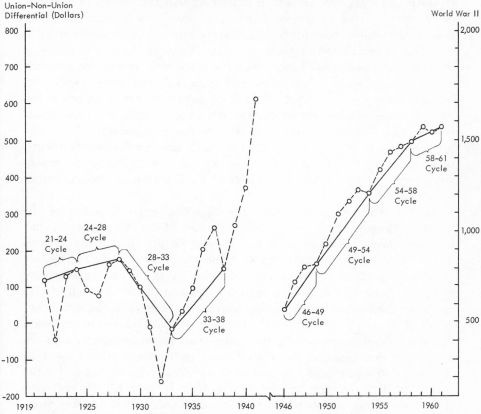

* In order to take account of changes in industrial mix through time 1954 weights were used throughout to standardize the estimates of compensation per full-time equivalent employee. Thus, these estimates abstract from shifts in industrial structure.

† The union sector is defined as consisting of mining, construction, manufacturing, and transportation, communications and public utilities types of employment.

‡ The nonunion sector is defined as consisting of wholesale and retail trade, finance, insurance, and real estate, and services types of employment.

SOURCES: U.S. Department of Commerce, Bureau of the Census, *Historical Statistics of the United States, Colonial Times to 1957*, Series D–685–D–719 (Washington, D.C.: U.S.G.P.O. 1960). U.S. Department of Commerce, *Survey of Current Business*, July, 1961 and July, 1964.

fairly narrow range and over the course of the business cycle the wage position of the union sector appears to be strongest at the trough of the cycle. Following 1933, there is a marked upward trend in the wage position of the union sector and in every full cycle (with the exception of the World War II years) the pattern of wage movements in the union sector over the cycle is exactly the opposite of that in the pre-1933 period. Consequently, it is difficult to account for the agreement between the behavior of the contemporary wage structure and the predictions generated by the theoretical discussion through the existence of a long-term pattern of behavior that transcends both periods of relative union strength and weakness. In fact, it is striking that the change in behavior of the wage structure occurs precisely at the point in time at which great structural changes which significantly affected the strength of trade unionism in the United States were taking place. In short, it is tempting to impute the post-1933 behavior of the wage structure to the presence of trade unions within a public policy framework which accepts collective bargaining as an instrument of national policy for resolving labor disputes. The temptation is even stronger when the evidence of a pronounced shift in the Phillips' curve for the United States is recalled. What has been said here is perfectly consistent with the conclusions developed in Chapter Six to the effect that the annual rate of change in money wage rates in the United States was about 5 percentage points higher after 1932.

The evidence with respect to the changing wage structure of the United States is quite persuasive as a test of the theory which has been advanced. However, it is not a complete test for the theory also has implications for the behavior of employment levels in the two sectors involved. Specifically, in the upward phase of the cycle the elasticity of employment with respect to aggregate demand should be much greater in the nonunion that in the union sector. Conversely, in the downward phase of the cycle the elasticity of employment with respect to aggregate demand should be greater in the union than in the nonunion area. In Table 7–2, estimates of the elasticity of employment with respect to sector aggregate demand are presented for various cycle phases for the period 1929–61 (except for the World War II years).[19] Six different downward phases are shown, one taking place before 1933 and five after.

In the five post-1933 downward cycle phases the elasticity of employment in the union sector averages 1.55. On the other hand, in the nonunion sector there is really only one comparable observation since in all four of the postwar downturns aggregate demand (measured in real terms) in the nonunion sector rises during the downswing. In that single case, the elasticity is —0.04. To this observation might be added one instance in which aggregate demand in the nonunion sector falls on an upswing of the cycle (1946–48). In that case, the elasticity is —3.07. Admittedly, the observations which are available are few, but what ones there are seem to be quite consistent with the theory. Further, a comparison of the post-1933 observations with the single available pre-1933 case reveals additional evidence of some fundamental structural change occurring about 1933. In the downward swing between 1929 and 1933

---

[19] For the reasons noted in footnote 18, the analysis runs only through the year 1961.

the elasticity of employment in the union sector is 0.65 while that in the nonunion is 0.37. Thus, in this single case the elasticity in the union sector is significantly lower than in the post-1933 observations while the elasticity in the nonunion sector is quite a bit larger.

The data for the upward cycle phases provide no pre-1933 observations and six post-1933 cases. In these the elasticity of employment in the union sector averages 0.46. As noted earlier, there are more than six instances in which aggregate demand rose in the nonunion sector

TABLE 7–2

Elasticities of Employment with Respect to Aggregate
Demand during Different Phases of Business Cycles,
Union* and Nonunion† Sectors of Economy,
United States, 1929–61

Years	Union Sector	Nonunion Sector
Downswings of Business Cycle		
1929–1933	0.65	0.37
1937–1938	0.71	−0.04
1948–1949	1.65	0.50‡
1953–1954	0.97	1.56‡
1957–1958	0.88	0.77‡
1960–1961	3.56	0.53‡
Upswings of Business Cycle		
1933–1937	0.39	0.49
1938–1941	0.41	0.62
1946–1948	0.64	−3.07§
1949–1953	0.69	0.56
1954–1957	0.25	0.54
1958–1960	0.39	0.53

* Defined as mining, construction, manufacturing, and transportation, communications and public utilities types of employment.
† Defined as nonagricultural employment less employment in union sector.
‡ Both aggregate demand and employment rose.
§ Employment rose even though aggregate demand declined.
Source: U.S. Department of Commerce, *National Income Supplement, 1957* and *Survey of Current Business*, July, 1961 and July, 1964.

over the course of a cycle phase. Five of these occur in the normal upward swings in the business cycle and four happen during a general downswing in economic activity. In these nine instances the average elasticity of employment is 0.89 which is almost twice that of the union sector in similar situations. This is in agreement with the predictions that follow from the earlier discussion.

To summarize, the data describing employment changes appear to be quite consistent with the theory of union-nonunion interrelationships in the labor market although they are not as overwhelming as the wage structure evidence. Nevertheless, the combination of wage structure and employment change data does seem to be a rather powerful test of the theory which has been advanced. At the least, it would seem that a prima facie case for its acceptance has been developed.

VII. CONCLUSIONS

The evidence presented in this chapter provides a plausible explanation for the pronounced post-1932 shift observed in the Phillips' curve for the United States in Chapter Six. That shift would seem to be the result of an upward bias having been imparted to wage levels by the major institutional changes of the 1930's which granted exclusive collective bargaining rights to trade unions in the United States. These changes appear to have produced a significant shift in the behavior of the union-nonunion wage structure in the United States. As a consequence, the union-nonunion wage differential has progressively widened and, given some limitation on the amount of downward wage flexibility in the non-union sector of the economy, the rate of change in money wage levels associated with a given level of unemployment has risen. The end result is a much more substantial inflationary bias in the American economy.

chapter EIGHT

The Structure of Unemployment in the American Economy[1]

O NE of the most intriguing questions related to the functioning of American labor markets in the post-World War II period is whether what is thought of as the "structure" of unemployment in the United States has been changing. This issue was first raised in the early 1960's when it was felt by some that unemployment rates were showing a tendency toward a secular drift upward.[2] There was some evidence that this was the case, for the average level of unemployment in each of the three postwar business cycles that occurred between 1948 and 1960 was successively higher—being 4.2 percent from 1948 to 1953, 4.4 percent from 1953 to 1957, and 5.9 percent from 1957 to 1960. This upward movement of the average unemployment rate was explained in some quarters as being the result of unemployment levels among certain subgroups of the labor force being on the increase relative to unemployment levels in general. The broad tenor of this argument was that the increasing pace of technological advance and the demand by employers for higher levels of skill and education were creating groups of workers who were finding it increasingly difficult to successfully compete in American labor markets. This argument came to be known as

[1] The material presented in this chapter draws very heavily on a study co-authored with Zachary Dyckman of the Center for Naval Analyses. His permission to use the material in this form is gratefully acknowledged.

[2] See, in particular, Killingsworth (101).

the "structural change hypothesis" and a substantial controversy developed around it with the other side arguing that all that was involved in the upward drift in unemployment rates was an inadequacy of aggregate demand.[3] However, this is for the most part past history: the bulk of the evidence which was developed favored the inadequate demand side of the argument and, certainly, the performance of the American economy in reducing the aggregate level of unemployment below the 3.5 percent level during the later 1960's does not fit the picture painted by the structural change advocates. More specifically, evaluations of the occupational, industrial, and geographic structure of American unemployment do not reveal any tendency for the composition of unemployment to be changing to any significant extent.[4] However, in one respect the resolution of this argument was not so clear-cut; there is some evidence to suggest that some significant changes have been taking place in the age-sex composition of American unemployment.[5] Further, despite the very favorable unemployment experience of the late 1960's, there are some disturbing indications of secular drift in the aggregate unemployment rate. A comparison of unemployment levels in 1953 and 1966–67 is enlightening along these lines. In those years, unemployment among what can be thought of as the prime labor force group—white males aged 25–54—was approximately 1.8–1.9 percent. Also, these are years in which standard indices of utilization of productive capacity show roughly the same levels of utilization.[6] Despite these indications that these two time periods are very similar with respect to the adequacy of aggregate demand in the economy, the aggregate unemployment rate in 1966–67 was approximately 1 percentage point higher than it was in 1953. The question is, "Why, and what significance does this phenomenon have for the American economy?"

In order to answer these questions, it will be necessary to know the extent to which the increase in the aggregate unemployment rate that has been noted between 1953 and 1966–67 is concentrated in certain subgroups of the labor force. Given the evidence which suggests possible changes in the age-sex composition of unemployment, it would seem

---

[3] For a good review article on the controversy, see Lipsey (123). Several studies which favored the inadequate demand thesis are cited in footnote 9 of Chapter Seven. Examples of those who favored the "structural change" hypothesis are Killingsworth (101) and Stoikov (180).

[4] See Gallaway (62), Kalachek (95), and Zaidi (217).

[5] See Demsetz (35).

[6] Comparison of 1953 and 1966 levels of capacity utilization show that the Federal Reserve Board Index for manufacturing stood at 94 for 1953 and 91 for 1966 while the Wharton Index of utilization for the industrial sector was 92 in 1953 and 94 in 1966 and for the industrial and service sectors combined was 93 and 94. For details of these indices, see DeLeeuw (34), as well as Klein and Gallin (102).

appropriate to focus on the behavior of unemployment levels among these groups. If it should be found that unemployment is becoming increasingly concentrated in particular age-sex groups, it will be necessary to raise the further questions: (1) Why have these increases occurred? and (2) How permanent are they likely to be?

I. HIGHER UNEMPLOYMENT AND CHANGING LABOR FORCE COMPOSITION

It is known that different demographic groups exhibit widely varying unemployment rates. For example, women, teen-agers, and nonwhites generally experience greater unemployment than white adult males. Perhaps some, or all, of the rise in the unemployment rate associated with what approximates full employment (the full-employment unemployment rate) is attributable to greater growth in the labor force sectors that experience the highest unemployment rates. It is possible to test this hypothesis, which assumes a stable structure of sector unemployment rates, by dividing the labor force into sectors along demographic lines and forming an array of 28 sectors, dimensioned by sex, color, and age (seven classifications). An unemployment rate which standardizes for changes in the relative numbers of the various groups in the labor force can then be constructed by assigning each of the 28 1953 sector unemployment rates the labor force weight which is appropriate in 1966 and summing the product of the weights and the unemployment rates. Algebraically,

$$\bar{U} = \sum_{i=1}^{28} \frac{(U_i)_{1953} \, (LF_i)_{1966}}{(LF)_{1966}} \tag{1}$$

where $\bar{U}$ is the standardized unemployment rate, U_i and LF_i are sector unemployment and labor force, respectively, and LF is the total labor force.

When the above-described procedure is employed, the resultant sum is 3.1 percent.[7] Thus, the increase in unemployment that can be attributed to the relative increase in size of high unemployment labor force sectors is approximately 0.2 percent, a small but significant fraction of the 1 percentage point increase observed between 1953 and 1966. An examination of Tables 8–1, 8–2, and 8–3 reveals which demographic groups caused the 0.2 percentage point rise in unemployment that is attributable to changing labor force composition. The bulk of the in-

---

[7] The source of all U.S. labor force and unemployment data is U.S. Department of Labor (206).

TABLE 8–1
1953 Sector Unemployment Rates
(percent)

Sector	Age-Group							
	14–19	20–24	25–34	35–44	45–54	55–64	65–	All
White males...........	7.2	4.5	2.0	1.8	2.0	2.7	2.3	2.6
White females.........	6.6	4.1	3.1	2.3	2.3	2.5	1.4	3.1
Nonwhite males........	7.6	8.1	4.3	3.6	5.1	3.6	3.1	4.8
Nonwhite females......	8.5	5.5	4.9	3.5	2.1	2.1	1.6	4.1

SOURCE: U.S. Department of Labor (206).

TABLE 8–2
1966 Sector Labor Forces as Percentage of Total Labor Force Group

Sector	Age-Group							
	14–19	20–24	25–34	35–44	45–54	55–64	65–	All
White males.........	5.14	5.45	11.50	12.84	11.93	8.11	2.50	57.48
White females.......	3.92	4.05	4.84	6.35	6.73	4.33	1.12	31.34
Nonwhite males......	0.67	0.80	1.41	1.41	1.18	0.77	0.21	6.47
Nonwhite females...........	0.43	0.60	1.01	1.12	0.91	0.51	0.13	4.72

SOURCE: U.S. Department of Labor (206).

TABLE 8–3
1953–66 Percentage Increases in Sector Labor Forces*

Sector	Age-Group							
	14–19	20–24	25–34	35–44	45–54	55–64	65–	All
White males..............	59	58	−8	5	18	13	−18	11
White females.............	75	49	7	23	61	82	37	42
Nonwhite males............	80	57	−7	10	17	35	−14	17
Nonwhite females..........	54	43	16	27	53	83	62	38

* The 1953–1966 percentage increase in the total civilian labor force was 21 percent.
SOURCE: U.S. Department of Labor (206).

crease is due to relative increases in the female, teen-age, and 20–24 age-group labor forces.[8]

[8] Certain additional standardizations were attempted in an effort to adjust for changes in labor force composition arising out of an increased proportion of teenagers being enrolled in school and a greater proportion of females in the labor force being married in 1966 as compared to 1953. The standardization to adjust for the change in the relative number of married females showed that this had no impact on the aggregate unemployment rate. On the other hand, the adjustment for the change in the proportion of teen-agers enrolled in school rather paradoxically indicates that it should have led to a reduction in the unemployment rate among

II. HIGHER UNEMPLOYMENT AND CHANGES
IN SECTOR UNEMPLOYMENT

It has just been shown that a small portion of the 1953–66 rise in the full-employment unemployment rate can be attributed to changing labor force composition. Clearly, the remainder must be due to increases in either some or all sector unemployment rates. It has already been noted that there is one large demographic group, white males aged 25–54, which did not experience any secular rise in unemployment (henceforth, the unemployment rate among this group will be referred to as the white male prime rate). It appears, then, that there has not been a general worsening of unemployment since 1953, but increases in unemployment occurred in only some sectors. One way to ascertain which unemployment rates have risen is by regressing annual observations of sector unemployment rates against the white male prime rate and time. Using the white male prime rate instead of the aggregate unemployment rate as an independent variable eliminates a built-in time trend effect but does not lessen its effectiveness as a proxy for aggregate economic activity. Using 25 of the 28 sector unemployment rates as dependent variables (the remaining three sectors constitute the white male prime sector), the regressions appearing in Table 8–4 are obtained. The R^2's are high, with most being above 0.85 and only three below 0.50. Estimated time trends appear in Table 8–5. Teen-age unemployment rates have the largest and most statistically significant time trends. Among teen-agers, female unemployment time trends are larger than males', and nonwhite time trends are larger than white time trends. All teen-age rates are very responsive to white male prime unemployment. With the exception of the 55–64 age-group, all female unemployment rates exhibit positive time trends, while most adult male time trends are negative. There has been some increase in unemployment among those 65 and over.

A more concise view of the changing unemployment structure can be had by examining the more aggregative regressions reported in Table 8–6. These broad labor force sectors, along with the white male prime sector and those sectors followed by an X in Table 8–4, exhaust the labor force. Nonwhite male unemployment has no trend, white female

---

this group. However, such a standardization is suspect for the increase in the percentage of teen-agers enrolled in school probably also involves lower levels of general ability among such a group due to individuals being enrolled in school in 1966 who are farther down the ability hierarchy than those enrolled in 1953. If this is true, it is not legitimate to assume that the proportion of those enrolled in school can change without altering the unemployment rate among such individuals. Unfortunately, this is precisely the assumption which must be made to carry out the standardizations that have been performed here.

unemployment has a relatively small positive trend, and nonwhite female unemployment has a large positive trend.

In order to ascertain each sector unemployment rate's contribution to the increase in the full-employment unemployment rate, the 1953–66 time trends are multiplied by the 1966 labor force weights. These estimated change-in-sector unemployment rates are not "pure" in the sense

TABLE 8–4
Sector Unemployment Regression Estimates, 1953–66,
by Age, Race, and Sex

Dependent Variable	Constant*	Time	Prime Unemployment Rate	R^2
White Male				
14–19 X	3.71	0.28	1.88	0.89
	(4.7)	(6.2)	(9.1)	
20–24 X	0.75	−0.03	2.21	0.94
	(1.2)	(0.8)	(13.7)	
55–64 X	1.03	0.00	0.89	0.93
	(4.0)	(0.2)	(13.0)	
65 and over X	1.03	0.03	0.82	0.87
	(3.4)	(1.9)	(10.4)	
White Female				
14–19 X	4.20	0.41	1.17	0.88
	(5.2)	(8.7)	(5.5)	
20–24	1.48	0.17	1.16	0.90
	(3.3)	(6.4)	(9.7)	
25–34	1.08	0.07	1.09	0.93
	(3.4)	(3.9)	(12.9)	
35–44	0.84	0.07	0.92	0.90
	(2.6)	(3.5)	(10.5)	
45–54	0.94	0.01	0.82	0.94
	(4.3)	(1.1)	(14.3)	
55–64	1.71	−0.04	0.64	0.78
	(4.5)	(1.8)	(6.4)	
65 and over	0.72	0.08	0.51	0.58
	(1.4)	(2.8)	(3.7)	
Nonwhite male				
14–19 X	1.17	1.09	3.21	0.89
	(0.6)	(9.2)	(5.9)	
20–24	3.10	−0.08	3.41	0.85
	(2.1)	(0.9)	(8.6)	
25–34	−0.89	0.00	3.18	0.92
	(0.9)	(0.0)	(12.1)	
35–44	0.14	−0.03	2.40	0.91
	(0.2)	(0.7)	(11.3)	
45–54	0.79	−0.05	2.12	0.95
	(1.6)	(1.7)	(16.1)	
55–64	1.18	0.03	1.98	0.61
	(0.8)	(0.3)	(4.8)	
65 and over	−0.35	0.20	1.94	0.54
	(0.2)	(1.8)	(3.9)	

TABLE 8–4 (Continued)

| Dependent Variable | Coefficients* | | | |
	Constant*	Time	Prime Unemployment Rate	R^2
Nonwhite Female				
14–19 X...........	6.06	1.50	2.14	0.89
	(2.3)	(10.0)	(3.1)	
20–24.............	1.41	0.51	3.06	0.76
	(0.7)	(4.2)	(5.4)	
25–34.............	3.72	0.16	1.50	0.53
	(2.5)	(1.8)	(3.8)	
35–44.............	−0.24	0.21	1.86	0.84
	(0.3)	(4.0)	(7.7)	
45–54.............	1.56	0.14	0.89	0.43
	(1.4)	(2.1)	(2.9)	
55–64.............	1.68	−0.02	0.94	0.47
	(0.7)	(0.3)	(3.6)	
65 and over........	0.15	0.03	1.05	0.39
	(0.1)	(0.5)	(3.2)	

* Values in parentheses are *t*-values associated with parameters.

that they include a multiplicative effect of change in relative sector labor force and change in sector unemployment rate.[9] The sector unemployment effects on the total unemployment rate appear in Table 8–7. The sum of the estimated unemployment contributions is precisely that portion of the 1 percentage point difference between the 1953 and 1966 unemployment rates that is not explained by changing labor force composition—0.8 percentage points. Three-fourths, or 0.6 percentage points,

---

[9] The multiplicative effect is quite small. Two types of forces operate to change the aggregate unemployment rate. The compositional changes multiply the 1953 unemployment rate by a factor $(1 + dC)$ where dC denotes the rate of change in unemployment due to compositional factors. The noncompositional changes also act in a multiplicative fashion to increase the full-employment unemployment rate to $(1 + dS)$ times its 1953 level where dS denotes the rate of change in unemployment due to sectoral increases in unemployment. Together, they increase the full-employment unemployment rate to $(1 + dC)$ $(1 + dS)$ times its 1953 level. Since the total value of $(1 + dC)$ $(1 + dS)$ is 1.345 and dC is 0.069, the following expression can be solved for dS:

$$1.345 = (1 + 0.069)(1 + dS)$$

The result is 0.258 which would produce a change in the full-employment unemployment rate between 1953 and 1966 of 0.75 percentage points from this source. Thus, the multiplicative (or interaction) factor accounts for 0.05 percentage points or about 5 percent of the total change.

TABLE 8–5
Estimated 1953–66 Time Trends in Sector Unemployment Rates, by Age, Race, and Sex
(percent)

Sector	14–19	20–24	25–34	35–44	45–54	55–64	65–	20+
White males..........	3.6	−0.4	...	...	...	−0.1	0.4	...
White females..........	5.3	2.1	0.9	0.8	0.2	−0.5	1.1	0.5
Nonwhite males........	14.1	−1.4	0.0	−0.4	−0.6	0.4	2.6	0.0
Nonwhite females......	19.5	6.7	2.0	2.7	1.8	−0.2	0.4	2.2

SOURCE: Table 8–4.

TABLE 8–6
Large Sector Unemployment Regression Estimates, 1953–66

Sector	Coefficients*			
	Constant	Time	Unemployment	R^2
White female............	1.22	0.04	0.88	0.88
Aged 20 and over......	(3.6)	(2.2)	(9.8)	
Nonwhite male..........	0.28	0.00	2.62	0.94
Aged 20 and over......	(0.6)	(0.0)	(12.5)	
Nonwhite female........	1.67	0.17	1.51	0.75
Aged 20 and over......	(1.6)	(2.9)	(6.0)	

* Values in parentheses are *t*-values associated with parameters.

TABLE 8–7
Sector Unemployment Contributions to 1953–66 Rise in Aggregate Unemployment Rate

Sector	Age-Group					
	14–19	20–24	55–64	65+	20+	25–54
White male........	0.185	−0.021	−0.004	−0.011	...	−0.036
White female......	0.246	...	...	...	0.151	...
Nonwhite male............	0.096	...	...	...	−0.001	...
Nonwhite female..........	0.084	...	...	...	0.094	...

SOURCE: Tables 8–4 and 8–6.

is caused by rising teen-age unemployment and, despite the nonwhite teen-age labor force constituting only 1.1 percent of the total civilian labor force, the rise in this sector's unemployment rate is responsible for almost 0.2 percentage points. The remainder, or 0.2 percentage points, is accounted for by increased female unemployment.

III.   IMPLICATIONS OF THE INCREASES
IN SECTOR UNEMPLOYMENT RATES

The findings to this point strongly support the thesis that there have been some significant changes in the structure of American unemployment. In particular, they are quite consistent with the frequently made contention that the labor market position of the relatively unskilled and uneducated has been deteriorating in the post-World War II United States.[10] This is especially true in the case of teen-agers who are, for the most part, relatively unskilled and uneducated and who account for the great bulk of the increase in the full-employment unemployment rate. The magnitude of the teen-age unemployment problem can be gauged from the fact that the unemployment rate among teen-age males in 1953 was 7.3 percent and by 1966 it had risen to 11.2 percent. Projecting ahead, a similar upward drift in the unemployment rate of this group would lead to about 15 percent of teen-age males being unemployed in 1980 and a full-employment unemployment rate of at least 4.5 percent—or even more. Such a set of circumstances would create substantial problems for the American economy. Consequently, it is appropriate to examine whether the changes that have been observed in teen-age unemployment rates are likely to continue into the future. Since the focus of most of the arguments relating to the labor market position of the relatively unskilled and uneducated implies a negative shift in the demand for the labor of this group relative to its supply, an appropriate point of departure for explaining the sources of the apparent worsening of the labor market position of teen-agers may well be an examination of the influences on the demand for labor among subgroups such as teen-agers (and, for that matter, groups such as nonteen-age females).

Perhaps the simplest formulation of a demand relationship for labor in a particular subgroup of the labor force is

$$D_i = f(Y), \frac{dD_i}{dY} > 0 \qquad (2)$$

where D_i denotes the demand for labor in the ith subgroup and Y represents the level of aggregate demand in the economy (measured, say, by gross national product). The rationale for this relationship is quite straightforward: the aggregate demand variable simply attempts to measure shifts in the demand for subgroup labor as the result of economic growth. Of course, it is hypothesized that there is a direct relationship between subgroup employment and overall economic activity.

---

[10] One of the strongest advocates of this position is Killingsworth (**101**).

Relationship (2) is an overly simplified explanation of conditions in a subgroup labor market in that it in no way takes into consideration changes on the supply side of the market nor does it appear to consider the impact of variations in wage rates on the quantity demanded of subgroup labor. Actually, the latter can be implicitly assumed away in (2) by postulating that there is no change over time in wage rates for subgroup labor relative to wage levels for the economy as a whole. However, this is a rather debatable assumption. In an effort to incorporate both wage and supply considerations into (2) it can be modified as follows:

$$D_i = f(Y, S_i/E), \frac{\delta D_i}{\delta Y} > 0 \quad \text{and} \quad \frac{\delta D_i}{\delta (S_i/E)} > 0 \qquad (3)$$

where S_i denotes the number of workers in the ith subgroup in the civilian labor force and E indicates employment among nonteen-age males. Note the positive sign posited for the partial derivative of D_i with respect to (S_i/E). The thesis underlying this relationship is that as the supply of subgroup labor relative to employment in the prime labor force group (represented by nonteen-age male employment) increases, there is downward pressure on wage levels of the subgroup which leads to an increase in the quantity demanded of such labor. Thus, the impact of changes in subgroup relative wage levels that results from shifts in the supply of subgroup labor are included in the analysis.[11] This is certainly consistent with formal theory, although one might wish to argue that minimum wage laws and the like will limit the operation of this normal adjustment mechanism in certain subgroup labor markets. To take account of this possibility, an explicit minimum wage variable can be introduced into (3). For this purpose, the ratio of the aggregate wage rate (w) to the federal minimum wage rate (w_m) is used.[12] It is hypothesized that a positive relationship exists between this variable and D_i.

In addition to the relationships already embodied in (3), it might also be useful to include three other variables in the demand equation: (1) the level of nonteen-age male employment itself, (2) a time drift variable (t), and (3) a labor force composition variable reflecting the changing proportion of the labor force enrolled in school for teen-agers

---

[11] One may naturally ask, "Why not use wage levels directly in the demand equation?" Unfortunately, annual data for wage levels on an age basis are not available. Consequently, the impact of variations in relative wage levels among subgroups on their labor market position must be introduced in an indirect fashion.

[12] The minimum wage variable is calculated by dividing hourly wage levels in the private sector by the federal minimum wage applicable in a given year. In cases where two minima exist during a year a weighted average is used. Data for hourly wage levels in the private sector are taken from U.S. Department of Labor (207).

and, in the case of nonteen-age females, the increasing importance of married women in the labor force. Including these produces:

$$D_i = f(Y, S_i/E, w/w_m, E, t, C), \frac{\delta D_i}{\delta Y} > 0, \frac{\delta D_i}{\delta S_i/E} > 0, \frac{\delta D_i}{\delta w/w_m} > 0,$$

(4)

$$\frac{\delta D_i}{\delta E} > 0, \frac{\delta D_i}{\delta t} < 0, \frac{\delta D_i}{\delta C} < 0,$$

where C represents the labor force composition variable and the other symbols retain their previous designations.

The inclusion of the variable E in addition to the ratio S_i/E in the relationship requires some justification. Actually, the rationale of including both variables is that S_i/E is designed to capture the effect of movement along the demand curve for labor and E, by itself, attempts to measure a shift in the demand curve in addition to that already implied by changes in Y. The reasoning underlying the former has already been developed. In the latter case, it can be argued that there is some "normal" mix of relatively unskilled subgroup employment and the more skilled prime employment which exists in the economy. Consequently, changes in the number of workers employed in the prime labor force group may well produce a shift in the demand curve for subgroup labor. At the same time, there might or might not be a change in the ratio S_i/E and a movement along the demand curve.

With respect to the time variable, a negative time drift is hypothesized in line with what has been noted previously with respect to the behavior of subgroup unemployment rates. Admittedly, inclusion of a time drift variable is something of a confession of ignorance. However, it may be defended on at least two counts. First, it is useful to know whether such a time drift does exist independent of the other variables that have been introduced and, second, it may be maintained that the time drift variable serves as a proxy for a widening education gap between certain of the subgroups (teen-agers, for example) and the remainder of the labor force.[13]

Finally, some discussion of the labor force composition variable is necessary before it is possible to proceed to the empirical evaluation of the relationships shown in (4). Two of the more significant developments in the post-World War II period have been the increase in the

---

[13] Such a possibility is very real for teen-agers in that there is a limit to the number of years of education they can achieve and *still* be a teen-ager. However, in the society as a whole education can increase without being subject to this constraint. Consequently, as education continues to increase in a fashion which requires commitment of time beyond the teen-age years, the possibility of an educational gap which is unfavorable to teen-agers becomes more and more pronounced.

proportion of teen-agers in the labor force who are enrolled in school and the increase in the percentage of females in the labor force who are married. It can be argued that these groups exhibit a much higher degree of labor force mobility which leads to higher levels of frictional unemployment among them.[14] If this is the case, as the relative importance of these groups increases there could be a negative effect on observed levels of teen-age and female employment which are the measures of the quantity demanded of labor which will be used. The labor force composition variable is designed to measure this. In the case of teen-agers, it will be the proportion of them in the labor force who are enrolled in school while among nonteen-age females it will be the proportion of the female labor force which is married.[15]

IV. SOME EMPIRICAL RESULTS

The discussion of the previous section provides a basis for an empirical exploration of the demand for subgroup labor. Proceeding in a direct fashion, a simple linear least squares regression equation depicting the relationships shown in (4) might be estimated. Such a regression would take the form:

$$D_i = a + bY + c(S_i/E) + d(w/w_m) + eE + ft + gC + u \qquad (5)$$

where u denotes a random error term and the other symbols retain their previous designation. However, since the only available source of data is time series information, there are severe technical problems in estimating this equation, both from the standpoint of possible serial correlation and multicolinearity among the independent variables. Consequently, (5) is estimated in first differences form in order to minimize these difficulties. The first difference form of (5) is

$$\Delta D_i = a' + b\Delta Y + c\Delta(S_i/E) + d\Delta(w/w_m) + e\Delta E + g\Delta C + u' \qquad (6)$$

Note that there is no time variable as such in (6). This is due to the fact that if the time variable is constructed in the usual fashion, i.e., by assigning the numeral one to the first year's data, two to the second, etc., Δt is a constant. Actually, if the time variable in (5) is signficant, it will be reflected in (6) in the form of a nonzero intercept

---

[14] In addition, this hypothesis is attractive on the grounds that increased school enrollment may siphon off the relatively more capable young people from the labor market and in the process produce a deterioration in the quality of the labor being supplied to the market by teen-agers. Such a case can be more easily made for males whose aggregate labor force participation rate fell between 1953 and 1966. At any rate, the hypothesis is certainly worth consideration.

[15] The data for calculating this variable are taken from U.S. Department of Labor (208) Table B–1 of the Statistical Appendix.

term. This explains why the specific intercept term, a', is included in (6).[16]

When a regression of the form shown in (6) is estimated from available data covering the period 1947–66 for teen-age males, the results are:[17]

$$\Delta D_{mt} = -67.9606 + 3.9768 \ \Delta Y + 339.4403 \ \Delta(S_{mt}/E)$$
$$\phantom{\Delta D_{mt} = -67.9606} (3.20) (8.82)$$
$$- 0.0199 \ \Delta(w/w_m) + 0.0955 \ \Delta E - 0.3651 \ \Delta(C_s)_{mt} \qquad (7)$$
$$ (0.05) (3.02) (0.77)$$
$$R^2 = 0.94$$

Generally speaking, the results are highly significant in a statistical sense. Over 90 percent of the variance is explained in a first difference type regression and three of the five regression coefficients for the independent variables are significant at or beyond the 1 percent level. However, two of the coefficients are not significant at any acceptable level: those associated with the minimum wage and proportion of teen-age males enrolled in school (denoted by $(C_s)_{mt}$) variables.[18] Consequently, (7) was reestimated without these variables with the following results:

$$\Delta D_{mt} = -72.7684 + 3.9288 \ \Delta Y + 341.3794 \ \Delta(S_{mt}/E)$$
$$\phantom{\Delta D_{mt} = -72.7684} (3.31) (9.24)$$
$$+ 0.0943 \ \Delta E, R^2 = 0.94 \qquad (8)$$
$$ (3.11)$$

Omission of the two insignificant variables has little effect on the

---

[16] If there were no other factors at work, the constant term in (6) would be equal to e (the coefficient of the time drift variable in (5)). However, since the change in aggregate demand variable is expressed in absolute terms and not as a growth rate, some negative time trend may appear as the result of technological change. For example, if there were no change in any of the independent variables (including real gross national product), advances in productive techniques would reduce the overall demand for labor which (given the assumption of no change in E) would have to be absorbed by marginal labor force groups such as teen-agers. Thus, the presence of a significant time trend does not in itself demonstrate demand deterioration due to unusual factors being operative in the markets for subgroup labor. The magnitude of the time drift is crucial for this matter.

[17] The value in parentheses beneath each regression coefficient is the t-value associated with that coefficient.

[18] It can be argued that the insignificance of the minimum wage variable is due to its impact already being measured by one of the other variables. Specifically, the (S/E) variable functions as a measure of the pressure on wage levels to change. Consequently, if minimum wages are a factor, they would tend to reduce the size of the coefficient of this variable. This argument receives support from other evidence which strongly suggests that minimum wages do have a differential employment effect in subgroup labor markets. A detailed analysis of these effects is contained in Chapin and Adie (29). The results reported there are summarized in Adie and Chapin (30).

TABLE 8-8

Changes in Demand for and Relative Supply of Teen-Agers, by Sex, and Nonteen-Age Women, Change in Real Gross National Product, and Change in Employment of Nonteen-Age Males, 1947–66

Years	ΔD_{mt} (000's)	ΔD_{ft} (000's)	ΔD_{fmt} (000's)	ΔE (000's)	ΔY billions of $	$\Delta \dfrac{S_{mt}}{E}$	$\Delta \dfrac{S_{ft}}{E_f}$	$\Delta \dfrac{S_{fmt}}{E}$
1947–1948	111	8	581	605	13.8	0.0012	−0.0032	0.0112
1948–1949	−216	−101	200	−579	0.4	−0.0018	−0.0052	0.0181
1949–1950	97	−51	688	592	31.2	0.0007	−0.0105	0.0116
1950–1951	−30	89	748	230	28.1	−0.0048	−0.0037	0.0123
1951–1952	−79	−10	387	−46	11.7	−0.0014	−0.0037	0.0070
1952–1953	11	−27	208	718	17.7	−0.0017	−0.0044	−0.0040
1953–1954	−140	−89	−166	−661	−5.8	0.0009	0.0005	0.0154
1954–1955	96	64	1002	891	31.0	0.0005	−0.0037	0.0105
1955–1956	157	151	766	690	8.1	0.0023	0.0058	0.0110
1956–1957	−33	31	283	24	6.4	0.0000	0.0002	0.0064
1957–1958	−119	−89	−8	−829	−5.2	0.0016	−0.0024	0.0200
1958–1959	190	97	481	857	28.1	0.0025	0.0013	−0.0030
1959–1960	120	13	581	276	11.8	0.0031	0.0045	0.0113
1960–1961	35	190	192	−202	9.5	0.0027	0.0067	0.0141
1961–1962	101	81	395	473	32.6	−0.0002	0.0024	−0.0011
1962–1963	2	−39	564	436	21.2	0.0014	−0.0046	0.0090
1963–1964	173	93	646	636	29.0	0.0024	0.0004	0.0067
1964–1965	360	199	728	535	34.4	0.0070	0.0052	0.0069
1965–1966	360	404	877	245	33.3	0.0065	0.0131	0.0138

Source: U.S. Department of Labor (208).

coefficients of the other three variables and the proportion of the variance which is explained remains unchanged. The basic data used to estimate (8) are provided in Table 8–8.

The significant results shown in (8) provide a basis for evaluating the causes of the increase in male teen-age unemployment in the past as well as the future prospects for the labor market for this group. First, it is possible with this information to evaluate the possibility that the upward drift in the unemployment rate among male teen-agers is the result of a deficiency of demand for such workers. Of course, in one sense

FIGURE 8–1

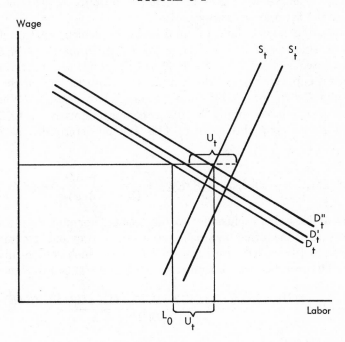

there has to be a lack of demand for teen-agers but it is just as valid to say that there is an excess supply of these workers. What we propose to do here is to establish specific definitions which will enable us to distinguish between a lack of demand and an excess supply in some meaningful fashion. To illustrate the definitions, Figure 8–1, which depicts the supply and demand conditions in a hypothetical teen-age labor market, is useful. In that diagram, the solid curves labeled S_t and D_t delineate the supply of and demand for male teen-age labor. A wage rate w_0 is posited which produces employment L_0 and unemployment U_t. Now, introduce a shift in the supply curve to S'_t where S'_t is just sufficient to keep the ratio S_t/E constant at wage rate w_0. It is presumed that this is a secular supply shift and that E itself is increasing. This implies a shift in the demand curve D_t—a shift which will be due to the change in E as well as any change in gross national product (Y). The magnitude of this demand shift will be crucial in the attempt to distinguish between a lack of demand for and an excess supply of teen-age labor. If the demand shift is to, say, D'_t, the demand for labor will not be sufficient to avoid either a fall in the wage rate w_0 and/or an increase in unemployment. This is called a deficiency of demand situation. On the other hand, if the demand shift is to D''_t, the demand for teen-age labor will be such that it will produce either an increase in w_0 and/or a decrease in unemployment. In such a case, an increase in unemployment could only occur if the actual shift in the supply curve were greater than the shift to S'_t. This is what is meant by the term excess supply.

The question now is how to empirically implement these definitions so as to be able to say whether the upward drift in male teen-age unemployment rates between 1953 and 1966 was the result of a lack of demand or an excess supply or both. This can be done with the use of the regression results shown in (8) by simply asking the question, "What level of male teen-age labor supply in 1966 is compatible with the 1953 unemployment rate among this group?" This can be determined as follows: let

$$\Delta (S/E)_{53\text{-}66} = (S/E)_{66} - (S/E)_{53} = \frac{(D)_{53} + \Delta D}{(1 - U_t)(E)_{66}} - (S/E)_{53} \quad (9)$$

where D and S refer exclusively to the demand for and supply of male teen-agers and the other symbols retain their previous meanings.

Now, from (8) we have an expression for ΔD which can be substituted into (9). The resultant expression can then be rearranged to produce

$$\Delta (S/E)_{53\text{-}66} = \frac{(D)_{53} + Na + b\Delta Y + d\Delta E - (1 - U_t)(E)_{66}(S/E)_{53}}{(1 - U_t)(E)_{66} - c} \quad (10)$$

where N denotes the number of years in the time interval under consideration. If we assume U_t at the 1953 level, (10) can be used to estimate the change in (S/E) between 1953 and 1966 which would be compatible with no upward drift in the male teen-age unemployment rate. This estimate can then be used to calculate the 1966 supply of male teen-age labor which the changes in E and Y would permit without there being an increase in U_t. If this value is *lower* than that which would maintain a constant value for (S/E), a deficiency of demand for male teen-age labor would be indicated. However, if it is *higher*, this would be suggestive that the secular drift in male teen-age unemployment is necessarily the result of increases in labor supply which are both larger than those which would maintain a constant value for (S/E) but are also larger than those which the increases in demand would tolerate without any increase in unemployment. This is precisely what was called an excess supply condition in Figure 8–1.

When the actual estimate of $\Delta(S/E)_{\Delta U_t=0}$ is calculated the result for teen-age males is $+0.0118$ which yields an estimated $[(S)_{66}]_{\Delta U_t=0}$ of 3,637,000 teen-age males. By comparison, if (S/E) had remained constant, $[(S)_{66}]$ would have been 3,122,000. According to the previous definitions, this implies an excess supply condition in the male teen-age labor market. The full extent of the excess supply of such labor may be gauged by the fact that the actual supply in 1966, $[(S)_{66}]_a$, was 4,474,000. Thus, $[(S)_{66}]_a$ exceeded $[(S)_{66}]_{\Delta(S/E)=0}$ by 1,352,000 workers and $[(S)_{66}]_{\Delta U_t=0}$ by 837,000 workers. Considering this bulge in the supply of male teen-age labor, it is really remarkable that even more unemployment did not develop among this group. For example, if $[(S)_{66}]_a = [(S)_{66}]_{\Delta U_t=0}$, the total amount of unemployment would have been 269,000 while actual 1966 unemployment was only 502,000. Thus, a difference between $[(S)_{66}]_a$ and $[(S)_{66}]_{\Delta U_t=0}$ of 837,000 only produced an increase in unemployment of 233,000 which means that about 72 percent of the excess supply (over and above $[(S)_{66}]_{\Delta U_t=0}$) of male teen-age labor was absorbed by the labor market through its normal adjustment mechanisms. The proportion of the difference between $[(S)_{66}]_a$ and $[(S)_{66}]_{\Delta U_t=0}$ which is absorbed in this fashion reflects among other things (1) the substitutability of male teen-age labor for the more skilled nonteen-age male labor and (2) the degree of wage flexibility in the market for such labor.

The general picture created by this discussion of the teen-age male labor market is one of general excess supply. This should not be surprising in view of the rather high birthrates which marked the immediate post-World War II period. The impact of such birthrates on relative labor supplies was accentuated by the relatively low birthrates that marked the immediate pre-World War II era. As a consequence of these factors, the value (S/E) rose from 0.0715 in 1953 to 0.1025 in 1966 which is simply a greater increase than present labor market mechanisms could accommodate without any increase in unemployment rates.[19]

If we accept the excess supply explanation for the upward drift in male teen-age unemployment rates between 1953 and 1966, the recent drop in birthrates would seem to suggest that the trend observed between 1953 and 1966 may be a temporary one. Evidence that this may be the case is given by the Census Bureau's projections of population and labor force for 1980. Using series B estimates the value of (S/E) can be estimated to be about 0.0954 in 1980[20]—a decline of 0.0071 from the 1966 level. This would seem to bode well for the future. To further explore the possibility that the time drift in male teen-age unemployment

---

[19] For a good description of the cycle of population growth which underlies this phenomenon, see Richard A. Easterlin (46).

[20] See U.S. Department of Labor (208), pp. 204 and 210.

is transitory, the relationship shown in (8) can be used to estimate the change in gross national product which would be necessary to produce in 1980 the 1953 male teen-age unemployment rate. The expression which yields this value is

$$\Delta(Y)_{U_t = (U)53} =$$

$$\frac{(S/E)_{80}(1 - U_t)_{53}(E)_{80} - Na - d\Delta(E)_{66-80} - c\Delta(S/E)_{66-80} - (D)_{66}}{b} \quad (11)$$

where all symbols retain their previous meaning. This calculation yields an estimate of the increase in real gross national product which would be necessary to return the male teen-age unemployment rate to its 1953 level of $277 billion. Such an increase requires only a 2.6 percent annual growth rate in the American economy which would certainly seem feasible in light of our recent experience. Consequently, it would seem that a reasonably optimistic view may be taken with respect to the prospects for improving the labor market position of male teen-agers.

But, what about the matter of labor market conditions affecting both female teen-agers and female nonteen-agers? To analyze these the procedure used in assessing the male teen-age labor market can simply be replicated. Commencing with teen-age females, the same type regression shown in (8) was estimated except that the ratio of the supply of female teen-age labor to employment among female nonteen-agers is substituted for the (S/E) variable used earlier.[21] The results are:

$$\Delta D_{ft} = -25.2272 + 4.6058 \ \Delta Y + 173.16 \ \Delta(S_{ft}/E_f) - 0.0077 \ \Delta E,$$
$$\quad\quad\quad (3.55) \quad\quad\quad (8.55) \quad\quad\quad\quad (0.23) \quad\quad\quad (12)$$
$$R^2 = 0.88$$

Again, the results are quite significant, particularly for a first difference relationship, with almost 90 percent of the variance being explained and the coefficients of two of the three independent variables being significant at the 1 percent level. The coefficient for the E variable is not significant but it was retained in the regression for the sake of consistency in the models being used. When this regression is employed to estimate the 1966 supply of female teen-age labor which would be consistent with the 1953 unemployment rate $([(S_{ft})_{66}]_{\Delta U_{ft}=0})$, the result is a value of 2,964,000. This

---

[21] One could argue just as well that the supply variable should be one that measures the availability of female teenagers relative to the prime male labor force group. However, since it is difficult to maintain on an a priori basis that one variable is superior to the other, the choice was made on the basis of the pragmatic consideration of "goodness" of fit. When regressions similar to (7) were estimated, the school enrollment and minimum wage variables again were not significant. Therefore, they have been dropped from the regression and the form shown in (8) is all that is reported.

compares with a value of 2,663,000 for $[(S_{ft})_{66}]_{\Delta(S/E)=0}$ and an actual labor supply of 3,354,000. Thus, a situation similar to that found in the case of male teen-agers also exists among female teen-agers, namely, an excess supply of female teen-agers relative to 1953 conditions. The one fundamental difference in this case is the impact this excess supply has had on unemployment levels. Whereas, the normal functioning of the labor market was able to absorb 72 percent of the difference between $[(S)_{66}]_a$ and $[(S)_{66}]_{\Delta U_t=0}$ in the case of males, it could accommodate only 40 percent of this difference among females. This probably reflects a lower degree of substitutability of teen-age female labor for other types of labor in the economy.

Looking ahead to 1980, it can be calculated that in order to return the female teen-age unemployment rate to its 1953 level an increase in real gross national product of $299 billion would be required. This is somewhat greater than that required for teen-age males but it still involves an annual growth rate of only 2.8 percent between 1966 and 1980. Again, this does not appear to be an impossible goal to achieve. Consequently, the same optimistic view warranted with respect to the male teen-age labor market would appear to be appropriate for the female teen-age labor market.

Finally, with respect to nonteen-age female labor (which was the other source of an increase in the full-employment unemployment rate between 1953 and 1966), the same basic regression was estimated with the following results:[22]

$$\Delta D_{fnt} = -119.5435 + 10.2808\ \Delta Y + 311.2544\ \Delta(S_{fnt}/E)$$
$$(3.41) \qquad\qquad (5.89)$$
$$+ 0.5010\ \Delta E,\ R^2 = 0.89 \qquad (13)$$
$$(5.51)$$

Again, about 90 percent of the variance is explained and all three of the regression coefficients are significant at the 1 percent level. Thus, the model seems to perform about equally well in explaining behavior in all three of the subgroup labor markets which have been considered. Similarly, when the past and future status of this market for labor are evaluated, the results are like those found in the case of teen-agers. Specifically, the value of $[(S_{fnt})_{66}]_{\Delta U_{fnt}=0}$ is 22,257,000 as compared to a value of 19,157,000 for $[(S_{fnt})_{66}]_{\Delta(S/E)=0}$ and an actual supply of 24,426,000. Thus, again, an excess supply situation is indicated. In fact, the difference between the actual supply and the 1953 unemployment rate supply is 2,169,000 workers. That this excess did not produce an even greater drift

---

[22] When minimum wage and proportion of married females in the labor force variables are included in the regression, they are not significant and, consequently, have been omitted from the regression results which are reported.

in the nonteen female unemployment rate is due to the fact that the market was able to absorb 87 percent of this excess supply. This relatively large adjustment response is probably attributable to a much greater degree of substitutability between nonteen female and nonteen male labor than exists between teen-age and nonteen male labor. At any rate, this substantial adjustment response undoubtedly has eased the stresses and strains on the labor market generated by the excess supply of female nonteen labor.

The similarity between the situation prevailing in the nonteen female and teen-age labor markets is confirmed when the change in gross national product required between 1966 and 1980 to return the nonteen female unemployment rate to its 1953 level is calculated. The result is a value of $243 billion which would require an annual growth rate of about 2.3 percent in this period. Thus, the status of the nonteen female labor market generates an even more optimistic picture than that found in the teen-age labor markets.

V. CONCLUSIONS

The main thrust of this chapter has been in the direction of providing answers to three inquiries: (1) Has there been an upward drift in the full-employment unemployment rate in the United States? (2) if so, What are the causes of such a drift?, and (3) What are the prospects with respect to any change in the full-employment unemployment rate between now and 1980? The answer to the first of these questions is a clear and unequivocal "yes." Between 1953 and 1966 the full-employment unemployment rate apparently increased by 1 full percentage point which is about a 33 percent increase. Twenty percent of this increase, or 0.2 percentage points, is attributable to changes in the demographic composition of the labor force. The other 80 percent results from relative increases in unemployment rates in the teen-age and nonteen-age female sectors of the labor force.

The answer to the second question involves an analysis of the reasons for the upward drift in unemployment rates in the teen-age and nonteen-age female labor markets. The framework of that analysis emphasizes distinguishing between excess supply and deficiency of demand conditions in these markets. On the basis of the definitions of excess supply and deficiency of demand that have been developed, it is clear that the increases in unemployment rates between 1953 and 1966 among teen-age males and all females are the result of substantial excess supplies of labor in those markets. Among teen-agers this excess supply is the aftermath of a demographic wave passing through the population due to the high birthrates of the immediate post-World War II period and the low birthrates of the immediate pre-World War II years. In the case of nonteen females, the bulge in supply is the result of increases in labor force participation among females.[23]

The significance of the excess supply explanation lies in the fact that future increases in labor supply will be much less substantial among teen-agers due to recent declines in birthrates and less among nonteen females because of anticipated greater stability in female labor force participation rates.[24] Consequently, it is not surprising to find that, when estimates are developed of the change in gross national product (in real terms) which would be required to reduce unemployment rates among these subgroups to their 1953 levels, the growth rates necessary to accomplish this objective by 1980 seem reasonably capable of being achieved. Specifically, the range of such estimates varies from a low of 2.3 percent for nonteen females to a high of 2.8 percent for teen-age females. Overall, this suggests that the upward drift in the full-employment unemployment rate which is due to increases in sectoral unemployment rates is essentially a transitory phenomenon and that with only modest growth rates the drift will reverse itself between now and 1980 as the pressure from the supply side of these sectors eases. Further, as these supply adjustments take place, about one half (or 0.1 percentage points) of the 1953–66 increase in unemployment which has been attributed directly to changes in demographic weights will also be eliminated. This suggests that the 1980 full-employment unemployment rate will be about 3 percent rather than the 4.5 percent mentioned earlier as a possible full-employment unemployment rate. This is certainly a much more optimistic appraisal of the overall status of the labor market than that which is obtained by a simple extrapolation of the 1953–66 trends in sector unemployment rates and suggests that at least from the labor market side there will not be changes in the next few years which will make more difficult the choice between unemployment and price inflation in the American economy.

---

[23] Between 1948 and 1966 the civilian labor force participation rate for females 16 years of age and over rose from 31.3 percent to 39.2 percent. Since there was no change to speak of in female labor force participation rates among the 16–19 age-group, this increase reflects almost entirely a shift in the degree of labor force attachment among nonteen females. Data are from U.S. Department of Labor (208), p. 205.

[24] The Census series B population projections indicate an expected change in the female labor force participation rate between 1965 and 1980 of about 3 percentage points. This is in contrast to the observed increase between 1948 and 1966 of almost 8 percentage points. See U.S. Department of Labor (208), p. 268.

chapter NINE

Hidden Unemployment in the American Economy

I N Chapters One and Two extensive references were made to the phenomenon of cyclical variations in the labor supply within the United States. These variations involve the operation of what are more popularly called "discouragement" and "added worker" effects among members of the labor force—concepts that have a substantial history in the literature of economics commencing with Woytinsky's (216) speculations about aggregate labor supply during the depths of the Great Depression of the 1930's. The recent work of Dernburg and Strand, Tella, and Barth, among others, has done much to clarify the operation of these effects with their general conclusion being that depressed economic conditions cause workers to leave the labor force (the "discouragement" effect) more rapidly than they induce them to enter (the "added worker" effect). Further, their research has rather clearly indicated that certain labor force subgroups experience these effects much more strongly than do other groups. In particular, the very young, the elderly, and females have been shown to be quite susceptible to the operation of the "discouragement" effect.[1]

The findings of this recent research are of particular importance since they imply that certain subgroups of the labor force are more seriously affected than others by cyclical variations in the general level of economic activity. Such differential sensitivity raises the intriguing question of

---

[1] In particular, see Dernburg and Strand (37).

TABLE 9–1

Interregional Flows of Labor, 1957–58, White Male Workers Employed in both 1957 and 1960

Region of Major Job in 1957	Total	Region of Major Job in 1958									
		New England	Middle Atlantic	South Atlantic	East North Central	East South Central	West North Central	West South Central	Mountain	Pacific	Not Employed
Total...............	282,543	18,683	62,819	30,768	62,036	12,926	21,678	21,249	9,801	32,772	9,811
New England.........	19,503	18,100	417	124	120	13	20	20	13	50	626
Middle Atlantic......	64,658	292	60,668	688	562	104	136	91	73	255	1,789
South Atlantic.......	31,363	90	479	28,574	431	270	88	128	44	115	1,144
East North Central...	65,076	90	674	633	59,934	449	372	233	130	394	2,167
East South Central...	13,161	29	84	306	187	11,701	51	144	28	41	590
West North Central...	22,650	20	125	116	364	40	20,520	241	169	210	845
West South Central...	22,133	21	108	145	135	195	174	19,261	223	204	967
Mountain............	10,014	6	49	56	96	28	132	202	8,678	330	437
Pacific.............	33,985	35	215	126	207	126	185	229	443	31,173	1,246

SOURCE: Social Security Administration, One Percent Continuous Work History Sample.

why it occurs. Fortunately, the labor mobility data derived from the social security records which were used in exploring patterns of geographic movement of labor are also useful for examining the phenomenon of labor force withdrawal in the face of a downturn in the business cycle. This is due to the fact that data similar to those for the period 1957–60 are available for the period 1957–58 for exactly the same sample of workers.[2] The significance of this lies in 1958's being a year which can be considered to be the peak unemployment year for the 1957–60 business cycle. Table 9–1 shows the appropriate data for white male workers in the economy.[3] For our purposes, the column entitled "not employed" is of primary importance since, for the most part, the workers recorded as being "not employed" in 1958 have, in reality, withdrawn from the labor force.[4] Thus, these workers in a very real sense represent individuals who have chosen to withdraw from the labor force in the face of the economic adversity of the 1958 cycle downturn. As such, they are indicative of the operation of the "discouragement" effect in the American economy.[5] However, since the sample of workers is defined

---

[2] Remember that only workers employed in both 1957 and 1960 are included in the sample.

[3] To refresh the memory, workers are classified by region of major job, where region of major job is defined as the region of employment in which a worker received the greatest amount of wages in employment covered by the Old Age Survivors Disability and Health Insurance system. Similarly, the classification by industry of major job shown in Table 9–3 is determined in the same fashion.

[4] There are three possible reasons why being recorded as not employed in 1958 may not reflect labor force withdrawal. First, an individual could have been employed in 1957 and entered military service in that year, been in the military throughout 1958, and then left the military in time to become employed during 1960. Second, workers might be employed in employment covered by the OASDHI system in 1957 and during that year might leave such employment and shift to noncovered employment, remain there during 1958, and then might move back into covered employment before or during 1960. And last, workers employed in 1957 could have become unemployed in that year, remained in that status all through 1958, and then become reemployed before or during 1960. From various data it can be estimated that the absolute "maximum" impact of these factors could account for perhaps one half of the observed nonemployment in 1958. However, this is a maximum possible impact and would require a very special set of conditions. My own feeling is that about one fourth of the observed nonemployment might be attributable to these factors. For further details about the maximum possible impact of these factors, see Gallaway (59, chap. 8).

[5] The fact that a part of the observed nonemployment in 1958 does not reflect labor force withdrawal raises the possibility that the data for nonemployment do not accurately reflect the operation of the discouragement effect. In particular, the fact that 3.47 percent of the sample is nonemployed in 1958 raises some questions: the actual decline in the labor force participation rate of white males in 1958 was only 0.5 percentage points, and Barth's (5) results suggest that the increase in aggregate male unemployment of 2.7 percentage points between 1957 and 1958 would have produced a decline of only 1.04 percentage points in their labor force participation rate. However, certain adjustments need to be made before the 3.47 percent figure can be considered to be strictly comparable with normal labor force participation rates. First, the sample includes workers employed at any time during

in such a way as to not include workers who were not employed in 1957 but were in 1958, no information is provided on the operation of the "added worker" effect. This presents no major complication in that the available evidence clearly indicates that the discouragement effect dominates the added worker effect.[6]

The data of Table 9–1 provide some insight into regional differences in the operation of the discouragement effect. For example, the maximum effect is found in the East South Central States where 4.48 percent of

---

both of the years 1957 and 1960. Restricting the sample to this group means that about 58 percent of the average male labor force in 1958 is considered. Thus, the 3.47 percent nonemployment would, of itself, produce only about a 2 percentage point change in labor force participation rates. Second, if our estimate is correct that 25 percent of our observed nonemployment does not reflect labor force withdrawal, we would expect only about a 1.5 percentage point change in labor force participation rates from this source. Last, the standard annual measures of labor force participation rates are averages of monthly "point in time" estimates as contrasted with the sample data which measure employment that occurs at any time during the year. Consequently, it is possible—indeed quite likely—that individuals observed as nonemployed in 1958 have sought employment during a part of the year and, thus, would be counted in the labor force in the point in time estimates, while still being recorded in the OASDHI sample as nonemployed. This group would consist of those officially measured as unemployed during part of the year but not during all of the year. If the average duration of unemployment is about 13 weeks, we should probably adjust the estimate of the effect on labor force participation of nonemployment in 1958, as recorded in the sample, by an additional 10 to 20 percent. This would reduce the estimated impact to about 1.2–1.3 percentage points, which begins to be roughly comparable with Barth's estimates of the impact of the 1958 cycle swing on labor force participation. At least, the estimates are not outlandishly in disagreement although there is probably still an element in the estimates which, even after corrections, does not reflect labor force withdrawal in the sense that is implied in the concept of the discouragement effect.

The likely presence of a nondiscouragement effect component in the data does not generate any problems if it is random in nature. However, if it is not, it could call into question any empirical relationships that are developed. To test for the randomness of this component the Barth (5) and Dernburg and Strand (37) findings were used as a basis for comparing the variation observed in the OASDHI measure of nonemployment with the variation they find in the operation of the discouragement effect. The expectation is that, if the data at hand do reflect the operation of the discouragement effect and the nondiscouragement effect component is truly random, observed variations in the OASDHI measure of 1958 nonemployment should be systematically related in a positive fashion to the variations in the operation of the discouragement effect observed by others. When Barth's coefficients for his discouragement effect variable for different age classes are compared with our percentage of nonemployment in 1958 by age class (in those instances where his results are statistically significant—ages 16–64) a correlation between the two of +0.81 is found. This is significant at the 1 percent level. Similarly, when a comparison is made between variations in our nonemployment measure and the Dernburg-Strand estimates of the combined impact of the discouragement and added worker effects by age class, a correlation of +0.74 is found. These results indicate that the OASDHI data behave generally in accord with what would be expected on the basis of other investigations. This suggests that the nondiscouragement effect component is essentially a random one.

[6] See Barth (5) and Dernburg and Strand (37).

the males employed in both 1957 and 1960 were not employed in 1958 while the minimum effect is 2.77 percent in the Middle Atlantic States.[7] Similarly, substantial differences in the magnitude of this effect can be observed when different age and industry of major job in 1957 comparisons are made. In Table 9–2 data describing age differences in the percentage of sample workers not employed in 1958 are shown for white males.[8] These comparisons are quite reassuring, for the differences they show are strikingly consistent with those found in both the Dernburg-Strand and Barth estimates of age variations in the combined impact of the discouragement and added worker effects.[9] This is indicative that

TABLE 9–2
Percent of Male White Workers Employed in 1957
but Not Employed in 1958, by Age

Age	Percent Not Employed in 1958
Less than 20	18.82
20–24	6.78
25–29	4.47
30–34	2.86
35–39	2.45
40–44	2.50
45–49	2.25
50–54	2.22
55–59	2.25
60–64	2.55
65 and over	3.95

SOURCE: Social Security Administration, One Percent Continuous Work History Sample.

the estimates of nonemployment in 1958 which have been presented are reasonably accurate indicators of the relative impact of the discouragement effect.

Some further insight into the pattern of variation in the percentage of sample workers who were not employed in 1958 can be obtained from Table 9–3 which shows this percentage for white males by industry of major job in 1957 of the workers concerned. The data contained in this table indicate a substantial amount of variation across industry of employment in 1957. Thus, another dimension is added to the matter of differential sensitivity to variations in general levels of economic ac-

---

[7] The percentages themselves are not shown in Table 9–1. They are: New England, 3.21; Middle Atlantic. 2.77; South Atlantic, 3.65; East North Central, 3.33; East South Central, 4.48; West North Central, 3.73; West South Central, 4.37; Mountain, 4.36; and Pacific, 3.67.

[8] The focus is restricted to white males due to limitations of sample size in the extended analysis and because the relationships developed here simply do not hold for Negro males. This will be discussed in more detail in Chapter Eleven.

[9] See footnote 5 for details.

TABLE 9–3
Percent of Male White Workers Employed in 1957 but Not
Employed in 1958, by Industry

Industry	Percent Not Employed in 1958
Agriculture.............................	11.28
Mining.................................	3.15
Construction...........................	4.90
Manufacturing	
Durable goods.......................	2.14
Nondurable goods....................	2.12
Transportation, communication,	
and public utilities.....................	2.02
Wholesale and retail trade................	4.20
Finance, insurance, and real estate.........	2.37
Services................................	4.79
Government.............................	5.01

SOURCE: Social Security Administration, One Percent Continuous Work History Sample.

tivity. In fact, such substantial variations have been shown in the degree of response of the sample workers to the economic downturn of 1958 that one's curiosity is piqued as to what underlies these differences.

To answer that question we turn first to the theoretical foundation of the phenomenon of the discouragement effect—a foundation which arises rather naturally out of the formal theory of individual behavior in the labor market. Assume that workers attempt to maximize a utility function with leisure and income arguments. For purposes of ease of discussion such a utility function is depicted by the indifference map of Figure 9–1 in which L_0 represents the maximum amount of leisure available to an individual in the time period under consideration, T_0 indicates the amount of nonwork related or transfer payment income available to an individual if he chooses not to work,[10] and L_0Y_0 is an income opportunity constraint whose slope is determined by the wage rate available to the individual in his current employment. In order for a worker to be included in the sample data under discussion here the wage rate he faces in the market in 1957 must be great enough to place him on a higher indifference curve than that which he can attain simply through the receipt of the transfer payment income T_0. Such a situation is indicated in Figure 9–1 and the equilibrium combination of income and leisure is Y_eL_e. This may be viewed as representing a worker employed in the year 1957.

At this point, we may introduce a downturn in the business cycle which increases the general unemployment rate and leads to a displace-

---

[10] This should not properly include unemployment compensation benefits, since it is generally the intent of this system to provide economic support for those still in the labor force but unable to find employment.

FIGURE 9–1

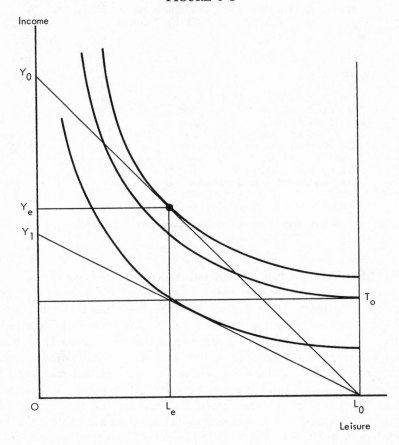

ment from employment of certain workers. Those affected in this fashion are faced with the necessity of locating another job at a time when job opportunities are not particularly abundant. As a consequence, it can be anticipated that the "search" costs implicit in locating a new job may be fairly substantial where by "search" costs we mean such things as the time and personal effort which must be expended in the search process as well as any money costs incurred therein. In addition, it is highly likely that if an individual's efforts at finding another job are not immediately fruitful, his perception of the wage rate that he can effectively command in the labor market will be altered in such a fashion as to lead him to believe he can only find work at a lower wage rate than that which he was receiving in his previous employment. The impact of both of these factors, i.e., the "search" costs and changing perceptions of the effective wage, is to cause the income opportunity constraint shown in Figure 9–1 to either shift or rotate downward, say, to the position L_0Y_1. Quite obviously, if this rotation or shift is substantial enough and if the individual has available to him certain nonwork related sources of transfer payment income (T_0, for example), a position will be approached at which the worker feels that it is in his own best interest to withdraw from the labor force rather than continuing to seek work.[11] Such a situation is depicted in the case of the income opportunity constraint L_0Y_1 of Figure 9–1.

The foregoing discussion suggests the theoretical fashion in which the discouragement effect operates to shift workers out of the labor force during downswings in the general level of economic activity. At this point, it is interesting to speculate about the differential impact of the forces which underlie the discouragement effect on different subgroups of the labor force. To begin, it might be noted that some of these groups may, on the average, have different leisure-income preference functions and that because of this it requires less of a shift in the income-opportunity constraint to move them out of the labor force. Or, it might be argued that various subgroups will have different amounts of transfer payment income available to them relative to their work related income and, consequently, will be differentially sensitive to the impact of changes in the income-opportunity constraint. Examples of this might be females and very young members of the labor force who may have substantial access to what can be thought of as intrafamily transfer payments. In short, they may well have access to the income of a primary wage earner and, as a result, be more willing to withdraw from the labor force than a primary earner himself.

While these speculations about the nature of the sources of differential discouragement effects in the American economy suggest some interesting hypotheses, they do not exhaust the range of possible explanations for the varying intensity of the discouragement effect. In particular, the hypotheses described to this point ignore one very important potential source of variation in the degree to which the discouragement phenomenon affects subgroups of the labor force, viz, differences in the position of the income-opportunity constraint prior to its being shifted by the pressures of the business cycle downturn. In short, it is quite possible that the discouragement effect has a much more substantial impact on individuals whose wage rate in their previous employment was relatively low. This might be expected on several counts. First, individuals with low levels of wages in their previous employment are apt to be relatively unskilled and the likelihood of a relatively unskilled individual finding another job during a business cycle downturn is undoubtedly less than that for a highly skilled worker. Consequently, the search costs for other

---

[11] As the income opportunity constraint is rotated and/or shifted, the worker is moved toward the boundary case of all leisure and no work, i.e., labor force withdrawal.

employment are probably greater and the tendency for the worker's perception of the wage rate he can command in the labor market to change is likely to be greater in the case of workers with low initial earnings levels. Second, the fact that those who are relatively low wage are prone to be relatively unskilled suggests the possibility that the incidence of unemployment is greater among this group. Therefore, it would not be surprising to discover that the operation of the discouragement effect would be stronger among those with low earnings levels.[12] And last, the very distinct possibility exists that transfer payment income will produce a greater "replacement" of a worker's earnings in those cases where those earnings are relatively low. One would expect this to be the case, for example, in those instances where transfer payments are of the general assistance type[13] and in those instances where the payments are in the form of intrafamily transfers this would also be a very likely situation.

To summarize, a number of possible hypotheses for explaining the differential incidence of the discouragement effect in the American economy have been suggested. What remains is to empirically test, where possible, the validity of the alternative hypotheses.

I. A FRAMEWORK FOR EMPIRICAL TESTING

The hypotheses which have been advanced to this point can be grouped into two basic categories: (1) those that involve explaining differential discouragement effects on the basis of variations in leisure-income preference functions or differing levels of transfer payment income that are available in the absence of work activity, and (2) those that emphasize the initial position of the income-opportunity constraint as the factor accounting for differences in the impact of the discouragement effect. Classifying the hypotheses in this fashion is convenient in that the data that are available to us are of such a character as to permit roughly distinguishing empirically between hypotheses of these broad types. Specifically, the availability of 1957 mean earnings level information for various subgroups of the data sample provides a fairly good measure of the nature of the income opportunity constraint facing workers in these groups in the year prior to the cycle downturn of 1958. Consequently, by assessing the impact of 1957 earnings levels as a factor

---

[12] Quite clearly, a relatively unskilled worker is at a distinct disadvantage in a "loose" labor market where employers are in a position to be much more selective in their choice of workers. Consequently, when relatively unskilled workers are displaced from jobs in a cycle downswing, the likelihood of their becoming reemployed is undoubtedly much less than it is for more skilled workers.

[13] Since general assistance payments are geared to providing some minimum standard of living *irrespective* of previous earnings, the replacement of earnings is greater for those with limited earning capacity.

in explaining the incidence of nonemployment in 1958 in the various subgroups of the data sample, it is possible to obtain some idea of the relative importance of 1957 earnings levels and the subgroup classification itself in explaining differences in the level of 1958 nonemployment.

The available data provide information for white males by industry of employment in 1957 (10 industries) and 11 age-groups (five-year categories) for the nine Census regions. Thus, for a single region it is possible to consider simultaneously the observations for all 10 industries and the 11 age-groups and estimate a regression of the form

$$H = a + bw_0 + cA + dU_a + eU_I + u \qquad (1)$$

where H denotes the percentage of nonemployment among sample workers in 1958, w_0 is 1957 earnings for the subgroup, A is an age variable, U_a represents age-group unemployment, U_I industry unemployment, and u is a random error term. The unemployment variables are included in the regression because the theoretical discussion indicated that one of the possible reasons why the initial position of the income-opportunity constraint might be related to the discouragement effect was that subgroups with lower incomes might have greater amounts of initial unemployment as the result of the cycle downturn. If this is the case, all the 1957 earnings level may be measuring is the relative incidence of unemployment among subgroups as a result of a decline in economic activity, i.e., it may be no more than a proxy for the actual level of subgroup unemployment. Thus, it would be somewhat tautological to say that the discouragement effect is greater whenever the amount of unemployment that occurs among a group of workers is greater. Therefore, the unemployment variables are included to discriminate between the impact of differential unemployment rates and 1957 earnings levels in the regression.[14] The results of regressions for each of the nine regions are summarized in Table 9–4.[15] The age variable takes the value of three for the less than 20 age-group, one for the 20–24 classification, two for the 65 and over group, and zero for all others. The rationale of this variable is that the empirical studies cited earlier have indicated that the operation of the discouragement effect is much stronger in the

---

[14] Obviously, no regional unemployment variable is required since the data are analyzed by individual region.

[15] The values in parentheses beneath the regression coefficients are t-values. The variable A is called an age variable although it obviously does not measure age in the strictest sense of the term. Several age variables were employed in various regression equations but none worked as well as that used here. For example, a simple 1 through 11 age dummy was tried (similar to that employed in the analysis of interindustry mobility patterns) and a matrix of one-zero dummies using $N - 1$ dummies (where N equals the number of age classes) was introduced. The first produced poor results while the dummies in the second case introduced substantial multicolinearity and made it difficult to discriminate between the impact of the age and age unemployment variables.

TABLE 9–4

Regression Analysis of Nonemployment in 1958, White Male Workers, by Region

Region	Constant	Coefficients					R^2	F-Value
		1957 Earnings	Age	Industry Unemployment	Unemployment	Age Unemployment		
New England	11.7815	-0.0018 (4.9661)	2.670 (4.3247)	0.1338 (1.1500)		-0.3817 (1.6074)	0.51	29.1489
Middle Atlantic	11.0169	-0.0022 (8.2101)	0.627 (1.4711)	0.2296 (2.8376)		0.0999 (0.5671)	0.72	71.9336
South Atlantic	11.1417	-0.0023 (6.4016)	1.038 (1.8800)	0.1953 (1.8559)		0.1030 (0.4704)	0.61	42.7082
East north central	11.6988	-0.0022 (5.0872)	0.907 (1.2088)	0.0110 (0.0772)		0.3883 (1.2925)	0.54	33.1210
East south central	10.3662	-0.0020 (4.4673)	1.884 (1.7413)	0.0468 (0.3439)		0.1612 (0.4656)	0.48	26.3071
West north central	8.8588	-0.0018 (5.1346)	1.849 (3.1012)	0.0526 (0.4656)		0.2755 (1.2165)	0.62	45.5832
West south central	7.9942	-0.0019 (6.1289)	1.906 (3.4876)	0.1885 (1.8085)		0.3808 (1.8238)	0.70	64.4265
Mountain	19.9454	-0.0031 (6.5290)	2.407 (3.1682)	0.2141 (1.4162)		-0.9615 (3.7189)	0.47	25.5921
Pacific	4.3833	-0.0016 (1.9686)	3.091 (2.3905)	0.4647 (1.9005)		0.4276 (0.8245)	0.35	15.9618

less than 20 age-group, followed, in order, by the 65 and over and the 20–24 age classes.[16]

The regressions confirm the importance of the 1957 earnings level in explaining 1958 nonemployment. In all nine regressions the earnings variable is significant (in eight cases at the 0.1 percent level and in one at the 1 percent level). The age variable is significant at the 5 percent level or beyond in seven of the nine regressions and has the expected positive sign in all cases. Among the unemployment variables the industry variable performs best in explaining the incidence of hidden unemployment, having the correct sign in all cases and showing significance at the 5 percent level or beyond in four instances, while age unemployment has the correct sign in seven instances but in only one of those seven is it significant at the 5 percent level.

Similar results are obtained when the data are grouped by age and regressions are estimated for each of the 11 age-groups in the form:[17]

$$H = a + bw_0 + cU_I + u \qquad (2)$$

where the symbols retain their previous meaning. The results (Table 9–5) indicate that the earnings variable is significant at the 1 percent level or beyond in all cases, while the industry unemployment variable is significant at the 5 percent level or beyond in six instances and in all cases the signs are in the expected direction.

The results obtained with the individual region and age-group regressions can be generalized by combining the data and estimating the following regression:[18]

$$H = 9.1965 - 0.0019\ w_0 + 17.30\ A + 0.1759\ U_a + 0.2004\ U_I,$$
$$(13.21) \qquad (6.74) \qquad (2.06) \qquad (3.72) \qquad (3)$$
$$R^2 = 0.50$$

Regression (3) indicates clearly that 1957 earnings levels are the primary explanation for differences in levels of nonemployment in 1958.[19] It is not, however, the only significant factor. The age variable is significant at the 0.1 percent level as is the industry unemployment variable.

---

[16] For example, Dernburg and Strand (37), p. 80, estimate that a change in employment of 1,000 will produce corresponding changes in the labor force of 88 among those aged 14–19, 39 among those aged 65 and over, 26 among those aged 20–24, and negligible changes in the other age-groups.

[17] Note that no regional unemployment variable is included in these regressions although one would seem appropriate. Such a variable was constructed from estimates of unemployment by state contained in the U.S. Department of Labor (208), p. 208, and was included in the regressions. However, it was not significant.

[18] Only 986 observations are available for 1957, rather than 990 (9 regions, 10 industries, and 11 age-groups) due to the absence of workers in four cells (mining in the under 20 age-group in four regions).

[19] When the variables are introduced in a stepwise fashion, introducing the earnings variable by itself yields an R^2 of 0.4519.

TABLE 9-5
Regression Analysis of Nonemployment in 1958, White Male Workers, by Age

		Coefficients			
Age Class	Constant	1957 Earnings	Industry Unemployment	R^2	F-Value
Less than 20.....	23.2150	−0.0221 (2.49)	0.6703 (1.52)	0.0808	3.65
20–24..........	15.4882	−0.0047 (7.06)	0.0346 (0.35)	0.3922	28.06
25–29..........	15.8569	−0.0037 (10.06)	0.1166 (1.51)	0.5381	50.67
30–34..........	11.6518	−0.0022 (12.17)	0.1208 (2.43)	0.6362	76.06
35–39..........	10.0897	−0.0018 (11.58)	0.1533 (3.13)	0.6289	73.73
40–44..........	12.0472	−0.0021 (10.32)	0.1957 (2.73)	0.5771	59.36
45–49..........	8.6501	−0.0014 (10.91)	0.1124 (2.30)	0.6003	65.32
50–54..........	9.2934	−0.0015 (8.19)	0.0889 (1.33)	0.4585	36.83
55–59..........	10.4878	−0.0018 (9.47)	0.1624 (2.16)	0.5410	51.28
60–64..........	11.6051	−0.0023 (8.43)	0.2309 (2.45)	0.4831	40.65
65 and over.....	8.8624	−0.0020 (5.27)	0.5423 (4.41)	0.3508	23.51

Further, the age unemployment variable is significant at the 5 percent level.[20] Overall, these results suggest the validity of the hypothesis that earnings levels are an extremely significant factor in accounting for differences in the amount of labor force withdrawal occurring in various subgroups on the downswing of the business cycle.

II. CONCLUSIONS

The essential question explored in this chapter is whether the differential incidence of the discouragement effect, observed in various empirical studies, is systematically related to the potential earnings levels of individuals. The general conclusion is that there is a strong inverse relationship. The data suggest that this relationship is widespread, holding across and within region, age, and industry groups for white male workers.

These results suggest that while the phenomenon of hidden unemployment may be more heavily concentrated in certain subgroups, it is found among virtually all portions of the sample. This should serve to dispel any sanguine notions that hidden unemployment is a phenomenon of little significance in the prime labor force groups. While the results are

---

[20] Again, the regional unemployment variable was tried but was not significant.

not inconsistent with the previous research into this phenomenon, they do indicate that within the prime labor force group (namely, white males aged 25–54) variations in the incidence of hidden unemployment can be largely explained by differences in potential earnings levels. This has some interesting public policy implications—primarily, that the incidence of hidden unemployment falls disproportionately on the low-income level groups. Of course, this effect is reinforced by the fact that the burden of overt unemployment is also heaviest on these groups.[21] Consequently, the results argue for the effectiveness of maintaining high levels of aggregate demand and employment in improving the economic status of relatively low-income groups.[22]

In a more speculative vein it might be asked what could be done to reduce the sensitivity of workers to fluctuations in the general level of employment. If the theoretical arguments are correct, it would seem that much could be accomplished through reducing the search costs involved in locating another job. Of course, this is merely the familiar proposition that better labor market information will produce a more efficient utilization of labor resources. In the particular context of this discussion, however, reducing search costs by $1 would have the same effect as increasing by the same amount the present (discounted) value of the stream of potential earnings. That this might yield substantial results is indicated by the elasticity of hidden unemployment with respect to potential earnings levels. From regression (3) this elasticity can be estimated at the mean to be −1.23. Thus, reducing search costs by improving labor market information should yield a significant reduction in the incidence of hidden unemployment.

One other point needs to be made. In the theoretical discussion there was some speculation about the impact of the availability of nonwork related sources of income upon the labor force withdrawal decisions that generate hidden unemployment. Since the empirical results argue that individuals are sensitive to potential earnings levels in making this decision, it would appear that increasing the relative availability of nonwork income would operate to increase the incidence of labor force withdrawal and hidden unemployment among the groups represented in the sample. In short, the results presented here are certainly consistent with the body of recent literature which points to the importance and significance of incentive effects in the American economy.[23]

---

[21] In Gallaway (69), evidence is presented that indicates the impact of differences in unemployment rates on the incidence of poverty among American families.

[22] This is not to say that maintaining high levels of aggregate demand is a complete solution to the problems of low-income groups, although it certainly has a very substantial contribution to make. The pros and cons of this issue are explored in Aaron (1) and Gallaway (70).

[23] For example, see Brehm and Saving (18), Gallaway (64) and (65), Kasper (96), and Taussig (184).

chapter TEN

Poverty in the United States

THE question of poverty has acquired very substantial significance in our contemporary society. Over the past several years much has been said and written about poverty ranging from popular treatises to technical investigations of the subject[1] and out of this literature has come a very lively controversy over the appropriate policy approach to eliminating poverty. As representative of one line of thinking as to a viable economic policy for dealing with the problems of poverty, the following statement by Walter Heller is enlightening: "Clearly, we cannot rely on the general progress of the economy—or on job creating programs alone—to erase poverty in America" (192). The policy issue raised by this statement is strikingly similar to that encountered in Chapter Eight in the discussion of the structural change-deficiency of aggregate demand controversy, namely, whether stimulating aggregate demand will be effective in dealing with a particular economic problem.

Actually, the conceptual basis for the concern over the poverty question is essentially the same as that underlying that earlier issue—a belief in the minds of some that there are very substantial groups of individuals in the society who are relatively unaffected by the general level of economic activity that is found in the economy. In the case of the unemployment question the argument ran to the effect that the relatively unskilled

---

[1] In the more popular vein, see Harrington (83). Of a more technical nature, see Aaron (1), Gallaway (69) and (70), Mooney (139), Muth (143), and Thurow (189).

in the economy were becoming progressively more and more detached from the normal operation of the labor market. Similarly, as it has been articulated by many the poverty problem is deemed to be one that is due to large segments of the population being relatively detached from the normal functioning of market mechanisms in the United States. Thus, there is a great similarity in the intellectual basis for the two issues.

In a broader sense, the two controversies to which we have already referred reflect an even more general thesis that is currently enjoying some popularity in the United States although few professional economists would subscribe to it. That thesis holds that there are substantial changes taking place in the United States which are producing an alteration in the relationship between work activity and the receipt of money income.[2] The concept of a "deterioration in the work-income nexus" is actually espoused by some as a broad basis for arguing that substantial changes in the methods by which we distribute income in the United States are going to be required due to this alteration in the relationship between work activity and the obtaining of income. Otherwise, the thesis maintains, increasing numbers of people are going to find themselves out of the mainstream of American economic life and in what I prefer to call the "backwash" of our economic system.

The question now arises as to what is the basis for contentions of this type? On the theoretical side it is argued that this deterioration in the work-income relationship is being triggered by an increasing amount of automation in the economy which is adding to our capability to produce goods and services without any corresponding rise in the capacity to consume them. Such a thesis sounds strikingly like the underconsumptionist arguments that have frequently appeared in economic literature over the years. This is precisely what it is and, as such, there are rather compelling arguments to refute it.[3] However, it has also been the case that within the past 15 years or so certain empirical evidence has been capable of being interpreted as supporting the deteriorating work-income nexus thesis. First, there is the previously discussed upward drift in aggregate unemployment rates which we dealt with in Chapter Eight. But, beyond this, in the late 1950's and early 1960's there appeared to be a significant slowing in the rate at which individuals and families were being shifted out of the poverty income classification—a development which could be interpreted as being consistent with the changing work-income nexus proposition. However, before we can discuss these

---

[2] The most vociferous advocate of this position is Theobald (**187**).

[3] The underconsumptionist argument has had an amazing vitality through the years. Hints of it are contained in Malthus (**133**). A French contemporary, Simonde de Sismondi, argued this view quite strongly in (**174**). Later, Hobson in (**89**) and (**88**) makes the same contentions.

empirical developments, it is necessary to provide a working definition of what we mean by "poverty" in the United States.

I. "POVERTY" DEFINED

The precise meaning of poverty is difficult to determine in that some type of value judgment is required as to what is and what is not a poverty level of living. To begin, the question of defining poverty may be approached from either a relative or an absolute income standpoint. The relativistic approach to defining poverty presents the most problems in that the poverty cutoff line is related to the general level of income in the economy. In effect, this converts the problem of poverty into the more general issue of the equality of income distribution and, unless there is a significant change in income equality, there can be no alteration in the relative numbers of people in poverty. Further, a relativistic approach to the concept of poverty has no necessary connection with the "backwash" thesis discussed earlier. It is entirely possible for the equality of income distribution to remain the same without the backwash thesis being operative. In fact, the backwash notion may well require increasing inequality of income distribution for it to be meaningful although we cannot be certain of this.[4] Thus, a relativistic approach to defining poverty would seem to be something of a "trap" and no attempt will be made to define poverty in this sense.[5]

From the absolute standpoint some consensus has developed with respect to a working definition of a poverty "cutoff" income level. Initially, that consensus focused on the $3,000 of money income per family figure and most of the early estimates of poverty were based on that definition. However, a more sophisticated approach to the problem has been developed and the federal government today provides estimates of the percentage of families and individuals in poverty based on these definitions.[6] In general, though, the present definitions correspond very closely to what would be obtained with a simple $3,000 of family income (in real terms) boundary for delineating poverty.[7]

---

[4] Increasing inequality of income distribution would imply that those at the lower tail of the income distribution were sharing less than proportionally in general increases in income. This will be developed further in later parts of this chapter.

[5] A recent study of poverty which attempts the relativistic approach is the work of Ornati (**146**).

[6] These definitions derive from the work of Orshansky (**147**).

[7] The Orshansky type definitions result in some people being excluded from the poverty category who would be counted with a simple $3,000 cutoff. However, some who would not be counted as being in poverty with the $3,000 definition are counted with Orshansky's definitions. The two types of change apparently roughly cancel out one another.

II. POVERTY IN THE AGGREGATE

Using the accepted definition of poverty,[8] it is easy to see why the "backwash" thesis could have acquired some currency in the late 1950's and early 1960's. In Table 10–1 data are presented which detail the percentage of families in poverty in the post-World War II period. These data indicate that between 1947 and 1956 the poverty rate in the United States declined from 31.7 to 22.2 percent (9.5 percentage points). How-

TABLE 10–1
Percent of Families with Less Than $3,000 Annual Income (1963 prices), Median Family Income, and Unemployment Rate, United States, 1947–1968

Year	Percent of Families with Less Than $3,000 Annual Income	Median Family Income (Constant $)	Unemployment Rate
1947	31.7%	$3,896	3.9%
1950	31.2	3,961	5.3
1953	25.8	4,542	2.9
1954	27.4	4,458	5.6
1955	24.4	4,738	4.4
1956	22.2	5,051	4.2
1957	22.2	5,072	4.3
1958	22.5	5,052	6.8
1959	21.4	5,337	5.5
1960	20.9	5,451	5.6
1961	20.9	5,506	6.7
1962	19.7	5,651	5.6
1963	18.5	5,856	5.7
1964	17.9	6,077	5.2
1965	16.8	6,330	4.5
1966	15.2	6,631	3.8
1967	14.2	6,702	3.8
1968	12.8	7,122	3.6

SOURCES: Department of Commerce, U.S. Bureau of the Census, *Current Population Reports*, P-60 Series (Washington, D.C.: U.S.G.P.O., various years), and Department of Labor, *Manpower Report of the President* (Washington, D.C.: U.S.G.P.O., March 1970).

ever, between 1956 and 1961, the decline was only another 1.3 percentage points. Thus, the nine years from 1947 to 1956 saw an average decline of a little over 1 percentage point a year while the next five years produced an average decline of only about one-quarter of a percentage point a year in the poverty rate. Incidentally, the poverty issue began to be articulated at just about the end of this period of very minimal

---

[8] Using the $3,000 definition (in constant prices) has the advantage of permitting us to extend the analysis backwards to years when the present official definitions were not in use. Thus, more data may be brought to bear on the analysis of poverty issues.

changes in the incidence of poverty. For example, Michael Harrington's *Other America* (83) was published in 1962. Of course, this is a comparison which is slanted in the direction of showing a smaller average decline in the poverty rate for 1956–61 due to 1961 being a year of depressed economic conditions. However, even if the comparison is restricted to the 1956–60 period, the result is essentially the same as the average decline in the poverty rate over this interval was only about a third of a percentage point a year. Interestingly, this is almost the same time interval which brought into focus the structural change-deficiency of aggregate demand unemployment controversy. Thus, the similarity between the poverty question and the unemployment rate problem is found again. Consequently, it is not surprising that the same conceptual framework can be employed to shed light on the issues involved. The discussion of Chapter Eight pointed out that the phenomenon of high unemployment rates could be explained as either (1) the result of changes in the unemployment structure producing higher levels of unemployment even though the economy is at full employment, or (2) due to the economy deviating from full employment.

The same distinction can be made in the case of poverty except that the backwash notion substitutes for the structural change thesis. Consequently, it would seem that a straightforward test of the validity of the backwash notion would be to compare poverty rates through time with some measure (or measures) of aggregate economic activity. However, there are difficulties here that are much more substantial than those encountered in the testing of the structural change hypothesis. The primary problem is that of a nonlinear relationship between the poverty rate and the general level of income and in this case it is not possible to circumvent the nonlinearity in any workable fashion. To illustrate the nature of the problem consider Figure 10–1 which shows two income distributions with different median incomes (both higher than the poverty line). With a fixed poverty line, it is apparent that as the income distribution shifts progressively in the direction of higher median incomes relatively fewer people are "pulled" across the poverty line with succeeding shifts.[9] This implies that those at the extreme tail of the society's income distribution are definitely less intimately connected with the normal processes of economic growth than those who are in the middle of the income distribution. Thus, the existence of a nonlinear relationship between measures of general levels of income and the poverty rate is quite consistent with the phenomenon of the backwash thesis. Actually, what is important here is not whether it becomes more difficult to shift people across an absolute poverty line as the economy grows and expands but the degree of increase in the

---

[9] Anderson (125).

FIGURE 10–1

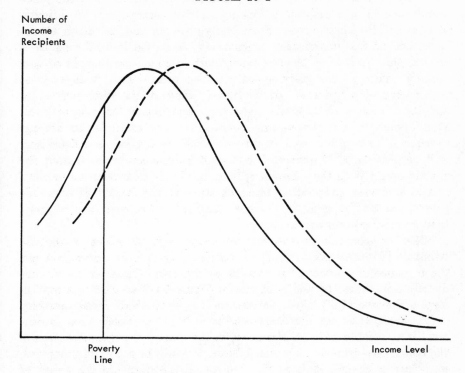

difficulty and the point at which the returns from economic growth in eliminating poverty render it relatively ineffective as a policy measure. It seems rather evident that many of those who initially became so concerned about the incidence of poverty in the early 1960's felt that we had reached that point at which economic growth had become relatively ineffective in eliminating poverty.[10]

III. THE RELATIONSHIP BETWEEN ECONOMIC GROWTH AND LEVELS OF POVERTY

The crux of the backwash issue is the effect on specific income levels of a general shift in the position of the income distribution brought

---

[10] For example, in congressional hearings (192), Walter Heller went on to comment:

"The new tax cut will sharply step up our rate of economic growth. By creating 2 to 3 million new jobs, it will open exits from poverty at a faster pace. But open exits mean little to those who cannot move—to the millions who are caught in the web of poverty through illiteracy, lack of skills, racial discrimination, broken homes, and ill health—conditions which are hardly touched by prosperity and growth."

about by economic growth. If the backwash proposition is valid, such a shift will have a differential impact on the income levels of different portions of the distribution. Specifically, the incomes of those at the lower end of the distribution presumably would be less affected by a general shift in income levels. Conceptually, this can be thought of as a "biased" shift in the distribution. On the other hand, it is possible to conceive of a "neutral" or "unbiased" shift in the distribution. By definition, such a shift would have the same impact on income levels at all points within the income distribution. For example, an average increase in income levels of 10 percent would be neutral as defined here if it resulted in a 10 percent increase in income levels throughout the distribution.[11] With these distinctions in mind it is clear that the validity of the backwash proposition turns on whether the impact of economic growth on the shape of the income distribution has been neutral, particularly at the lower income levels.

Whether economic growth has been neutral in its effect on the distribution of income is essentially an empirical matter. However, how can the presence or absence of neutrality be detected? Consider the income distribution shown by the solid line in Figure 10–2 which has a median level of income of Y_m^1. Now, let the income level which defines poverty status be B. It is not necessary here to indicate precisely what income level is associated with B. However, in the empirical implementation of the conceptual framework which follows, this will be done. At this point, introduce a general shift in the income distribution (as the result of economic growth) which displaces it to the position indicated by the dotted line of Figure 10–2. The extent of the shift in the distribution is measured by the difference between the median income levels of the two distributions $(Y_m^1 - Y_m^2)$. Further, if the shift is strictly neutral in its impact, each income level in the old distribution is multiplied by $1 + [(Y_m^1 - Y_m^2)/Y_m^1]$ or by $1 + \Delta Y/Y$.

The question at this point is a simple one: How will neutrality of economic growth be reflected in the proportion of income recipients falling below the poverty boundary B. Actually, if the shift in the income distribution is strictly neutral, the number of income recipients with incomes less than B in the new distribution will be exactly the same as the number in the old distribution with income levels less than $B/(1 + \Delta Y/Y)$. This follows from the fact that under conditions of strict neutrality all income levels are multiplied by $1 + \Delta Y/Y$. This suggests a straightforward method of determining whether an intertemporal shift in an income distribution is truly neutral in its impact on various parts of the income distribution. All that is required is to esti-

---

[11] In effect, this amounts to saying that there is no change in the Lorenz curve which describes the income distribution when there is a general shift in that distribution as the result of economic growth.

FIGURE 10–2

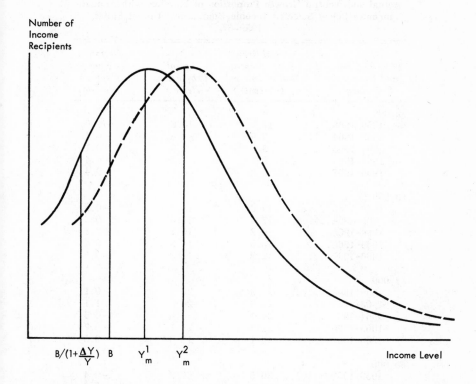

mate the proportion of income recipients with income less than $B/(1 + \Delta Y/Y)$ in the original income distribution and compare it with the proportion with income less than B in the new distribution. If the two are equal, the shift has been neutral with respect to income recipients with incomes less than B. However, if the proportion expected under the assumption of neutrality is less than the actual proportion, the income shift is biased against this portion of the income distribution and vice versa. All that remains now is to examine income distributions in the United States to determine whether shifts in them have been neutral with respect to various income groups.

Before implementing the empirical test of neutrality of economic growth which has been suggested it is necessary to choose a specific value for the income boundary B. Given the concern with the problem of poverty and the backwash thesis, it was decided to evaluate the neutrality proposition at four different levels on the low end of the income distribution: $2,000, $3,000, $4,000, and $5,000. In addition, it was felt that it would be useful to evaluate the neutrality of economic growth with respect to the high-income portion of the income distribu-

TABLE 10–2
Actual and Neutral Growth Proportion of Families with Annual Incomes below Selected Income Boundaries, United States, 1959–67

Time Interval and Income Boundary	Neutral Growth Proportion at End of Interval (Percent)	Actual Proportion (Percent)	Deviation (Actual − Neutral) (Percent)
$2,000			
1959–1963........	11.2	10.6	−0.6
1963–1964........	9.9	9.5	−0.4
1964–1965........	8.8	8.9	0.1
1965–1966........	8.1	7.7	−0.4
1966–1967........	6.8	6.4	−0.4
$3,000			
1959–1963........	19.0	18.5	−0.5
1963–1964........	17.4	17.6	0.2
1964–1965........	16.2	16.1	−0.1
1965–1966........	13.9	14.3	0.4
1966–1967........	12.8	12.3	−0.5
$4,000			
1959–1963........	27.3	27.2	−0.1
1963–1964........	24.9	26.0	1.1
1964–1965........	24.1	23.8	−0.3
1965–1966........	21.8	21.1	−0.7
1966–1967........	19.1	18.6	−0.5
$5,000			
1959–1963........	36.6	36.2	−0.4
1963–1964........	34.0	34.6	0.6
1964–1965........	32.2	31.7	−0.5
1965–1966........	29.2	28.2	−1.0
1966–1967........	25.6	25.1	−0.5
$15,000			
1959–1963........	94.4	94.5	0.1
1963–1964........	93.7	93.8	0.1
1964–1965........	92.5	92.4	−0.1
1965–1966........	90.7	90.8	0.1
1966–1967........	88.8	87.8	−1.0
$25,000			
1959–1963........	98.9	98.9	0.0
1963–1964........	98.7	99.0	0.3
1964–1965........	98.6	98.6	0.0
1965–1966........	98.3	98.3	0.0
1966–1967........	97.8	97.5	−0.3

Source: Department of Commerce, U.S. Bureau of the Census, *Current Population Reports—Consumer Income*, P-60 Series (Washington, D.C.: U.S.G.P.O., 1960–68).

tion. Therefore, the necessary calculations have been made for the $15,000 and $25,000 income boundaries.

The results for the period 1959–67 for families in the United States are presented in Table 10–2 and are extremely enlightening. Turning first to the low-income portion of the income distribution, it seems to be clear that there are systematic deviations of the actual proportion of families with incomes below the boundaries evaluated from the proportions expected assuming neutrality of income shifts. However, the deviations are *not* in the direction suggested by the backwash hypothesis. Quite the contrary—in 15 of the 20 cases reported in Table 10–2 for the low-income level values of *B*—the actual proportion of families with income levels below the chosen value of *B* is *less than* that which would be associated with neutrality of income shifts. This argues that the relationship between general increases in income levels and changes in income levels among low-income families is biased in favor of the low-income groups.

The findings with respect to the upper end of the income distribution are somewhat different from those obtained at the lower end of the distribution. For the most part the results shown in Table 10–2 suggest that economic growth is neutral with respect to the upper end of the income distribution.[12] Specifically, in 7 of the 10 high-income cases reported the deviation of the actual proportion of income recipients below the selected values of *B* from the neutral growth proportions are 0.1 percentage points or less and there is no consistency in the signs of the deviations.

IV.   SOME ADDITIONAL EVIDENCE

There is an alternative method of approaching the question of the relationship between the poverty rate in the United States and the amount of economic activity. It involves comparing the behavior of the poverty rate in the economy with some measure of the general level of economic performance in an effort to determine how changes in the overall economy alter the incidence of poverty. For example, we could explore the relationship between the poverty rate and median family income in the United States. However, before this is attempted it is necessary to specify quite precisely the form of the relationship we would expect to find between a measure such as median family income and the poverty rate. There has been some extended discussion of the techni-

---

[12] A different technique for extrapolating between the limits of the income classes is used at the upper end of the income distribution than at the lower. At the lower end a strictly linear technique is used but at the upper end the extrapolations are made on the basis of the relationship implied in the Pareto curve. For a brief discussion of the rationale of this technique, see Miller (**135**).

cal aspects of this problem in various sources[13] and it has produced a general consensus to the effect that the most appropriate form of the relationship would seem to be the following:

$$P = aM^b u \tag{1}$$

where P denotes the poverty rate, M represents median family income (in real terms) and u is a random error term.

Using the data of Table 10–1 a least squares regression of the form shown in (1) was estimated with the following results:[14]

$$\log P = 6.68394 - 1.43944 \log M, \; R^2 = 0.98 \tag{2}$$
$$(26.40)$$

These are highly significant explaining 98 percent of the variance in the relationship. However, an examination of the residuals of the regression reveals that the relationship shown in (2) systematically understates the incidence of poverty in high unemployment rate years and overstates it when unemployment is low. Consequently, an unemployment rate variable was added to the regression and it was reestimated with the following results:

$$\log P = 6.66799 - 1.42472 \log M + 0.09764 \log U,$$
$$(41.74) \qquad\qquad (3.79) \tag{3}$$
$$R^2 = 0.9921$$

where U signifies the level of unemployment.

In this case both of the independent variables are highly significant and over 99 percent of the variation in aggregate levels of poverty is explained. As a further test of the validity of the relationship shown in (3) the same regression was estimated using only the 1947–64 data and the results are then used to predict the 1965–68 poverty rates.[15] A comparison of the predicted and actual rates is shown in Table 10–3 and it indicates that there is a tendency for the 1947–64 regression results to overpredict the level of poverty in subsequent years.[16]

Given these results the question now is what will explain the divergence of the actual aggregate poverty rate from the one predicted on the basis of the 1947–64 relationship between poverty and levels of

---

[13] Aaron (1), Gallaway (70), and Muth (143).

[14] The numbers in parentheses beneath the regression coefficients are their t-values.

[15] A similar approach is used in Gallaway (70), using a regression estimated with 1947–60 data to predict poverty rates for 1961–64. In that case the predicted and actual poverty rates were quite similar.

[16] This overprediction might suggest that the appropriate regression form for estimating expression (2) is the semi-logarithmic one used in Gallaway's original piece (69). However, it seems clear from the interchange between Aaron and Gallaway and Muth's (143) work that this is not the case.

median family income and unemployment. As a first step in assessing the nature of the forces producing this discrepancy it is useful to compare the regression results obtained using the 1947–64 data with those shown in (3). Such a comparison shows that there has been a sizable shift in the values of the regression parameters. First, the elasticity of poverty with respect to median family income is higher in the 1947–68 regression by an amount equal to almost three standard errors of that coefficient. Similarly, the elasticity with respect to the aggregate unemployment rate has increased by over two standard errors. This suggests a fundamental structural change in the relationship between poverty and the variables M and U in the years 1965–68. As a crude measure of this type of shift, a time variable (t) has been incorporated in (3). It takes

TABLE 10–3
Predicted and Actual Poverty Rates, United States, 1965 through 1968

Year	Poverty Rate (Percent)	
	Actual	Predicted*
1965..............	16.8	16.4
1966..............	15.2	15.3
1967..............	14.2	15.1
1968..............	12.8	13.9

* Predicted rates calculated from equation (3).

the value one for the years 1947 through 1963, two for 1964, three for 1965, etc., through six for 1968. Its inclusion in (3) produces the following:

$$\log P = 6.19552 - 1.31654 \log M + 0.05372 \log U - 0.03951 \log t,$$
$$ (25.00) (2.29) (2.48) (4)$$
$$R^2 = 0.9941$$

The time drift variable is statistically significant at the 5 percent level and indicates a systematic negative drift in the aggregate poverty rate. However, even more interesting is the fact that the regression parameters associated with M and U are approximately the same in (4) as they are in the 1947–64 regression. Specifically, the earlier elasticity of poverty with respect to median family income is −1.33262 compared to the −1.31654 of (4) and the respective unemployment coefficients are 0.04356 and 0.05372. This would indicate that the time drift variable does capture whatever structural change there has been. However, there is something inherently unsatisfactory in explaining a phenomenon in terms of just a time drift variable. This amounts to confessing one's ignorance (although it is sometimes necessary), for the true source of the variation in the dependent variable has not been specified. The question, though, is what might be substituted for the time drift variable? A brief consideration of the function of the variables already included in (4) suggests a possibility. The median family income variable is designed to capture the impact of overall shifts in the income distribution on poverty levels while the unemployment variable would be expected to reflect the effect of shifts in the distribution of income that result from the greater impact of changes in unemployment on the lower tail of the income distribution. It can be argued, however, that the unemployment rate is an imperfect measure of this effect due to the operation of the "discouragement effect" in the American economy.[17] Evidence has already been presented which indicates that this effect is relatively strong among the lower income groups.[18] Consequently, labor force entry and withdrawal as the result of changing general levels of unemployment may be having an effect on the aggregate poverty rate which is not measured in the regressions reported thus far. In the period 1964–68 this would operate in the direction of reducing the poverty rate more rapidly than anticipated since unemployment rates fell consistently. If this argument is accepted, the need for an additional variable measuring shifts in the income distribution is indicated. An obvious choice in this respect is the Gini coefficient for evaluating the equality of income distribution.[19] When this variable is added to (4) the result is:

$$\log P = 6.39259 - 1.29172 \log M + 0.04535 \log U$$
$$ (24.11) (1.13) \tag{5}$$
$$- 0.65161 \log G - 0.03251 \log t, \ R^2 = 0.9959$$
$$ (2.13) (1.87)$$

where G denotes the Gini coefficient.

Interestingly, the Gini coefficient variable is statistically significant with the expected negative sign. Even more enlightening, though, is the fact that there is little change in the other parameters although the unemployment coefficient is no longer significant. The insignificance of the unemployment coefficient is expected since the unemployment variable also measures shifts in income distribution. Perhaps the most striking thing, however, is the continued significance of the time drift variable.[20] This indicates that the structural change under discussion is the

---

[17] The operation of this effect has been so well documented in the previous chapters that no further citations seem necessary.

[18] See, for example, Chapter Nine.

[19] The Gini coefficients are calculated using the technique described in Miller (**135**), pp. 220–21.

[20] Since we are hypothesizing a priori a negative sign for the time drift coefficient, a one-tailed test of significance is appropriate.

result of factors other than those measured by the other independent variables in the regression equation.

The presence of a structural change in the poverty-economic activity relationship is quite consistent with the earlier evidence concerning a bias in the impact of economic growth on the status of low-income families. That material indicated that during the 1960's economic growth produced a greater degree of upward movement in income levels at the low end of the income distribution than would have been expected if growth were neutral in its impact on the income distribution. The question posed by such results is why has the structural change that has been observed occurred? A number of speculative answers might be advanced. For example, perhaps the complex of social programs growing out of the "war on poverty" issue has been producing a reduction in poverty levels in excess of that which would be the natural outgrowth of increases in the general level of income in society. Or, it could be that the unexpected decline in the aggregate poverty rate has a basis in some aspect of the long cyclical upswing in economic activity of the 1960's which has not been measured in our analysis. At any rate, the structural shift is there and indicates that the society's progress in eliminating poverty has been better than we had any right to expect as of the early 1960's.

V. THE FUTURE PROSPECTS

Clearly, the record with respect to poverty elimination in the 1960's has not borne out the rather dismal predictions made by many at the beginning of the decade.[21] In fact, by 1968 the poverty rate among American families had been pushed below the levels predicted for 1980 by the Council of Economic Advisers in 1964 assuming economic growth conditions such as those which existed between 1957 and 1962.[22] This is an impressive "speeding-up" of the elimination of poverty, no matter how accomplished. However, the important question now is what can be expected in the future in regards to further reduction in poverty levels. One way to approach answering this question is to project median income levels and unemployment rates into the future and from these predict aggregate poverty rates. Of course, this assumes that the parameters of the regression equations we have estimated are stable which, in view of the evidence presented to this point, does not seem that unreasonable once the time drift factor is corrected for in the regressions.

---

[21] In the early years of the concern about poverty the basic orientation of most of the commentary was focused on the reluctance of the poverty rate to dip below the 20 percent level. Obviously, such concern has proven to be extremely ill-founded.

[22] The Council of Economic Advisers' projections were presented in (32). They predicted a poverty rate of 13 percent in 1980 assuming 1957–62 growth conditions.

Probably the most straightforward way to depict the relationship between future poverty rates and income levels is to assume some unemployment rate and then calculate poverty rates for various levels of median family income assuming that the time drift factor does not continue to operate.[23] Assuming away any further time drift in the overall poverty rate means that the calculations will yield estimates of future poverty rates which are maximal in character. The necessary arithmetic has been done for four different unemployment rates (3, 4, 5, and 6 percent) and the results are shown graphically in Figure 10–3. From this diagram it can be seen that a 10 percent poverty rate is associated with a real median family income level (in 1963 prices) of about $9,000 (assuming a 3 to 4 percent unemployment rate). However, the important question is when such a level of real family income could reasonably be achieved. To determine this the income levels shown in Figure 10–3

FIGURE 10–3

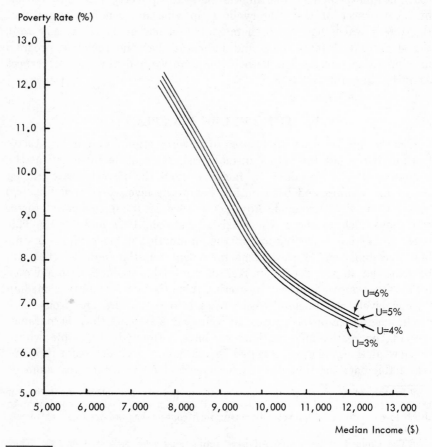

---

[23] Regression equation (4) was used for this purpose.

need to be expressed in terms of the growth rate in median family income necessary to achieve it in a specific time period or the number of years required to reach such a level with a given growth rate. Some insight into the combinations of growth rates and/or time required to achieve, say, a 10 percent poverty rate can be obtained from Figure 10–4 which shows the poverty rates which would be associated with 2, 3, and 4 percent rates of growth in real median family income between 1970 and 1990. In all cases, a 4 percent unemployment rate is assumed.[24] The 4 percent growth rate in real median family income corresponds roughly to the rate maintained in the 1960's, the 3 percent rate with that between 1957 and 1956, while the 2 percent rate is closer to the immediate post-1956 period rate which generated the rather low poverty elimination rates of that period.

The relationships shown in Figure 10–4 indicate that a 4 percent

FIGURE 10–4

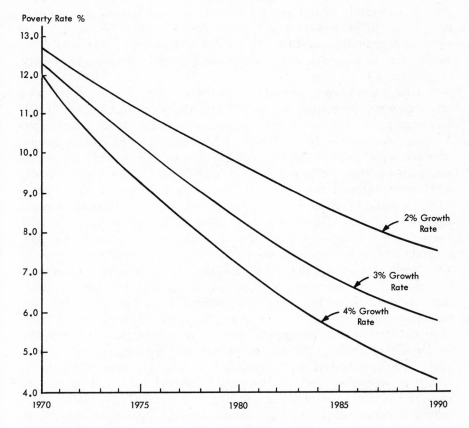

---
[24] The time drift is assumed to be zero.

growth rate in real median family income would produce a 10 percent poverty rate in about 1974, a 3 percent rate would give this result about 1976, whereas a 2 percent rate would lead to such a poverty level in about 1979. Clearly, differences in growth rates in median family income will have a very substantial impact on the poverty rate but this still leaves unanswered the basic question of whether the returns from economic growth warrant placing further confidence in its capacity to eliminate poverty. There are various ways of viewing this question. First, one can assess the contribution a difference in growth rates in real median family income will make to eliminating poverty at a given point in time. For example, from Figure 10–4 it can be seen that in 1975 the difference in the incidence of poverty which would result from a 3 percent growth rate instead of a 2 percent rate is about 8 percent (0.9 percentage points). By 1980 the difference is of the magnitude of approximately 14 percent (1.4 percentage points) and by 1990, 24 percent (1.8 percentage points). Similarly, the respective differences in the incidence of poverty as the result of a 4 percent growth rate versus a 2 percent rate are: 1975—19 percent (1.8 percentage points); 1980—36 percent (2.6 percentage points); and 1990—74 percent (3.2 percentage points). This would seem to suggest that the returns to growth in eliminating poverty are substantial.

A second approach is to evaluate the year-to-year change in the poverty rate which accompanies a specific growth rate in real median family income. Again, Figure 10–4 is useful for it shows that if the relationship between median family income and the poverty rate remains stable, over the period 1970 to 1980 the poverty rate will fall about 0.5 percentage points a year with a 4 percent growth rate. On the other hand, a 3 percent growth rate will yield an average decline in the poverty rate of about 0.4 percentage points and a 2 percent rate about 0.3 percentage points a year. Given that over the past few years we have been averaging a 1 percentage point a year decline in the poverty rate, this suggests that as we approach the 10 percent poverty rate level the going will become slower and slower as far as eliminating poverty is concerned. Consequently, if one views a 10 percent poverty rate as unacceptably high, it would seem that there are definite limitations as to how far economic growth can go in eliminating poverty. However, at the same time it seems clear that growth still has something to offer from the standpoint of ridding the society of poverty. Remember, only a few years ago the potential role of growth in eliminating poverty was being greatly downgraded—yet, in the period 1961–68 about 40 percent of existing poverty was eliminated and largely because of the greatly accelerated economic growth of the period. Specifically, approximately 85 percent of the decline in poverty in this period appears to be the direct result of economic growth and about 15 percent is due to the time drift phenomenon.[25]

To summarize, the available evidence with respect to the relationship between economic growth and the incidence of poverty suggests that growth has a powerful influence on the incidence of poverty but that its present successes in eliminating poverty lessen its future effectiveness in this respect. Specifically, it appears that as the poverty rate begins to approach 10 percent the impact of growth becomes progressively more and more diluted. Consequently, it is possible to conceive of a backwash phenomenon in operation once the poverty rate is pushed into the 5 to 10 percent range. However, this is a far cry from what was meant by the concept of backwash when it was initially advanced.[26]

---

[25] The portion of the overall decrease in poverty assigned to growth is the difference between the actual poverty rate in 1961 and the predicted rate in 1968 divided by the difference between the actual 1961 and actual 1968 rates. The remainder is attributed to the time drift factor.

[26] This does not mean that the backwash phenomenon may not be operative in certain subgroups of the population. In the next few chapters this possibility will be explored in the context of discussions of the economic status of nonwhites, the aged, and women in the United States.

chapter ELEVEN

The Economic Status
of Nonwhites

INCREASINGLY, there is evidence that perhaps the most important problem facing our contemporary society is that of the political, social, and economic status of nonwhites in America. The dimensions of the economic difficulties presently being encountered by nonwhites are rather clearly reflected in some very simple and straightforward statistics. First, nonwhite income levels are markedly lower than those of whites. As of the 1960 decennial census (1959 income levels) nonwhite males had a median income that was only 52 percent of that of white males.[1] Further, over the period 1950 to 1960 there was little sign of any improvement in their relative income position.[2] Nonwhite females are somewhat better off than males but, even so, their median income level was only 60 percent of that of white females in 1959.[3] On the positive side, some signs of improvement in this situation can be detected in the post-1959 period. As of 1968 median incomes of nonwhite men had risen to about 60 percent of those of white males while nonwhite females had improved their relative income position to almost 80 percent.[4]

The relatively poor income position of nonwhites in our society reflects

---

[1] The median income of Negro men in 1959 was $2,254 compared to $4,337 for white men. See U.S. Department of Commerce (205).

[2] Batchelder (6) presents evidence on this point. The ratio of Negro male to white male income was 0.52 in both the 1950 and 1960 censuses.

[3] The median income of Negro women in 1959 was $905 compared to $1,509 for white women. Source: same as cited in footnote 1.

[4] Source: U.S. Department of Commerce (197), Table 37.

in part their tendency to suffer substantially higher levels of unemployment than whites. Table 11-1 presents data which indicate that unemployment rates among nonwhites in post-World War II America are typically about twice those of whites. Such high levels of unemployment among nonwhites make a very substantial contribution to the relatively poor income position of the nonwhite. However, this is only one aspect

TABLE 11-1
Unemployment Rates, by Race, United States,
1954-69
(percent)

	Unemployment Rate	
Year	White	Nonwhite
1954	5.0	9.9
1955	3.9	8.7
1956	3.6	8.3
1957	3.8	7.9
1958	6.1	12.6
1959	4.8	10.7
1960	4.9	10.2
1961	6.0	12.4
1962	4.9	10.9
1963	5.0	10.8
1964	4.6	9.6
1965	4.1	8.1
1966	3.3	7.3
1967	3.4	7.4
1968	3.2	6.7
1969	3.1	6.4

SOURCE: U.S. Department of Labor (209), Table A-5.

of the problem of unemployment, viz, overt or measured unemployment. In addition, one must take into consideration the impact of the phenomenon of "hidden unemployment" that was discussed in detail in Chapter Nine. Data similar to those presented in that chapter indicate quite clearly that this effect is much stronger among nonwhites than among whites.[5] Thus, not only do nonwhites suffer from higher unemployment rates than do whites but there appears to be a tendency for them to withdraw from the labor force in much greater numbers in response to high levels of unemployment. This phenomenon merely reinforces the impact of increased unemployment on nonwhite income levels.

One further simple statistic is helpful in developing an appreciation

---

[5] In the sample taken from the social security records, the percentage of Negro males employed in both 1957 and 1960 who were not employed in 1958 was 5.6 percent compared to 3.6 percent for all males. The same percentages for Negro and all females are 9.0 and 6.9, respectively. See Gallaway (61), chap. 9.

of the difficult economic position of the nonwhite in America. In the previous chapter, the impact of poverty in our society was discussed at the aggregate level but there was no treatment of the relative incidence of poverty among various population subgroups. However, in this chapter we are interested in the relative amounts of poverty found in certain of these subgroups. Table 11–2 summarizes the data relating to the inci-

TABLE 11–2
Percent of Families with Less Than $3,000
Annual Income (1963 Prices), by Race,
United States, 1947–68

| Year | Percent of Families with Less Than $3,000 Income | |
	White	Nonwhite
1947	27.8	66.1
1950	28.0	62.4
1953	22.7	52.8
1954	24.3	53.6
1955	21.6	51.6
1956	19.4	50.4
1957	19.5	49.8
1958	19.6	51.5
1959	18.2	49.3
1960	18.1	44.9
1961	18.0	46.4
1962	16.8	43.9
1963	15.7	43.1
1964	15.5	37.8
1965	14.5	37.3
1966	13.5	33.2
1967	12.6	31.6
1968	11.1	29.1

Source: U.S. Department of Commerce (197).

dence of poverty by race in the post-World War II period and they indicate quite clearly, and not unexpectedly, that nonwhites constitute a vastly disproportionate number of those considered to be in poverty by currently accepted standards. Roughly, the nonwhite sector of our society provides about one fourth of those defined as being in poverty despite their making up only about one tenth of the population.

I. HOW MUCH PROGRESS HAVE WE MADE?

While it is clear that there are still substantial economic differentials between whites and nonwhites in the United States, there are some suggestions that progress is being made in eliminating them. Take, for example, the tendency for the income levels of nonwhites to rise relative to those of whites during the 1960's. Detailed information on the relative income of nonwhite males, nonwhite females, and nonwhite families is presented in Table 11–3. These confirm the earlier observations to the

TABLE 11–3
Relative Income of Nonwhite Families, Nonwhite
Males, and Nonwhite Females, United States,
1947–68

	Relative Income*		
Year	Families	Males	Females
1947..........	0.51	n.a.	n.a.
1948..........	0.53	0.54	0.49
1949..........	0.51	0.49	0.51
1950..........	0.54	0.54	0.49
1951..........	0.53	0.55	0.46
1953..........	0.57	0.55	0.59
1954..........	0.51	0.50	0.55
1955..........	0.56	0.53	0.54
1956..........	0.53	0.52	0.58
1957..........	0.54	0.53	0.58
1958..........	0.51	0.50	0.59
1959..........	0.52	0.47	0.62
1960..........	0.55	0.53	0.70
1961..........	0.53	0.52	0.67
1962..........	0.53	0.49	0.67
1963..........	0.53	0.52	0.67
1964..........	0.56	0.57	0.70
1965..........	0.55	0.54	0.73
1966..........	0.60	0.55	0.76
1967..........	0.62	0.63	0.78
1968..........	0.63	0.59	0.79

* Ratio of nonwhite to white median income in each group.
SOURCE: U.S. Department of Commerce (197).

effect that since the late 1940's there has been a modest improvement in the relative income position of nonwhite males (mostly in very recent years), a steady and substantial increase in the relative income of nonwhite females, and some improvement in the position of nonwhite families. The last of these is the most significant from the standpoint of analyzing the extent to which the relative economic position of nonwhites has changed in recent years in that it describes the total income position of nonwhites more completely than the other measures. Consequently, the behavior of this statistic will be explored in greater depth.

The studies of Becker, Rayack, Batchelder, and Anderson suggest that the relative income position of nonwhite families may be quite sensitive to variations in economic activity.[6] This suspicion is confirmed when the data for nonwhite families are displayed graphically as is done in Figure 11-1. The general pattern of behavior of the relative income position of nonwhite families shows an increase from 1947 to 1952, followed by a decline through the remainder of the 1950's, some stability (at about 53 percent) in the early 1960's, and then an increase in the past few years.

The period of decline in nonwhite relative income corresponds roughly with the somewhat high unemployment and low growth rates that marked the American economy in the post-Korean War period while the upsurge in very recent years has occurred during a period when the economy has been experiencing substantial growth rates and a rather tight labor market. At the same time, a brief examination of Figure 11-1 also suggests that there may well have been some secular improve-

FIGURE 11-1
Ratio of Nonwhite to White Median Family Income

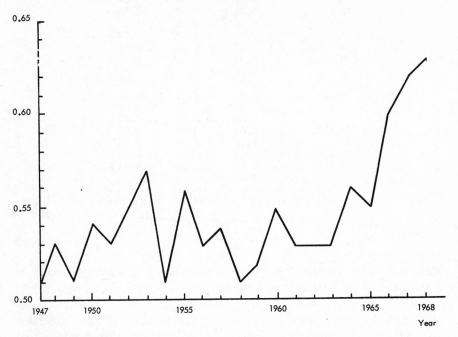

------

[6] Becker (**10**) and Rayack (**157**) conclude that during the relatively prosperous period of the 1940's the relative position of Negroes improved. Batchelder (**6**), p. 548, asks the question, "Can exhortation ever be as effective a means to Negro advance as is buoyant demand?" Anderson (**125**) finds that median income of families with a nonwhite head are quite sensitive to variations in per capita personal income. In fact, median income of this group rises and falls almost 50 percent more rapidly than per capita income during variations in the business cycle.

ment in the relative income position of nonwhite families in the post-World War II period. At least, the level of nonwhite relative income in 1953 and 1966 is consistent with this possibility. As noted earlier, these two years are fairly similar from the standpoint of the extent to which the American economy was functioning at near capacity.[7] Consequently, if the only factor affecting nonwhite relative income is fluctuations in economic activity, it would be expected that the relative income of nonwhites vis-à-vis whites would be approximately the same in these two years. Yet, the level of relative nonwhite family income is about 3.5 percentage points higher in 1966 than in 1953.

With this consideration in mind, a regression equation of the following form was estimated using the data of Table 11–3:

$$R = a + bU + ct + u \tag{1}$$

where R denotes the relative income of nonwhite families, U is the aggregate unemployment rate for the economy, t is a time variable, and u is a random error term. The unemployment variable is used as a measure of resource utilization in the economy and the general looseness or tightness of the labor market. Time (t) is quantified by indexing the years 1947 through 1968 from 1 to 22 in chronological order. The results of estimating the regression shown in (1) are:[8]

$$R = 0.59127 - 0.01855\ U + 0.00367\ t, R^2 = 0.76 \tag{2}$$
$$(5.12) \qquad\qquad (5.98)$$

Both of the regression coefficients are significant at the 2.5 percent level as is the coefficient of determination. This indicates that the relative income position of nonwhite families in the post-World War II United States has been responsive to fluctuations in the general level at which the economy has been operating and has also shown a secular drift upward as shown by the positive sign of the time variable in (2). Specifically, the coefficient associated with the unemployment variable indicates that a 1 percentage point change in the aggregate unemployment rate will be accompanied by a little less than a 2 percentage point change in the opposite direction in the relative income position of nonwhite families. Since the unemployment rate varied from 3.0 to 6.8 percent in the period under consideration, this means that the relative income position of nonwhite families varied by from 6.5 to 7.5 percentage points between 1947 and 1968 as the result of this factor. This implies that there are distinct limits to how much improvement in the relative income position of nonwhites can be expected from keeping the economy operating at high levels. In fact, the 1968 level of nonwhite relative

---

[7] See Chapter Eight for details. This judgment is based on the behavior of standard capacity utilization indices.

[8] The values in parentheses beneath the regression coefficients are t-values.

income may reflect almost the maximum impact of high levels of economic activity.[9]

Turning now to the performance of the time variable in regression (2), it is heartening to find that there is some positive drift upward in the level of nonwhite relative income through time. However, before attributing too much significance to this, the magnitude of the time drift needs to be taken into consideration. Actually, it is so small that it affords little cause for optimism about possible improvements in the relative income position of nonwhites. After all, it only amounts to about a 0.3 percentage point improvement in the relative income position of nonwhites each year. At that rate, it would take over a century to eliminate the existing disparity between white and nonwhite income levels.

The rather modest size of the time drift variable coefficient is surprising in one respect but not in another. On the one hand, given the tremendous strides made in closing the quantitative gap in education between whites and nonwhites in the post-World War II era, greater progress in eliminating the income differential might have been expected. Roughly, in this period over two thirds of the difference in median years of education was eliminated.[10] However, if we refer back to the material presented in Chapter Eight, it is possible to detect indications of little, if any, improvement in nonwhite economic status as far as the behavior of their unemployment levels is concerned. In Table 8–4 of that chapter, information on the age-sex-race structure of unemployment is presented. For nonwhite males the data presented there indicate a very stable unemployment structure except for the teen-age (14–19) group which has experienced a relative worsening of its position over time. What this means is that there has been no improvement in the relative unemployment position of nonwhite males. Further, in the case of teen-age members of this group the same optimistic view that emerged from the general analysis of the teen-age unemployment question in Chapter Eight is not warranted. When the same analysis is done for just nonwhite teenagers the conclusion is reached that there has been a relative deterioration in the demand for their services in the labor market and that unless an almost prohibitively high growth rate in the general economy is maintained the problem of high unemployment among teen-age nonwhites

---

[9] Thurow in (**189**, p. 50) points out that there are distinct limits to the effect of high levels of growth on relative income levels of nonwhites. He notes, correctly I think, that the sensitivity of nonwhite income levels to swings in economic activity noted by Anderson (**125**) reflect cyclical factors and do not indicate what would happen under conditions of sustained steady economic growth.

[10] In October, 1952, median school years completed by nonwhites was 7.6 and by whites 11.4. As of March, 1969, the respective figures were 11.3 and 12.4. Source: U.S. Department of Labor (**209**), Table B–9.

will be a permanent feature of the American scene.[11] With respect to nonwhite females, they appear to have actually lost ground relative to white females as regards the incidence of unemployment. While, in general, the structure of unemployment has shifted adversely for females the shift is more pronounced for nonwhite than for white females.

The very slight improvement in the relative economic position of nonwhites is reflected in the performance of the poverty rate among nonwhite families. Referring again to Table 11–2, the data shown there indicate that there has been little change in the relative incidence of poverty among nonwhites. Throughout the post-World War II period the nonwhite poverty rate is fairly consistently about two-and-one-half times larger than the white rate.

II. CAUSES OF ECONOMIC DISTRESS AMONG NONWHITES

The picture painted to this point is one of relative economic deprivation among American nonwhites. This rather naturally suggests the next question to be discussed, viz, Why do nonwhites have second-class economic status in our world? A number of possible answers come quickly to mind but perhaps the most widely advanced ones are some variation on the theme of racial discrimination. Actually, the rubric "discrimination" encompasses a great variety of possibilities. In a very general sense discriminatory practices may be dichotomized into (1) those that take place prior to entry into the labor market and (2) those that occur subsequent to labor market entry. The first of these rather obviously includes the broad area of differences in the availability of educational opportunity to whites and nonwhites. For example, from the standpoint of pure quantity of education nonwhites in the United States until very recent years had a median level of education that was about two years less than that of whites.[12] In general, the difference is greater among older nonwhites but it persists across most age-groups as can be seen from the data of Table 11–4. Such quantitative differences in the amount of education available to nonwhites are magnified by qualitative shortcomings of nonwhite education in many areas (such as still or formerly segregated southern schools and northern urban "inner area" facilities).[13] Beyond the matter of current educational opportunity for nonwhites,

---

[11] For details of this argument, see Gallaway (72).

[12] The gap in education declined from 3.8 years in 1952 to 1.8 years in 1966 and to 1.1 years in 1969. Source: U.S. Department of Labor (209), Table B–9.

[13] For a discussion of the possible magnitude of these qualitative differences, see Coleman, et al. (31). The findings of this study suggest that one year of education for nonwhites is the equivalent of about three quarters of one year of education for whites.

TABLE 11–4
Median Years of Education, 1960, White and
Negro Males, by Age

Age	Median Years of Education	
	White	Negro
14–24	10.8	9.6
25–29	12.4	10.5
30–34	12.2	9.7
35–39	12.2	8.9
40–44	12.0	8.3
45–49	10.7	7.4
50–54	9.8	6.8
55–59	8.8	6.0
60 and over	8.4	4.7

SOURCE: U.S. Department of Commerce, Bureau of the Census, *Census of Population*, 1960, *United States Summary, General Social and Economic Characteristics* (Washington, D.C., U.S.G.P.O., 1961).

premarket discrimination may also be occurring indirectly through the inheritance of cultural attitudes which reflect the lack of educational opportunity in past generations.[14] The nonwhite child reared in a family where the parents have relatively meager educational attainments may well fall so far behind children reared in homes where the parents are better educated that he finds it extremely difficult to maintain the same pace of educational advancement. Such an inherited cultural lag merely reinforces the impact of relative unavailability of education for nonwhites. Consequently, it adds to the effect of quantitative differences in educational opportunity and further emphasizes the fact that the mere quantitative differences in educational opportunity understate the extent of premarket discrimination in American society.

The phenomenon of market discrimination against nonwhites has been extensively analyzed[15] and, in general, two variations of such discrimination can be considered. First, there is the possibility that nonwhites working in the same employment as whites receive lower wage rates than whites. This variant can be thought of as wage discrimination and can be contrasted with labor market practices of an exclusive nature, i.e., those that lead to nonwhites not being employed in certain lines of economic activity. Some studies suggest that the exclusion variant of discrimination against nonwhites is the dominant one and, certainly,

[14] The possibility of cultural differences between white and Negro families is treated extensively by Moynihan (141).

[15] See Becker (10) and Krueger (107) for the best theoretical discussions. In a more empirical vein, the studies cited in footnote 6 are worth noting as well as Dewey (38) and Katzner (97).

to the extent that collective bargaining agreements exist in American industry it would seem highly unlikely that overt wage discrimination would be the major form of providing nonwhites with smaller economic rewards than those available to whites.[16]

On the other hand, the exclusion variant of discrimination would seem to be relatively easy to practice through the expedient of simply not hiring nonwhites when job openings are available or dismissing them whenever reductions in employment must be made. In particular, the latter practice would be easily implemented if nonwhites were only hired whenever the labor market was extremely tight, for nonwhites would then tend to be workers with less seniority than whites. When viewed in these terms the exclusion variant of economic discrimination bears a striking resemblance to the "last-hired-first-fired" thesis which is frequently advanced to account for levels of nonwhite unemployment.[17] Very simply, that thesis maintains that nonwhites are not hired until the labor market becomes sufficiently tight to make it too costly for employers to ignore the availability of nonwhite labor and are then dismissed whenever the labor market becomes loose again.[18]

The last-hired-first-fired form of nonwhite exclusion from job opportunities is only one manifestation of this phenomenon. There is, in addition, what could be thought of as the "never-hired" type of exclusion. This may be particularly appropriate in certain white-collar or professional areas where nonwhite employment is quite minimal or nonexistent.[19] Of course, these low levels of employment in certain occupations may also reflect educational discrimination but, on the basis of available evidence, it is quite difficult to explain the relative lack of nonwhite employment in many fields on the basis of just this factor. Rather, there does seem to be a systematic tendency for nonwhites to be excluded from employment in many areas with consequent effects on their levels of income.[20]

A few further comments are in order with respect to possible sources of the relatively low levels of nonwhite income in the United States. To this point we have been emphasizing elements which are the product of discriminatory behavior on the part of the white majority of America's

---

[16] Dewey (38) found little evidence of open-wage discrimination.

[17] For a summary of the "last-hired-first-fired" proposition, see Gilman (77).

[18] Scully and Gallaway have found evidence to support the "last-hired-first-fired" thesis in (171). However, they also found evidence to suggest that the phenomenon also operates in other nonprime labor force groups and that nonwhite male adults appear to suffer least from its impact.

[19] For a detailed description of the pattern of occupations held by nonwhites, see Hiestand (86).

[20] Later in this chapter an explanation for the presence of exclusion of nonwhites will be suggested in the process of testing for the presence or absence of pure market discrimination.

population. This involves an implicit assumption on our part that the nonwhite portion of our population is basically seeking the same objectives as the remainder of the society. In short, it assumes the non-existence of a distinctive nonwhite subculture in the United States. Now, there is some evidence to the effect that such a subculture may exist.[21] Admittedly, it is extremely difficult to disentangle the effects of discriminatory action by whites on nonwhite behavior from any possible cultural differences. For example, we previously alluded to the possible impact of differences in the educational attainments of nonwhite parents upon the capacity of nonwhite children to compete educationally with other children. Should this be considered to be the product of past discriminatory behavior on the part of whites or treated as a symptom of the existence of a nonwhite subculture?

In the case of potential educational differences it may be easy to answer that question in that there is some objective and quantifiable evidence of past discriminatory practices which would seem to offer an explanation for the difficulties encountered by the nonwhite child. However, is the answer so clear when the question under consideration is the source of differences in the response of nonwhites to labor market stimuli? Such differences apparently do exist[22] and it is possible that they are purely the result of different behavior patterns being forced upon nonwhites by the white majority. On the other hand, it is quite possible that such behavioral differences reflect a distinctive nonwhite subculture and, if they do, it may be somewhat presumptuous of whites to assume that their particular set of cultural values should be the norm for all members of the society. At any rate, regardless of the difficulties inherent in identifying the sources of differences between nonwhite and white behavior patterns, it is appropriate to keep in mind the possibility that some of these observed differences are not purely the result of discriminatory behavior on the part of the white portion of the society.

In line with that possibility, if we are to consider the whole range of explanations of differences in white and nonwhite economic status, we ought to also deal with the contingency that there is something generic to nonwhites which renders them less productive than whites and thus less desirable as employees in an economic enterprise. Obviously, educational differences might produce such productivity differentials but the maximum estimate I have seen of the contribution of educa-

---

[21] See Moynihan (**141**).

[22] Such differences are marked. For example, Negroes do not respond in the same fashion to the stimuli hypothesized to affect the incidence of hidden unemployment in Chapter Nine. Nor do they respond to the same factors as whites where labor mobility behavior is concerned. In general, where their labor market responses differ from those of whites, the difference operates to worsen their relative economic position in our society.

tional discrimination to the white-nonwhite income gap would argue that education accounts for about one third of the income differential.[23] The other two-thirds must be explained by other factors and a possibility here is that there are productivity differentials which do not have their roots in educational discrimination. Admittedly, this is a very controversial subject to even broach but objectivity dictates that even controversial hypotheses must be considered.

It is possible to conduct some exploratory testing of this hypothesis.[24] To begin, we can postulate that variations in average output among differing employments (where the same production function is involved)[25] are related to the capital-labor ratio in those employments, the average amount of education possessed by workers, and, if there are negative productivity impacts associated with the hiring of nonwhites, the proportion of nonwhites in the particular employment. Further, it can be argued that under such conditions employers might respond to the impact on productivity by either excluding some nonwhites from employment or paying them a wage which would be commensurate with the differences in productivity.[26] If employers respond in this fashion, it can be further reasoned that both wages and average productivity in those cases where exclusion is practiced will not be affected by variations in whatever employment of nonwhites takes place. But, where there is no exclusion of nonwhites from employment opportunities wages and productivity levels will be affected by variations in nonwhite employment. These propositions can be tested for the manufacturing sector of the American economy using data from the 1958 Census of Manufactures describing value added by manufacturing, wages, volume of capital employed, and the amount of labor used in different industries and different states along with estimates of human capital (i.e., education) possessed by workers in different states and industries in 1960.[27]

---

[23] Katzner (**97**).

[24] A considerably more detailed discussion of the testing process is contained in Gallaway and Scully (**75**). This manuscript is available as Research Paper No. 4, Department of Economics, Ohio University, Athens, Ohio.

[25] Theoretically, marginal productivity is the key magnitude to consider. However, data describing the marginal productivity of workers is simply not available. The use of average productivity is justified if industry production functions approximate the Cobb-Douglas form. In such a case the marginal product of labor is proportional to its average product.

[26] In effect, it can be argued that employers might choose to integrate their labor forces up to the point at which the marginal products of majority and minority group labor were equal. If productivity differentials unfavorable to the minority group exist, this will result in exclusion of the minority group. On the other hand, if employment of the minority group is expanded beyond this point in the face of unfavorable productivity differentials, wage differentials will result, assuming employers behave in a maximizing fashion.

[27] A brief description of the nature of these estimates may be found in Scully (**170**).

TABLE 11-5

Regression Results for Analysis of Discrimination against Nonwhites*

Regression Type	Dependent Variable	Regression Parameters					
		Constant	Capital/Labor Ratio	Human Capital/Labor Ratio	Percent Nonwhite Employment	R^2	Degrees of Freedom
No exclusion.........	Wages	4.0750	0.3255 (6.13)	0.2470 (4.29)	-0.1203 (4.56)	0.88	109
Exclusion.........	Wages	0.2766	0.0864 (2.76)	0.3220 (5.65)	0.0135 (0.68)	0.85	125
No exclusion.........	Productivity	-46.4859	2.3825 (5.95)	0.9542 (2.36)	-0.4094 (2.21)	0.86	109
Exclusion.........	Productivity	-4.2210	0.8842 (3.64)	-0.1234 (0.28)	0.0618 (0.40)	0.61	125

* Other variables are included in the regressions from which these parameters are taken. These are present to adjust for interindustry variations in production functions, the presence of other minority group labor inputs, and the presence of trade unions.

Source: Gallaway and Scully (**75**).

The latter enables us to control for differences in the educational accomplishments of workers. The results are summarized in Table 11–5.[28] They indicate that in industries where exclusion of nonwhites is the rule there are no wage or productivity differentials associated with variations in the employment of nonwhites.[29] However, when nonwhites are not excluded from employment significant negative wage and productivity differentials appear. Not only are they significant, but the ratio of the wage to the productivity coefficients is almost exactly equal to the ratio of wages to productivity in the industries where exclusion is not practiced. This would seem to suggest that the wage differentials which are detected in these industries have their basis in the productivity differentials which are observed.[30] Now, this is a significant finding but one which should be treated cautiously. The portion of the economy for which sufficient data are available to conduct the necessary tests is restricted to the manufacturing sector and there is always the possibility that variables which have not been sufficiently controlled for are affecting the results. Nevertheless, the evidence is sufficiently strong to at least warrant considering the productivity differential hypothesis as a possible explanation for white-nonwhite income differentials. Let me emphasize at this point that it would be presumptuous to consider it as being considered substantiated. However, it would be equally presumptuous to simply ignore this hypothesis.

III. CONCLUSIONS

The question of the relative economic status of nonwhites in the United States seems to be dominated by the tendency for the income differential between these groups to be rather unresponsive to changing conditions. Despite tremendous strides in eliminating the quantitative differentials in education, the enactment of fairly wide-sweeping equal

---

[28] Variables other than those shown in Table 11–5 are included in the regression equations to adjust for interindustry differences in production functions. These permit pooling the various industry and state observations.

[29] The criteria for distinguishing between industries that exclude nonwhites and those that do not is approximately 10 percent of total employment being nonwhite. Less than this indicates exclusion; more, nonexclusion. Generally speaking, the various manufacturing industries divide fairly clearly into those that practice exclusion and those that do not.

[30] Assuming strict Cobb-Douglas production functions, the labor share of income would be constant with maximizing behavior by employers. Consequently, comparing the actual share of value added by manufacturing accruing to labor with the ratio of the wage to the productivity coefficients shown in Table 11–5 will provide an indication of whether the wage differential associated with employing minority group labor is consistent with the productivity differential. If the ratio is about the same as the aggregate ratio of wage income to total value added, the wage and productivity coefficients are consistent with one another.

employment opportunity legislation, and a good many expressions of public concern about the economic status of nonwhites, only grudging progress seems to have been made in improving their relative lot. At first glance, this might seem to suggest that the charges of some that discrimination against nonwhites is extremely strong and pervasive are quite valid. However, some alternative explanations have been explored, particularly the possibility that there are productivity differentials between whites and nonwhites other than those that could be explained by differing amounts of education possessed by workers. What the source of these productivity differentials might be is a matter of speculation. However, whatever their source, if they exist, there are very substantial public policy implications. Specifically, the evidence which indicates a more than passing degree of consistency between wage and productivity effects of nonwhite employment implies that there is an economic rationale on the part of employers for the exclusionary and apparently discriminatory practices in which they engage. In short, it may well be that the source of discrimination in employment and wages lies not so much in subjective considerations of race that exist in employers' minds, but in the hard realities of the economic variables of costs and profits. The obvious consequence of such a possibility is that public policy approaches to the problem of disparities between white and nonwhite income levels which emphasize equal employment opportunity legislation and exhortation of the business community to abandon its "iniquitous practices" may not be particularly effective in that following these injunctions would impose economic costs on employers. Thus, it is possible that far from employers' being individuals who are willing to pay a price in terms of malallocation of resources to indulge their personal desires to discriminate against nonwhites, they are really engaging in standard maximizing practices which have the end result of creating differential levels of income by race. Certainly, if this is the case, the tendency for white-nonwhite income differentials to be so persistent is somewhat understandable.

chapter TWELVE

The Economic Status
of the Aged

IN recent years in the United States there have been repeated expressions of concern with respect to the economic condition of the aged portion of our population. One of the most recent examples of this are the 1969 hearings before the Special Committee on Aging of the U.S. Senate.[1] The essence of the concern is expressed in two basic propositions:

1. The existing levels of income available to the aged are not adequate to provide them with a satisfactory standard of living, and
2. The relative income position of the aged vis-à-vis the nonaged has been deteriorating over time and will continue to do so in the future.

These are rather serious complaints and, if true, they would suggest that the United States faces a fundamental social problem. However, let us see what the evidence is to substantiate these contentions.

I. THE NATURE OF THE INCOME OF THE AGED

The easiest to deal with of the two propositions relating to the economic position of the aged in the United States is the second one, i.e., that the relative position of the aged has been deteriorating over time. Consequently, it will be treated first. A straightforward comparison of the median income levels of families whose head is aged 65 or older

---

[1] For a summary of the positions developed during these hearings, see (50).

with the median income levels of all families suggests that there is some validity to the proposition that there has been a decline in the relative income position of the aged (see Table 12–1). In 1947 the income level of the aged was 60.4 percent of that of all families while by 1969 it had declined to about 50 percent. The bulk of this decline occurred between 1947 and 1960 (from 60.4 percent to 51.5 percent) and W. H. Locke Anderson (**125**) concluded that over this period income levels of the aged were not responsive in any fashion to variations in the

TABLE 12–1
Relative Income of Families with Head Aged 65 and over,
United States, 1947–69

Year	Ratio of Median Income of Families with Aged Head to Median Income of All Families (Percent)	Year	Ratio of Median Income of Families with Aged Head to Median Income of All Families (Percent)
1947	60.4	1959	52.3
1948	60.0	1960	51.5
1949	60.9	1961	52.7
1950	57.5	1962	53.8
1951	53.0	1963	55.4
1952	58.5	1964	51.4
1953	52.7	1965	49.7
1954	55.1	1966	49.1
1955	52.8	1967	48.5
1956	53.3	1968	53.2
1957	50.1	1969	50.9
1958	52.4		

SOURCE: U.S. Department of Commerce (**197**).

general level of economic activity. This would seem to be fairly conclusive evidence that the relative deterioration hypothesis has a substantial degree of validity and that aged Americans may truly be separated from the mainstream of economic activity, which is to say that they are prime candidates for being considered as being in the "backwash" of economic life in the United States.

Probing beneath the surface of the evidence which has been cited, however, reveals some interesting facets of the changes in the relative income position of the aged which make it less than self-evident that the observed decline in the relative income position of the aged should be interpreted as being indicative of a general worsening of their social welfare position. To begin, there are some very obvious reasons for the decline in the income position of the aged. Since 1947 there has been a substitution of income received from public and private retirement systems for work-related income. For example, this is reflected in an extremely large increase in the proportion of the aged receiving benefits under the Old Age Survivors Disability Health Insurance (OASDHI) system and the decline in the labor force participation rate of aged males. In 1947 only about 10 percent of the aged were recipients of OASDHI benefits and the labor force participation rate among aged males was 47.8 percent. Recently, it is estimated that almost 85 percent of the aged receive OASDHI benefits and the labor force participation rate for aged males is 27.2 percent.[2]

These rather sizable changes in the circumstances surrounding the receipt of money income by the aged offer an explanation for the failure of the income of aged families to move in conjunction with overall levels of income in the economy. While this in itself is interesting, it unfortunately does not shed much light on the matter of the social significance of this phenomenon for it does not attack the question of why these changes have been taking place. Why have elderly people more and more withdrawn from the labor force? Why have increasing numbers of them become recipients of increasing amounts of transfer payment income through both public and private retirement systems? One possibility is that they have been forced into these patterns of behavior by a lack of economic opportunity. If this is the case, the previously cited evidence suggests that the aged have been involuntarily isolated from the mainstream of American economic life. On the other hand, there is an alternative explanation for the changes which have occurred, namely, that the elderly have selected these new behavior patterns in preference to patterns which would have left them more in the mainstream of American economic life. If this is the case, the social significance of the low-income levels generated by the isolation of the aged from the normal processes of economic growth must be assessed in a different light. Consequently, it is important to determine whether the changes in the structure of the income of the aged have been voluntary or involuntary in character.

II. THE OLDER WORKER AND RETIREMENT— DECLINING DEMAND?

Essentially, the question of the nature of the changes in the economic behavior of the aged is a matter of determining whether the crucial factor is a relative decline in the demand for the labor of the elderly or a relative decline in the supply of such labor. The first of these possibilities can be formally analyzed with the assistance of the theory of economic discrimination. Commencing with Gary Becker's (10) con-

---

[2] The source of these data is U.S. Department of Labor (209), Table A–2 for the labor force participation rates, and Social Security Bulletin, September, 1969, Table Q–4 for the proportion of the aged receiving OASDHI benefits.

ception of economic discrimination as existing only in the presence of identifiable opportunity costs of either an objective (money) or subjective (utility) nature, it is easy to see why a relative decrease in job opportunities among the aged may be viewed as a special case of economic discrimination, for such a decline must be based on either increased money costs associated with employing older workers or a subjective preference on the part of employers for hiring younger workers.

To illustrate how the theory of economic discrimination applies to the question of whether there has been a relative decline in job opportunities for the aged, let us consider the working of the labor market under the following conditions:

1. There are significant numbers of both younger and older members of the labor force in the market.
2. Younger and older workers are homogeneous in all respects except age.
3. All factor and commodity markets are purely competitive.

Now, let the employer's money proceeds (M) for employing labor be denoted by

$$M = f(K, L) \tag{1}$$

where K represents the amount of capital and L the quantity of labor employed in the productive process.[3] In a general fashion the profits (P) obtained from employing a variable amount of labor with a fixed quantity of capital are given by[4]

$$P = f(K, L) - wL \tag{2}$$

where w denotes the wage rate paid to labor. Differentiating (2) with respect to L, setting the result equal to zero, and solving yields the familiar condition for profit maximization that the wage rate and the marginal productivity of labor should be equated.

Obviously, (2) makes no provision for distinguishing between young and old labor inputs. This can be accomplished by expanding (2) as follows:

$$P = f(K, L_y + L_o) - [w_y L_y + (w_y - d)L_o] \tag{3}$$

where the subscripts y and o denote young and old, respectively, and d represents the differential between the wage rates of younger and older workers. Some differential (d) is required or (3) is merely a trivial redefinition of (2).

---

[3] Expression (1) is assumed to be twice differentiable with negative second order derivatives.

[4] This abstracts from nonlabor costs such as fixed and variable material costs.

The question at this point is: "What determines the value of d?" Keeping within Becker's opportunity cost framework, d will obviously depend on the complex of additional costs which the employer must incur if he employs older workers. These costs (whatever their origin) operate to create in the mind of an employer a "taste" for discrimination against older workers. Symbolically, we can represent such a taste by the following function:

$$D = \phi(L_o) \tag{4}$$

where D denotes the money equivalent of the various costs (including subjective ones) associated with employing older workers. Now, expression (3) can be rewritten to incorporate the employer's taste for discrimination

$$P = f(K, L_y + L_o) - \phi(L_o) - [w_y L_y + (w_y - d)L_o] \tag{5}$$

In order to maximize P the employer should maintain a wage differential d which is equal to $\phi'(L_o)$, i.e., equal to his "marginal" taste for discrimination.[5] This, in turn, implies that the wage rate for younger labor should be equated with $f'(K, L_y + L_o)$, i.e., with the marginal product of young and old labor combined (remember the homogeneity assumption).

The impact of such maximizing behavior by all employers in a competitive market is dependent on the magnitude of the marginal taste for discrimination. For example, in an extreme case the marginal taste for discrimination may be sufficiently large to dictate a wage differential d that would reduce the wage of older workers to a point at which the supply of such labor would be zero. This might be the case if some institutional restriction such as a mandatory retirement age were in force. Under these conditions older workers would be excluded from the market even though they were willing to work at the prevailing wage for younger workers. In short, within the framework of our definition of unemployment they would be considered to be involuntarily unemployed. Admittedly, in the case of some of these workers the unemployment may be disguised by labor force withdrawal. However, if the phenomenon of exclusion is a significant factor in our economy, there should be a discernible change in the unemployment rate for older workers relative to that for younger workers.[6]

---

[5] The function $\phi(L_o)$ is assumed to have a nonnegative second order derivative. This is necessary in order for these maximizing "rules" to hold.

[6] Evidence such as that developed by Dernburg and Strand (**37**) indicates that the "discouragement" effect which produces labor force withdrawal is strong among the aged. However, it does not seem to be sufficiently strong to produce a zero change in unemployment levels among the aged in the face of their being displaced involuntarily from the labor market.

In addition to the exclusion case, we need to also consider the possibility of employers' possessing tastes for discrimination against older workers which are greater than zero but not sufficient to produce complete exclusion of older workers from job opportunities. In this case, older workers will still be employed but at a wage which is less than that of younger workers by the amount d. Examples of this type of situation might be instances in which employers are faced with additional monetary costs if they employ older workers, costs such as (1) retirement plan expenditures or (2) less-efficient work performance by older workers. In cases such as these, maximizing behavior by employers dictates that a wage differential unfavorable to older workers exist as compensation to the employer for these additional costs. In the absence of such a differential, older workers will not be hired.

One further comment on the end results of the presence of factors which operate to reduce the availability of job opportunities for the aged is in order. It should be realized that the two variants of discrimination against older workers that we have discussed in some instances may blend into one another. Take as an example, a situation in which an employer feels that there are certain monetary disadvantages associated with hiring older workers. As we have noted, before older workers will be hired under these conditions, a wage differential unfavorable to these workers must develop. However, it is entirely possible that the institutional framework of the labor market in question may prohibit the creation of such a differential. This could be the case in a market where there were collective bargaining agreements between employers and unions. These would be quite unlikely to contain any provisions permitting the creation of such a differential. As a consequence, the wage differential variant would simply be converted to an exclusion case, although this would in all probability only apply to new hirings. The existence of seniority provisions in most collective bargaining agreements would prohibit the systematic elimination of existing older employees.

The analysis of the working of economic discrimination (which is all that is implied in the argument that there has been an adverse shift in the demand for older workers) against older workers suggests two possible end results. Such discrimination will produce either (1) unemployment among older workers or (2) a wage differential which is unfavorable to older workers. These, in turn, argue that, if there has been a change between two points in time which has adversely affected the demand for older workers, this change will be accompanied by either (1) a worsening of unemployment among the aged relative to unemployment among younger workers or (2) a worsening of the relative wage position of older workers vis-à-vis younger workers.

On the basis of the preceding argument, it would seem that the declining demand hypothesis can be tested by examining the behavior of relative unemployment rates and wage levels among the aged. The first of these can be rather easily assessed by referring again to Table 8–4 of Chapter Eight. There, the unemployment rates for the aged by race and sex are regressed against the "prime" unemployment rate and time. The results are summarized in Table 12–2. They seem to indicate some evidence of positive time drifts in unemployment among the elderly relative to the prime labor force group. Collectively, these time drifts are sufficient to produce about an 0.7 percentage point upward drift in the unemployment rate of the elderly vis-à-vis the prime group between 1953 and 1966. However, a time drift of this proportion does not appear to be something exclusively associated with age. The analysis

TABLE 12–2
Time Drift in Aged Unemployment Rates, 1953–66,
by Sex and Race

Sex and Race	Time Drift Coefficient	t-Value	Total Drift 1953–66
White male............	0.03	1.9	0.39
White female...........	0.08	2.8	1.04
Nonwhite male........	0.20	1.8	2.60
Nonwhite female.......	0.03	0.5	0.39

SOURCE: Table 8–4, Chapter Eight.

presented in Chapter Eight dealt rather extensively with this phenomenon and from the data presented there it can be estimated that the unemployment rate for the nonaged nonprime labor force groups drifted upward by 1.3 percentage points over this period or almost twice as much as the drift in the aged rate. Of course, it can be argued that teen-agers are perhaps a special case and ought to be excluded. If this is done, the drift in the nonaged nonprime unemployment rate is 0.6 percentage points or about the same as that among the aged. Thus, what time drift there is in the unemployment rate of the aged is apparently part of a general phenomenon which is found among the nonprime labor force group as a whole. Consequently, on the basis of the behavior of aged unemployment rates, there would seem to be little grounds for arguing that there was some type of systematic discrimination against older workers in the labor market in favor of younger workers.

The wage aspect of the declining demand hypothesis is somewhat more difficult to test due to the paucity of data of the exact form which is required. Ideally, hourly wage rate data would be the best for this purpose but they are not readily available by age. Simple income data from the Census will not suffice in that they include transfer payments and do not distinguish between full- and part-time workers. The latter consideration is quite important, for the legal constraints upon earnings imposed upon recipients of social security benefits produce a shift toward part-time employment among the aged.[7] About the only data which are available that shed light on this question are various estimates of the annual earnings of full-time workers by age. They generally indicate that there has been little shift in the level of annual earnings of aged males relative to the earnings of nonaged men.[8] However, the data are somewhat sketchy. Even so, the totality of evidence which can be obtained (both on wages and unemployment) reflects adversely on the proposition that discrimination against older workers in American labor markets has produced a decline in the demand for the labor services of the aged.

III.   THE OLDER WORKER AND RETIREMENT— A SUPPLY SHIFT?

If we reject the demand shift explanation for the changes in the economic behavior of the aged, we would seem to be left with an explanation couched in terms of labor supply shifts. To substantiate such a contention, we can appeal to the conventional theory of consumer behavior. Very simply, that theory would argue that the impact of making available to the elderly a stream of transfer payment income (of the social security type, for example) would induce a reduction in the quantity of labor which they would supply in the market at various wage rates, a conclusion which is consistent with the actual behavioral changes previously mentioned. While such theoretical support for the supply shift hypothesis is helpful, it would be somewhat more reassuring if positive empirical evidence supporting the hypothesis were available.

One possible source of such evidence is cross-section data on a geographic basis relating labor force participation to the presence of transfer payment income. Such data are available from the Census and Social Security Administration. A conceptual framework for analyzing these data can be developed by considering the following relationship:

$$R = mB + n(1 - B) \tag{5}$$

where R denotes an aggregate labor force participation rate for the

---

[7] For a discussion of the impact of these constraints, see Gallaway (**71**).

[8] Evidence from the Social Security Administration relating to earnings levels of aged male workers employed in all four quarters of the year provide information which indicates that during the 1950's the wage income of such workers was consistently between 80 and 85 percent of earnings of all workers. See Gallaway (**68**). During the 1960's data describing incomes of full-time experienced aged workers show that they are about 80 percent of those of nonaged full-time workers. See (**50**).

aged, B is the proportion of the aged receiving old-age benefits under the social security system, m denotes the propensity to be a member of the labor force among recipients of retirement income, and n denotes the same propensity among nonrecipients.

Now, if n and m could be treated as constants across all sectors, it would be a simple matter to compare sectoral observations of R with sectoral observations of B. However, this is not the case: in fact, m and n would be expected to be quite variant from sector to sector due to differences in relative income opportunities, differences in industrial composition of sectors, differences in the degree of urbanization, and differences in cultural attitudes toward work.

A solution to this difficulty can be had by considering different time periods (indicated by subscripts t and $t + 1$) and expanding (5) to

$$R_t - R_{t+1} = m(B_t - B_{t+1}) - n(B_t - B_{t+1}) \tag{6}$$

or

$$\Delta R = m\Delta B - n\Delta B \tag{7}$$

Further, if m is assumed to be some invariant multiple (q) of n, (7) becomes

$$\Delta R = qn\Delta B - n\Delta B = n(q - 1)\Delta B \tag{8}$$

which transforms to

$$\Delta R/\Delta B = (q - 1)n \tag{9}$$

where $0 < q < 1$. This is the basic relationship we wish to explore. It can be tested by fitting

$$\Delta R/\Delta B = a + bN + u \tag{10}$$

where N represents the labor force participation rate among nonrecipients of transfer payment income (the empirical equivalent of n) and u is a random error term. Empirical evaluation of this relationship requires data describing ΔR, ΔB, and N for differing geographic areas. Data describing ΔR can be obtained from the 1960 and 1950 decennial censuses. In fact, the detail in the census data is sufficient to permit the calculation of labor force participation rates on an urban-rural basis which is helpful in eliminating one source of variation in the relationship. Consequently, in the analysis to follow, an urban-rural breakdown of labor force participation rates is used.

State by state data are not as easily obtained for the other two components of the regression. Beneficiary rates per 1,000 population aged 65 and over by state are available, but there is no breakdown by sex or by whether the beneficiaries are primary or secondary beneficiaries[9] or by their urban-rural status. This difficulty is not insurmountable since there is in all probability a strong correlation between changes in overall beneficiary rates and changes in the primary beneficiary rates by sex and by urban-rural status. However, the use of overall beneficiary rates will tend to weaken any observed relationship between $\Delta R/\Delta B$ and N. As for data describing N, probably the best estimate that might be used would be the state by state labor force participation rates, by sex, from a census prior to the great increase in the proportion of the elderly who receive social security benefits. The 1940 census was selected for this purpose in preference to the 1950 census in an effort to eliminate the impact of the phenomenon of regression toward the mean which would be present as the result of regressing a variable containing ΔR against one of the terms used in calculating ΔR.[10]

The data sources which have been described were employed to estimate a regression equation for urban males using the individual states (except Alaska and Hawaii) as observations with the following results:[11]

$$\Delta R/\Delta B = 0.1664 - 0.9472\ N, \quad R^2 = 0.46. \qquad (11)$$
$$(6.47)$$

The regression coefficient associated with N is statistically significant at the 1 percent level indicating a meaningful relationship between the dependent and independent variables.

The results of the regression of cross-section data are reassuring with respect to the existence of the suggested relationship between the receipt of transfer payment income by the aged and their labor force participation. While this is helpful, some positive evidence indicating the operation of the causal relationship suggested by the theory of consumer demand would be even more persuasive. As we noted, that theory argues that the presence of transfer payment income of the social security benefit type produces a substitution of leisure for income-producing work. Now, if this is true, *ceteris paribus*, differing levels of benefits relative to income should produce different degrees of substitution of leisure for work and different amounts of labor force participation. This possibility can be tested if it is possible to obtain a sufficient number of observations

---

[9] A primary beneficiary is the person on the basis of whose earnings record the Social Security Administration has entitled the individuals concerned to benefits. A secondary beneficiary is one who receives benefits as the result of another's earnings record, such as a dependent wife.

[10] This problem would be particularly acute if R_{1950} were regressed against $(R_{1950} - R_{1960})/\Delta B$. Consequently, the 1940 census was used to obtain estimates of N. This does not introduce any serious problem in that there was little change in the aggregate labor force participation rate among aged men between 1940 and 1950.

[11] The values in parentheses beneath the regression coefficients are t-values.

which satisfy the *ceteris paribus* conditions of the preceding statement. An obvious possibility here is geographical data such as that already employed. However, a group of observations by state that will meet the *ceteris paribus* conditions are not readily available. The complication is the sensitivity of state labor force participation rates to such factors as the level of unemployment in the state and its degree of industrialization, among other things.[12] To take account of these, it is necessary to include additional variables in the relationship which has been postulated. Consequently, the following expression is hypothesized to explain state by state variations in the labor force participation rate of aged males:

$$R = a + bM + cU + dE + u \qquad (12)$$

where M represents the ratio of annual benefits under the old-age benefits provisions of the social security legislation for males in 1959[13] to median earnings of male members of the experienced civilian labor force during 1959,[14] U is the percent of the population of a state living in urban areas in 1960, E is the percent of the labor force unemployed by state in 1960, and u is a random error term.[15] In line with the substitutive relationship which is postulated between labor force participation of aged males and the availability of retirement benefits, a negative sign is hypothesized for the variable M. The results of fitting (12) are:

$$R = 0.632 - 0.635\ M - 0.133\ U - 2.182\ E,\ R^2 = 0.38 \qquad (13)$$
$$(3.00)(3.11)(4.90)$$

Clearly, the relative benefits variable (M) is highly significant in a statistical sense with the expected sign. This lends substantial support to the hypothesis that the changes in economic behavior of the aged represent essentially a negative shift in the quantity of labor which they are willing to supply in the labor market at various wage rates.

The preceding findings argue (1) that the evidence suggesting that the aged are relatively isolated from the mainstream of American economic life is not surprising due to the great changes in the work patterns of the aged during the post-1947 period and (2) that these changes are primarily the result of a shift in the supply of labor forthcoming from the elderly. The obvious question now is, "What is the importance of these findings?" To answer the query, we must again take up the ques-

---

[12] For example, the level of unemployment affects aged labor force participation levels through the operation of the discouragement effect.

[13] SOURCE: *Social Security Bulletin; Annual Statistical Supplement,* 1959, Table 81.

[14] U.S. Department of Commerce (195), Table 140.

[15] This formulation of the relationship which is hypothesized to explain R was suggested in part by Taussig (184).

tion of the social significance of "voluntary" versus "involuntary" changes in work patterns. Presumably, in a relatively free market economy, an "involuntary" (i.e., strictly demand induced) change in the work patterns of a group that results in a relative reduction of their levels of income is indicative of a worsening of their general welfare. On the other hand, if the changes in work habits are "voluntary" in character (i.e., reflect a supply shift), then presumably the individuals who have made these decisions feel that their welfare is enhanced by their "new" behavioral pattern. In short, if I elect one combination of income and leisure to another, I "reveal" my preference for that combination and am therefore indicating that I am happier (or more satisfied or on a higher indifference curve) with it. In this instance, the fact that I elect a lower level of income does not indicate a decline in my welfare—quite the contrary; it would seem to indicate an improvement in welfare. Thus, the conclusion that the behavioral shifts among the elderly over the period in question are essentially "voluntary" in character implies quite strongly that the lower relative income levels implicit in these behavior patterns need not be interpreted as a sign that the elderly are lagging behind the rest of the economy in terms of their social welfare. A good case can be made that the elderly in the United States have in recent years elected to take a larger portion of their "real income" in the form of a commodity which is not priced through the market mechanism and, consequently, has no money equivalent assigned to it, viz, leisure. From this it would follow that the money income statistics which indicate that the aged are relatively isolated from the processes of economic change are not really demonstrating "poverty" in a welfare sense but merely "poverty" in a money income sense. Apparently, those among the elderly who have not elected the increase in leisure as part of their "real income" package have not suffered in a relative income sense.

IV. HOW ADEQUATE ARE INCOME LEVELS FOR THE AGED?

In the introduction to this chapter, two areas of concern about the economic status of the aged were noted. One has been dealt with but the other remains, namely, the contention that existing levels of income for the aged are not sufficient to provide them with a satisfactory standard of living. This argument implicitly involves a criticism of the existing system of income maintenance for the aged which is a combination of benefits under public and private retirement programs plus some amount of income derived from the ownership of assets and work activity. Usually, the major focus of this criticism is on the adequacy of the retirement benefits provided by our public retirement system. Whether these benefits in combination with other sources of income provide the aged with a generally satisfactory standard of living can only be answered by the aged themselves. Of course, in one sense people are rarely "satisfied" with their standard of living: rather, their conception of what is satisfactory in this respect tends to expand over time as income levels rise and general consumption standards are elevated.[16] What is considered to be merely "satisfactory" now would have been sumptuous, say, a quarter century ago. Consequently, it is quite difficult to evaluate in any purely objective fashion the proposition that contemporary programs for providing income to the aged yield unsatisfactory income levels for this group.

About the best we can do in this respect is to make certain observations about how the aged have responded to various income alternatives available to them. Presumably, the actual behavior patterns of the aged will reveal something about their perceptions of the adequacy of our public systems for providing the aged with income. To a sizable extent, this is what has been discussed in the preceding sections of this chapter. The evidence presented there argues that the aged have frequently chosen the receipt of income through the public retirement system in preference to receiving work-related income. This would seem to reflect favorably on the adequacy of this income relative to the alternative of continuing to rely solely on work-related income. Such a conclusion is reinforced by considering what has occurred in the wake of the expansion of the options available to aging individuals under the social security system in the early 1960's. Beginning in 1962, individuals aged 62 or over were granted the right to elect to "retire" under the social security system before reaching age 65 with appropriate reductions in the level of benefits which they receive. The response to this option has been dramatic. Over one half of the new benefit awards under the system at present fall in this category (see Table 12–3). Apparently, individuals who have not yet reached the "normal" retirement age of 65 tend to feel that even the reduced benefits offered under the existing social security system are sufficiently adequate to induce them to elect their receipt despite the restrictions on work activity which are involved in receiving benefits from the social security system. This would seem to imply that at least for large numbers of the aged the income generated by the benefits produced by our public retirement system are not so grossly inadequate as to be rejected by them. In fact, when faced with the alternative of re-

---

[16] For example, data presented in (50) indicate that the aged's concept of what they thought was a moderate standard of living increased about 30 percent more rapidly between 1950 and 1966 than did the general wage level. At the same time, in both of these years the old-age benefits for a September-December retiree would provide almost exactly the same proportion of that moderate standard of living. This suggests that aged income levels and the concept of a moderate standard of living move together. Details of this argument can be found in Gallaway (67), pp. 306–10.

TABLE 12–3
OASDHI Retirement Benefits Awarded to Men, with and without
Reduction for Early Retirement, 1962–66

Year	Number of Awards (000's)	Not Actuarily Reduced (000's)	Reduced (000's)	Reduced as Percent of Total
1962	722	299	423	59
1963	592	239	353	60
1964	524	200	324	62
1965	518	198	319	62
1966	491	146	345	70

SOURCE: (50).

ceiving this income with its restrictions on continuing to work full time they opt in large numbers for the retirement income. Of course, it should be kept in mind that this generalization does not apply to all the aged. Those that make the kind of choice described here amount to only about one half of the aged at present.

V. CONCLUSIONS

The evaluation of the economic status of the aged which has been presented suggests that some substantial strides have been made in the United States in improving their economic lot. Certainly, the finding that there has been a meaningful amount of "voluntary" substitution by the aged of leisure for work activity as the result of changes in the availability of income from the public retirement system of the country would indicate this. Consequently, the rather pessimistic arguments advanced by many with respect to the economic position of the elderly members of our society would seem to be somewhat unwarranted. This does not necessarily mean that we should be perfectly content with our present arrangements for providing income to the elderly. However, neither should we be wringing our hands in anguish and inaugurating changes in our present arrangements in an atmosphere of "crisis."

chapter THIRTEEN

The Economic Position
of Women

THROUGHOUT the 20th century in the United States there has been a persistent tendency toward increasing participation by women in the normal economic activities of the American economy. In particular, the tendency for increasing labor force participation on the part of women has been especially pronounced. In Table 13-1 comparative labor force participation rates for women by age are presented for 1890–1969. The pattern is clear. In every age category except 65 and over there has been an increase in the proportion of women engaged in what we call labor force activity. These increases have generated

TABLE 13–1
Labor Force Participation of Women, by Age, United States, 1890–1969
(percent)

Age	Year							
	1890	1900	1910	1920	1930	1940	1950	1969*
14–19........	24.4	26.8	28.1	28.4	22.8	18.8	22.5	32.4
20–24........	30.8	32.1	35.5	38.1	42.5	45.1	42.5	56.7
25–44........	15.6	18.0	21.0	22.5	25.4	30.2	33.0	46.8
45–64........	12.6	14.1	17.1	17.1	18.7	19.8	28.6	49.0
65 and over.......	8.3	9.1	8.6	8.0	8.0	5.9	7.6	9.9

* The 1969 rates are not strictly comparable with Long's which are derived from decennial censuses. The 1969 rates are from the Current Population Survey. Generally, the Current Population Survey participation rates are higher than those of the census.

SOURCES: Long (128); U.S. Department of Labor (209) Tables A-3 and A-7.

some very substantial problems for society. Initially, it raised the question of whether women needed special protective legislation to shield them from the rigors and dangers of certain types of occupations and employment. However, more recently the tendency has been to be concerned with whether women are receiving "equal" treatment with men. Both of these positions have a common denominator in that they revolve about the question of whether female inputs into the productive process, *ceteris paribus,* are homogeneous with male inputs.

The rather plentiful statistics describing the economic status of women engaged in the labor force in the United States argue quite strongly that employers do not regard them as being a factor of production which

TABLE 13–2
Relative Income of Families with a Female Head, United States, 1947–69

Year	Median Income of Families with Female Head as Percent of Median Income of Families with a Male Head	Year	Median Income of Families with Female Head as Percent of Median Income of Families with a Male Head
1947	70.0	1959	49.1
1948	63.1	1960	50.7
1949	66.1	1961	49.7
1950	56.1	1962	50.2
1951	57.9	1963	48.9
1952	55.2	1964	50.2
1953	56.3	1965	48.9
1954	53.1	1966	50.5
1955	53.6	1967	52.1
1956	55.5	1968	49.2
1957	53.6	1969	48.4
1958	51.8		

Source: U.S. Department of Commerce (**197**).

is strictly homogeneous with male labor. Rather, the evidence indicates quite persistent and substantial economic differentials between males and females. For example, simple income statistics for families headed by a female show that family income in these cases is markedly less than it is for families where the head of the family is male (see Table 13–2). Roughly, the ratio of female to male income shown in Table 13–2 is 0.50. Similarly, income data for all persons with income show that female income is only about one third of that of males.

One of the factors contributing to the discrepancy between male and female income levels in the United States is relatively higher unemployment rates among females. In Table 13–3 a comparison of unemployment rates of males and females by age group in 1969 is shown. In every age category the unemployment rate for females exceeds that of males.

TABLE 13–3
Unemployment Rates, by Age and Sex, 1969
(percent)

	Unemployment Rate	
Age	Male	Female
16–17	13.8	15.5
18–19	9.4	11.8
20–24	5.1	6.3
25–34	1.9	4.6
35–44	1.5	3.4
45–54	1.5	2.6
55–64	1.8	2.2
65 and over	2.2	2.3
All	2.8	4.7

SOURCE: U.S. Department of Labor (209), Table A-13.

This indicates that female unemployment levels are generally greater than those of males. In addition, from the treatment of the structure of unemployment presented in Chapter Eight it is clear that unemployment rates among females have been drifting upward over time relative to those of males. Even though this time drift in female unemployment rates apparently stems from a relative increase in the supply of women in the labor market, it implies that employers do not treat male and female labor as being strictly substitutes for one another in the process of production.

The unfavorable relative economic position of women in the American economy is also indicated by their pronounced tendency to suffer more from the "hidden unemployment" phenomenon. This is rather clearly shown, for example, by the Dernburg-Strand analysis of the incidence of the operation of the discouragement effect by age and sex and by data of the type which were analyzed in Chapter Nine. Dernburg and Strand concluded that women were approximately twice as likely to become "discouraged" and withdraw from the labor force as men with a given change in general employment conditions. Similarly, information from the records of the Social Security Administration for 1957–60 indicate that 6.9 percent of women employed in covered employment in both 1957 and 1960 were not so employed during the year of 1958 which was an economic downturn. This compares to 3.6 percent among men.

Finally, we can note the impact of differential economic treatment of women by observing the differences in the occupational distribution of males and females in the United States as of the 1960 decennial census.[1] Table 13–4 presents such a comparison for broad occupational

---

[1] A more complete discussion of these patterns may be found in Dale L. Hiestand (86).

TABLE 13–4
Occupational Distribution, by Sex, United States, 1960
(in 000's)

	Male		Female	
Occupation	Number	Percent of Total	Number	Percent of Total
Professional, technical, and managerial.....................	10,358	25.9	3,668	19.1
Clerical...........................	5,532	13.8	7,964	41.4
Skilled craftsmen..................	7,993	20.0	207	1.1
Semiskilled and laborers............	12,440	31.1	6,797	35.3
Farmers and farm laborers..........	3,703	9.3	611	3.2

SOURCE: Hiestand (86), Table II.

groups and it clearly shows that women appear to be systematically excluded from certain occupational groupings. In particular, relatively few women are found among the managers, officials, and proprietors group while relatively large numbers of females are employed in the clerical occupations. This would seem to substantiate the notion that there is a tendency for women to be shifted into the more menial occupations and out of those that involve responsibility and decision-making authority. At least, that is how data of this sort would be interpreted by the supporters of the current "women's liberation" movement.

I. THE INCIDENCE OF POVERTY AMONG WOMEN

The fact that women are treated differently economically in the United States has had some profound impacts on the relative magnitude of poverty among women. Table 13–5 shows estimates for the period

TABLE 13–5
Percent of Families with Female Head with Less Than
$3,000 Income in 1963 Prices, United States, 1947–68

Year	Percent with Less Than $3,000 Income	Year	Percent with Less Than $3,000 Income
1947.........	50.1	1958.........	51.0
1948.........	56.2	1959.........	51.3
1949.........	54.7	1960.........	48.8
1950.........	58.7	1961.........	49.0
1951.........	54.9	1962.........	47.5
1952.........	56.0	1963.........	47.1
1953.........	52.4	1964.........	44.2
1954.........	55.1	1965.........	43.7
1955.........	52.3	1966.........	40.5
1956.........	48.7	1967.........	38.2
1957.........	49.8	1968.........	38.5

SOURCE: U.S. Department of Commerce (197).

1947–68 of the poverty rate among families where the head of the family unit is a female.[2] When these are compared with the aggregate poverty rates for the same period it is fairly obvious that much less progress has been made in reducing poverty among this group than in society as a whole. This conclusion is confirmed by Anderson's (125) analysis for the period 1947–60 of the relationship between general levels of income and median income of families where the head of the household is female. He found that there was very little connection between the two. In fact, in this period the real median family income (in 1959 prices) of families with a female head rose only from $2,849 in 1947 to $2,928 in 1960. This amounts to a 2.8 percent increase while the same increase for all family units was 40.4 percent. The situation for female led families has improved somewhat since 1960 but there is still evidence of a differential sensitivity to variations in aggregate economic activity among this group. Whereas the aggregate poverty rate among all families in the United States declined by almost 40 percent, from 20.9 percent to 12.8 percent, the decrease in the poverty rate among family units whose head was a woman was only about one-half that (from 48.8 percent to 38.5 percent— a decline of about 20 percent).

The relatively grudging progress in reducing poverty among females is producing a shift in the composition of poverty in the United States. As of 1964 about 40 percent of the families with poverty levels of income had a female head.[3] If the trends in poverty elimination among females continue, that proportion will rise in the years ahead. In fact, by 1980 it is quite likely that this single category will account for almost 60 percent of the families with poverty levels of income.

II. WHY UNEQUAL ECONOMIC STATUS FOR WOMEN?

The brief introductory survey of the relative economic status of women in the United States seems to suggest a rather clear pattern of differential economic treatment of females. The interesting question this poses is, "Why?" Perhaps the most obvious answer is "discriminatory" attitudes on the part of predominantly male employers who for a variety of reasons feel that there are either subjective or objective costs associated with the employment of females. A possible source of such attitudes might be a purely subjective feeling on the part of men that women somehow pose a threat to the male domination of life and that, consequently, they should be treated differently in an economic sense. Or, to put a more generous interpretation on such attitudes, they might simply be the result of employers' feeling that males merit preferential treatment relative to females due to the greater "responsibility"

---

[2] In the discussion which follows the $3,000 of income in 1963 prices definition of poverty is employed.

[3] For a discussion of the distribution of poverty among various subgroups, see Aaron (1) and Gallaway's reply (70) to his remarks.

which society places on men, both psychologically and legally, to function as the "provider" or source of income for the family unit. Such reasoning tends to treat women as being typically "additional" suppliers of income to families and not as the primary source of family income. It is certainly true that females do tend to be "additional" sources of family income more frequently than do males. However, for the large group of women who function as heads of households this is obviously not true. Given the relatively high incidence of poverty that has been noted among such families, this raises some serious problems for the society.

While discrimination that is rooted in the functioning of the male ego receives the bulk of the attention when the issue of differential economic treatment of women is under discussion, there are some other possible sources of this treatment which ought to be considered. First, women do have a greater tendency to be "transient" in their labor force behavior. For a variety of reasons, they are simply less likely to be a "permanent" employee than men. Their labor force attachment is tied to a variety of factors.[4] If married, they may suddenly leave employment because of a change in their husband's labor force activity (such as a move to another geographic area). Or, they may withdraw from the labor force to have children and rear them. On the other hand, if an employer has unmarried female employees, he must bear in mind the possibility that their marital status is subject to change. However, how important is the matter of the tendency of women to be transient in their labor force attachment? Quantitatively, it is substantial. Some simple statistics taken from the Social Security Administration records used earlier indicate that of men and women employed at a particular point in time, the women in the group are over one-third more likely to be nonemployed at some point in the future.[5]

The next question which might be asked is, "Why does this affect employers' attitudes toward the hiring and employing of women?" The answer is almost all too obvious. When an employer hires an employee he typically undertakes some investment in "training" the individual to fit the exact needs of his enterprise. This training may be formal or informal. There is a learning period associated with almost any new job and, however this learning is accomplished, the worker is usually less effective and efficient during the period in which he is acclimatizing himself to his new employment. Consequently, an employer, in effect, "invests" in the training of a new employee. The return on that invest-

---

[4] See Cain (**24**) and Mincer (**136**) for analyses of the factors affecting female labor force participation.

[5] About 19 percent of men employed in 1957 were not employed in 1960, but 27 percent of women employed in 1957 were not employed in 1960. For details, see Gallaway (**61**), chap. 9, Tables 9–2 and 9–3.

ment depends very substantially on the length of time the individual remains in his employ. The longer the period of employment the greater the return and the more willing an employer is to make the necessary training investments. Therefore, if an employer is faced with a choice of hiring two different workers, a major consideration in his decision will be what he feels are the probabilities that the workers in question will be available to him for employment at various times in the future. If one worker is male and the other female, it is not arbitrary and capricious behavior on the part of an employer to prefer the male to the female on the grounds that he will have, on the average, a longer period of time in which to recoup his investment in training the employee. Thus, if his options are to hire either a male or a female at the same wage for a particular position, females may be systematically excluded from the employment in question. Of course, another possibility is that lower wage rates will be offered females for the same type of work. In this fashion, employers could increase the rate of return on their training investment and compensate for the briefer period of employment they anticipate with the hiring of a woman.

One other possible source of differential economic treatment of women remains to be discussed, namely, the possibility that in many employments they tend to be less productive than men. This could provide an additional economic rationale for the obvious disparities in the economic status of males and females in the United States. This potential source of what appears to be pure market discrimination against a minority group has been discussed previously in the chapter dealing with the economic position of nonwhites in American society. When introducing this possibility in the case of women, it should be kept in mind from the outset that we are not talking about productivity differentials based on differential investments in human capital of the formal education type. Clearly, we do not have the situation here of extensive premarket discrimination in the availability of education that has existed historically with nonwhites. Admittedly, certain very specialized types of education might not be available on the same basis to both males and females (such as medical training) but this will not explain the pervasiveness of the differential economic treatment of women. Thus, it would not seem to be reasonable to attempt to explain the economic status of women in terms of lower productivity resulting from a lack of formal education. An explanation of the productivity differential type clearly implies that female and male labor inputs into the productive process are not homogeneous. Such a possibility exists and, while extremely controversial, should be considered. To do this, the same basic framework that was employed in Chapter Eleven to evaluate the productivity differential hypothesis with respect to non-whites will be utilized.

To refresh our memory, the productivity differential proposition can be tested by assuming that average productivity of labor and wages in an industry and state are a function of the capital-labor ratio in the activity, the average amount of human capital possessed by the workers, and the proportion of minority group labor involved in the activity.[6] Also, it can be argued that employers may choose alternate modes of responding to the presence of productivity differentials by either practicing relative exclusion of the minority group or not excluding them and insisting on a wage differential which is unfavorable to the minority group. These hypotheses can be tested using the same data employed in Chapter Eleven to estimate the necessary multiple regression equations. The results are presented in Table 13–6 and are extremely interesting.

Let us look first at the productivity equations. In the industries where relative exclusion is not practiced a statistically significant productivity differential associated with employing females emerges. However, no such differential is found in the industries where females are relatively excluded from employment. This is the same result obtained in the case of nonwhites and suggests that where employers do not choose to engage in relative exclusion of females they must pay a cost in terms of the average productivity of their labor force. Thus, there do appear to be objective economic costs associated with the employment of women in American industry.

The wage relationships shown in Table 13–6 differ somewhat from those obtained in the nonwhite analysis. In those cases where relative exclusion is not practiced there is a very substantial wage differential associated with the employment of females. In fact, it is so substantial that it is difficult to justify it on the basis of the productivity differential which has been detected. According to the results obtained in the productivity expression, the coefficient of the female employment variable in the wage regression should be about three-fourths its actual size.[7] Taken literally, it suggests that the wage differential associated with female employment may be divided into two components—one that reflects the productivity differences associated with employing females and another that is the product of discriminatory behavior on the part of employers. Such an interpretation receives support from the wage regression for those activities where relative exclusion of females exists. Rather than showing no impact of minority group employment on wage levels, as was the case with nonwhites, it indicates a significant negative relationship between female employment and average wage levels. Since

---

[6] Again, see Gallaway and Scully (75) for details.

[7] The wage coefficient should be about 30 percent as large as the productivity coefficient assuming strict Cobb-Douglas production functions. This implies a value of about 0.32 for the wage coefficient. Actually, it is 0.44.

TABLE 13-6
Regression Results for Analysis of Discrimination against Women*

Regression Type	Dependent Variable	Constant	Regression Parameters			R²	Degrees of Freedom
			Capital/ Labor Ratio	Human Capital/Labor Ratio	Percent Female Employment		
No exclusion..........	Wages	-0.6767	0.0535 (1.81)	0.3146 (6.43)	-0.4443 (6.17)	0.86	108
Exclusion..........	Wages	-0.0690	0.2029 (4.41)	0.2724 (4.39)	-0.1415 (2.37)	0.85	126
No exclusion..........	Productivity	-0.6016	0.8888 (4.00)	0.3374 (0.77)	-1.0868 (2.02)	0.73	108
Exclusion..........	Productivity	-21.7777	1.6108 (3.50)	0.3374 (0.55)	-0.4761 (0.80)	0.64	126

* Other variables are included in the regressions from which these parameters are taken. These are present to adjust for interindustry variations in production functions, the presence of other minority group labor inputs, and the presence of trade unions.
Source: Gallaway and Scully (75).

there is no productivity differential to justify it, the lower wages for females that are implied by this result would seem to be the outcome of discriminatory behavior on the part of employers. It is also interesting to note that the size of the coefficient in question is roughly equal to the difference between the actual and expected coefficients in the no-exclusion wage regression (−0.14 compared to −0.44 − (−0.32) or −0.12).

Several qualifications should be added to the findings which have been reported here. First, the implication that there is a pure discrimination component in the male-female wage differential needs to be approached somewhat cautiously. The productivity levels which are used as the dependent variable in the regressions which have been reported reflect a single year's impact of female employment on productivity. Thus, they measure relatively short-run effects of female employment on productivity. However, in line with the earlier discussion of various sources of employers' aversion to hiring females, it is possible that over a longer period of time the effects of "transient" labor force behavior by women would be reflected in the productivity statistic. Second, the data which have been used to test the productivity differential hypothesis with respect to females is only for production workers in the manufacturing sector of the economy. Since the great bulk of female employment lies outside these areas, broad generalizations across the entire range of the economy can only be made with substantial reservations. Finally, in any analysis of this sort the possibility that the results are distorted by variables which have not been specified and incorporated in the regression equations cannot be ignored. However, it is not obvious what they might be.

III. CONCLUDING REMARKS

Our discussion of the economic position of women in the United States has yielded a number of interesting and provocative generalizations. Clearly, the available evidence indicates that women do receive unfavorable differential economic treatment in our society. Whether the barometer of economic well-being is income levels, unemployment rates, occupational distributions, or poverty rates the message is the same—women do not fare as well as men. The major problem that this seems to generate is in the area of the incidence of poverty. All of the available data argue quite strongly that poverty among families with a female head of household is quite prevalent and perhaps the most difficult to eliminate by the standard policy approaches that have been employed over the past decade. The social implications of this may be profound since the households in question contain a substantial proportion of "broken homes" and the like. If these families must often face low levels of income in addition to the problems which have created a household with a female head, the potentiality for social dislocation among its members is extremely large. Consequently, it can be rather convincingly argued that this is an area where concern over the incidence of poverty is truly warranted and one where there is little ground for optimism as things now stand.

Pushing beyond these broad generalizations, some specific conclusions with respect to the possible sources of the differential economic treatment of females can be set forth. While the available evidence is not of a conclusive nature, what information we do have implies that there are concrete objective costs of employing females which must be borne by employers. These take the form of productivity differentials which are associated with the employment of women. Apparently, employers respond to these differentials by either excluding some females from employment or by paying them a lower wage than they offer males. In addition, there also appears to be evidence of the consistent operation of a pure discrimination phenomenon in the case of females. Consequently, a case can be made that women are discriminated against economically in the United States although a substantial portion of the economic differentials which can be observed probably do not arise from this source.

chapter FOURTEEN

Rural and Urban "Ghettos": The Labor Market in Operation

A REMARKABLE thing has occurred in the United States. Within the memory of most living men this country has always been faced with something called the "farm problem" which is simply a euphemism to convey the fact that the economic returns to human endeavor in the agricultural sector of the American economy are markedly lower than in nonagricultural pursuits. However, there has now been added to this traditional dilemma what may be thought of as the "nonfarm problem," i.e., the phenomenon of urban decay and blight of both a physical and human type. Certainly, the outcry to do something about the problem of the cities is intense and, if one believes the estimates advanced by urban politicians, the solution to urban decay may involve the expenditure of not millions or billions but hundreds of billions or trillions of dollars.[1] Thus, at this point in time it might seem as if the entire nation is simply one large disaster area—both on the farm and off the farm. This is not quite the case, though, for what has essentially happened in the United States within the past 30 years is the development of a third broad area of society. No longer does the rural-urban distinction effectively categorize American life. Rather, what is

---

[1] This statement is predicated on mass media reports of the estimates made by the mayors of many large cities as to the amount of federal funds which might be required to alleviate the problems of their cities.

required is at least a trichotomy consisting of rural, central urban, and suburban (or ex-urban). As a result, contemporary America is much more stratified along economic lines than it was a quarter or a half century ago. Some simple statistics will suffice to illustrate the differences in the population composition of central urban and suburban areas. For example, median family income in 1960 in the central cities of urbanized places in the United States was $5,945 compared with $7,144 in the suburban portions of these areas. As a result, 17.6 percent of central city families had income levels below $3,000, contrasted to 9.9 percent in the suburban areas. Similarly, 1960 unemployment rates were higher in the central cities (5.5 percent versus 4.1 percent in the suburbs) and median years of education were lower (10.7 years versus 12).[2] Statistics comparing urban-rural areas would show differences of the same type in favor of the urban areas vis-à-vis the rural.[3]

Granted that there are pronounced economic differentials between various parts of American society, the significant questions are, "Why do they exist?" and "What is their long-term significance?" In line with the bias of this book toward explaining phenomena in terms of the operation of labor markets the discussion to follow will be organized about a consideration of (1) the labor market response to urban-rural economic differentials and (2) the role the labor market plays in producing the urban-suburban distinctions noted earlier.

I. THE FARM TO NONFARM MOVEMENT

The classic labor market response to economic differentials that is suggested by the discussion of labor mobility in Chapters Three, Four, and Five is a movement of individuals away from the low-wage toward the high-wage areas of the economy. That this has happened in the case of the agricultural portion of the American economy cannot be denied. Agriculture has traditionally been a low-wage sector and the proportion of the population associated with agricultural pursuits has been declining ever since the first population census in 1790. At that time about 95 percent of Americans were engaged in agricultural activity and today less than 10 percent are so involved. Further, the movement away from agriculture still continues. Table 14–1 presents data on the movement of male hired agricultural labor to other industries over the period 1957–60. They are taken from the sample of social security records employed in Chapters Three, Four, and Nine and they indicate a very substantial out-movement of workers from agriculture. Specifically,

[2] Source: U.S. Department of Commerce (204), Tables 151 and 152.

[3] For studies which highlight the persistence of urban-rural income differentials, see Hathaway (84), Johnson (92), and President's National Advisory Commission on Rural Poverty (154).

TABLE 14-1

Industry of Major Job in 1960 of Male Wage and Salary Workers Employed in Both 1957 and 1960, Classified by Industry of Major Job in 1957

Industry of Major Job in 1957	Total	Industry of Major Job in 1960										
		A	B	C	D	E	F	G	H	I	J	K
Total	312,773	8,512	6,635	28,421	77,204	44,313	23,204	63,528	12,552	32,434	14,379	1,591
Agriculture (A)	8,923	5,524	66	546	568	449	180	871	68	386	224	41
Mining (B)	7,397	95	5,022	452	512	286	156	434	50	216	135	39
Contract construction (C)	27,603	452	311	19,280	1,742	720	595	1,975	528	1,180	570	250
Durable goods manufacturing (D)	78,458	491	296	2,109	63,676	2,325	1,061	4,559	544	2,250	883	264
Nondurable goods manufacturing (E)	45,255	408	155	961	2,200	34,653	609	3,682	439	1,405	549	194
Transportation, communication, and public utilities (F)	22,507	168	143	568	733	421	17,906	1,282	163	694	295	134
Wholesale and retail trade (G)	65,950	778	322	2,470	4,712	3,680	1,594	45,598	1,116	4,003	1,301	376
Finance, insurance, and real estate (H)	11,215	47	28	361	275	217	105	680	8,778	502	173	49
Services (I)	30,019	304	119	874	1,693	937	670	3,107	594	20,778	809	134
Government (J)	12,373	153	48	322	403	257	206	671	172	736	9,369	36
Unknown (K)	3,073	92	125	478	690	368	122	669	100	284	71	74

SOURCE: Gallaway (**61**), p. 145.

of the 8,923 workers in the sample whose major job was in agriculture in 1957, 3,399 had their major job in nonagricultural employments in 1960. This represents an out-movement of 38 percent which is clearly substantial. Most of this out-movement was among the very young, two thirds of it occurring among those under age 40.[4]

Substantial out-movement of workers from agriculture would be expected to have some positive impact on the relative income position of agricultural workers. This is not the case, though, for the available data show almost no increase in the relative income of hired agricultural workers between 1957 and 1960. In 1957 the mean estimated earnings of these workers were 38.8 percent of those of all workers; in 1960, they were 39 percent. However, markedly different patterns may be observed when workers in agriculture in either 1957 or 1960 are grouped into the following categories: (1) those in agriculture in both 1957 and 1960 (stayers), (2) those in agriculture in 1957 but not in 1960 (out-movers), and (3) those in agriculture in 1960 but not in 1957 (in-movers). The 1960 mean earnings of the first group were 42.1 percent of the earnings of all workers in 1960. Thus, their relative earnings were about 3 percentage points above the level of relative earnings for all agricultural workers in 1957. However, the 1960 earnings of in-movers into agriculture were only 34.1 percent of 1960 earnings for all workers. From these data it is clear that the failure of relative earnings of hired agricultural labor to rise between 1957 and 1960 is not due to a lack of improvement in the relative earnings position of those who remained in agriculture. Rather, it is the result of an influx of workers from other industries whose relative earnings levels are markedly lower than those of stayers.

The in-flow of workers from the nonagricultural areas is quite substantial. Actually, despite a 38 percent gross outflow of workers from agriculture, the net change in agricultural employment in this sample was only 4.6 percent. Almost 3,000 workers moved into agriculture from nonagricultural jobs. In addition, there is every indication that agricultural employment is serving as a "safety valve" for individuals who encounter difficulties in nonagricultural labor markets. To begin, the markedly lower 1960 earnings levels of the in-movers would imply this. Also, the age distribution of the in-movers indicates that they are older than the out-movers. In fact, above age 40 there is actually a net movement of workers *into* agriculture. What is suggested by these data is that there is a systematic "adverse" selection of the agricultural labor force where the term "adverse" is used to denote a lack of economic success. The agricultural sector seems to serve as an employer of last resort

---

[4] Of the 3,399 members of the sample whose major job was in agriculture in 1957 but was not in 1960, 1,096 were over age 40.

for the unsuccessful in the nonagricultural areas. At the same time, it appears to export its more economically competent workers, particularly the young. It is interesting to note that the 1960 earnings of out-movers from agriculture were 47.4 percent of those of all workers while the earnings levels of out-movers from agriculture in the two youngest age-groups were about equal to those of all workers in those age-groups.[5]

The preceding discussion also offers an explanation for why the relative returns to human inputs into the agricultural sector have not improved markedly in this century. Apparently, what happens is that as succeeding generations of farm families are reared those more likely to be successful economically migrate out of agriculture in sufficient numbers to create job opportunities for those who have been relatively unsuccessful in the nonagricultural area. As these people flow into agriculture they depress wage levels and, in effect, a kind of steady state equilibrium is reached in which agricultural wage levels are a rather stable fraction of aggregate wage levels.[6] Of course, such a thesis implies a rather permanent state of depressed agricultural earnings accompanied by a process through which the labor force is "selected" to fit those wage levels. In a sense, this amounts to the creation of an agricultural "ghetto" (as that term is misused in contemporary America) consisting of those who are among the poorest equipped to compete in the labor markets of the society.

II.   THE LABOR MARKET AND URBAN ECONOMIC PROBLEMS

The major urban problems that seem to exist today involve the relative deterioration of portions of our urban areas. This has become a highly publicized phenomenon, if for no other reason than its existence in the large urban centers of the society where its presence is obvious to the communications media. At first glance, this problem may seem to be relatively unrelated to labor markets in the economy. However, a closer examination of this question reveals that labor market considerations play a significant role in its existence. As background, keep in mind that labor market decisions by individuals have a variety of dimensions, including wage rates, hours and place of work, and availability

---

[5] In the under 20 age-group earnings of agricultural out-migrants were 119.4 percent of those of all workers under age 20 and the comparable statistic for the age 20–24 group is 80.3 percent.

[6] Such a steady state equilibrium could result from a migration process of a stochastic type which converges to an equilibrium state. A very simple example could produce these results exist in the United States is argued in Gallaway (59) and Gallaway, Chapin, and Vedder (73).

of job opportunities. All of these factors contribute to the final choice of job which a person makes and thus influence significantly mobility patterns in the economy. For example, the fact that urbanized areas in the United States are typically high wage and provide abundant job opportunities serves to attract individuals into them, explaining in part the pronounced population shifts in the direction of urban areas. At the same time, these population shifts have been predominantly into the suburban portions of our cities.[7] Why have these movements been in this direction? Why have people chosen to live at extended distances from the centers of urban areas? The answers to these questions lie in the decision-making process involved in an individual's choosing where to live within a given metropolitan area.

From the purely economic standpoint, that decision has three components: the preference functions which embody individual attitudes toward living in different sections of an urban community, constraints in the form of budgetary and time limitations, and "prices" which reflect the various costs of residing in such areas. Much has been said about the preference functions of urban dwellers, with the emphasis being upon such negative factors as congestion, dirt, crime, Negroes, and so forth. However, very little attention has been paid to the other aspects of the location decision, particularly the possibility that intertemporal shifts in the constraints affecting that decision may contribute to the observed phenomenon of urban decay. This deserves particular attention in that there are two obvious sources of such shifts in these constraints. First, the budgetary constraint has been eased over time by the general increases in levels of real income that have characterized American society. Second, the time constraint has been shifted by the long-term decline in the length of the average workday and workweek, a decline which has produced a freeing of time for individuals to participate in activities other than work, including commuting if they so desire.

With these considerations in mind, it is now possible to assess the influence of the labor market on locational decisions, an influence which is twofold. First, there is the previously noted general phenomenon of the flow into urban areas. This is its interarea effect and needs little additional comment. However, in addition to the interarea effect, there is an intraarea effect which operates through the shifts in the constraints that influence the locational decision.

An example of the intraarea impact of the labor market on the locational decision is provided by the intertemporal shift in the budgetary

---

[7] Between 1950 and 1960, the average annual net migration for the suburban counties of the 38 largest standard metropolitan statistical areas was +24.2 percent, contrasted to +3.1 percent for the central counties of these areas. Between 1960 and 1964, these rates were +12.3 percent and +0.5 percent, respectively. See U.S. Department of Commerce (**196**).

constraint.[8] The specific impact of changes in this constraint depends on whether suburban living is an income elastic commodity. If it is income elastic, increases in real income levels will produce an increase in the amount of suburban living relative to urban living, *ceteris paribus*. On the other hand, if suburban living is income inelastic, increases in the budgetary constraint will lead to decreases in the relative amount of suburban living. If the former is the case, the long-run tendency for increases in real income in the society provides at least a partial explanation for the increased relative quantity of suburban living.[9]

In addition, the easing of the time constraint also has its impact on location decisions. However, in contrast to the shifting budgetary constraint, the impact of changes in the time constraint does not turn solely on the income elasticity of suburban living. Rather, the changes in the time constraint have both an income and price effect. For example, the greater availability of time obviously produces a pure income effect, but in addition, if time has diminishing marginal utility for individuals, there will also be an alteration of the relative prices of urban and suburban living. This has the effect of decreasing the relative price of suburban living because of the greater availability of time.[10] The combined effect of these shifts—assuming that urban and suburban living are normal goods—is to produce an increase in the relative quantity of suburban living desired by individuals.

The simple theoretical framework for relating changes in the labor market to the locational decisions of individuals has some very interesting implications for patterns of metropolitan area growth. To begin, if the proposition that suburban living is essentially an income-elastic commodity is accepted, it seems that the process of migration to the suburbs will be selective in an income sense; that is, those with more rapid improvements in income in urban centers will tend to move more rapidly toward the suburbs. In effect, this would suggest that an urban center throws off toward the suburbs in a centrifugal fashion those most likely to have high levels of earning ability, since these are the most able to afford suburban living. Thus, as migration into metropolitan

---

[8] For ease of discussion, the impact of shifts in the budgetary and time constraints is handled in a *ceteris paribus* fashion. However, in reality, these constraints operate in an interdependent manner. An excellent general treatment of this phenomenon is given by Becker (8). Casting the present discussion in *ceteris paribus* terms is sufficient for purposes of analyzing the general direction of changes produced by shifts in these two constraints.

[9] In Lansing and Mueller (113), there is limited evidence of the income elasticity of suburban living. Of those who have over $7,500 of income, 75 percent live more than 3.9 miles from the city center. Only 65 percent of those with less than $7,500 of income live beyond 3.9 miles.

[10] Given diminishing marginal utility of time, increasing the quantity of it available to the individual lessens the subjective cost of surburban living relative to urban living and thus alters the relative prices of urban and suburban living.

areas takes place, the urban center tends to receive, to begin with, the least competent economically because of the nature of the locational decisions which individuals make. Further, through time, among those who moved into the urban center itself, there will be a tendency for those who are most economically successful to move toward the suburbs. The result is once more a process of adverse selection of the population; this time, though, it is the population of the urban sector of a metropolitan area. This is what is commonly referred to by the expression "human decay" in discussing the problems of our urban areas.

The impact of the processes by which the population of urban centers of metropolitan areas is selected may well be reinforced by intertemporal shifts in individual preference functions for living location. In particular, as the selection process previously described develops and "human decay" in urban centers becomes more and more obvious, the preference functions of both those living in such areas and those migrating into metropolitan areas may shift in the direction of favoring suburban living over urban living. In addition, the deterioration in the human factor in central urban areas may have the effect of generating shifts in industry which accelerate the decline of central urban areas. For example, as the population in the central portion of a metropolitan area becomes less and less economically competent as the result of the selection process that has been described, industry may feel it is easier to obtain an efficient labor force if it locates closer to the more economically able population. Consequently, it may follow the migration to the suburbs, a phenomenon which may very well have the effect of reducing the relative price of suburban living even further in terms of both time and money considerations. To the extent this happens, the flow of population to the suburbs is reinforced. In effect, what has been described is a dynamic process through which the tendency for individuals to move toward the suburbs becomes progressively stronger and stronger. This merely accelerates the process of adverse population selection and the rate of human decay of central urban areas.

To this point, the discussion of urban problems has been purely in the speculative or theoretical vein. Although the result has suggested some intriguing generalizations about the origins of human decay in metropolitan areas, it would be helpful to have some empirical verification of the operation of the relationships which have been posited. What follows is far from a complete empirical examination of what may be thought of as the "exodus" explanation of human decay. However, it is an interesting case study. Specifically, as the result of a special 1965 survey of several areas in South Los Angeles, California, it is possible to explore some of the generalizations which have been developed. The significance of this particular locale for a discussion of contemporary urban problems becomes apparent when it is recognized that one of the areas in question is the Watts section, scene of the violent riots of 1965.

The data in question are the result of a special census survey of seven South Los Angeles neighborhoods: Central, Avalon, Exposition, Green Meadows, Watts, Florence, and Willowbrook. The survey was conducted in October of 1965 and developed data which are comparable to material from the 1960 Census. Thus, comparisons can be made between changes over this five-year period. The data are varied and are presented in a Technical Study of the Current Population Reports series.[11]

The areas in question are predominantly Negro in character and are becoming increasingly so: in 1965, 81 percent of the population in these neighborhoods was Negro, compared to 69.7 percent in 1960. As such, they have frequently been characterized as "ghettos." But perhaps of more importance than the racial composition of these areas is the behavior of certain economic statistics over the time period in question. In particular, the behavior of male labor force participation rates between 1960 and 1965 is striking. In the aggregate, these areas had a labor force participation rate among males 14 and over of 76.6 percent in April of 1960. This was about 4 percentage points less than the national average for all males in 1960.[12] However, in October of 1965 this rate was only 68.6 percent, a decline of 8 percentage points, compared with a decline in the national rate of about 3 percentage points.

The decline in male labor force participation rates in the individual neighborhoods was varied, ranging from 12.8 percentage points in the Central area to 5.9 percentage points in Willowbrook (see Figure 14–1). In addition, the range of male labor force participation rates was substantial. In 1965, the lowest rate was in the Watts area (57.9 percent) and the highest was in Green Meadows (72.9 percent). A substantial part of the difference in these rates can be explained by levels of unemployment in these areas. A significant negative relationship between unemployment rates in these areas and labor force participation rates exists (see Table 14–2 for data). This is suggestive of the frequently mentioned "discouragement" effect which operates in American labor markets. However, differences in unemployment rates will not account for the general decline in labor force participation rates between 1960 and 1965. This can be seen from Figure 14–2, which is a scatter diagram showing the relationship between unemployment rates and labor force participation rates by neighborhood for both 1960 and 1965. Clearly, there is a rela-

---

[11] U.S. Department of Commerce (**200**).

[12] The national labor force participation rates are taken from the statistical supplement to the *Manpower Report to the President* (**208**) prepared by the U.S. Department of Labor.

FIGURE 14–1
Los Angeles Special Census Area

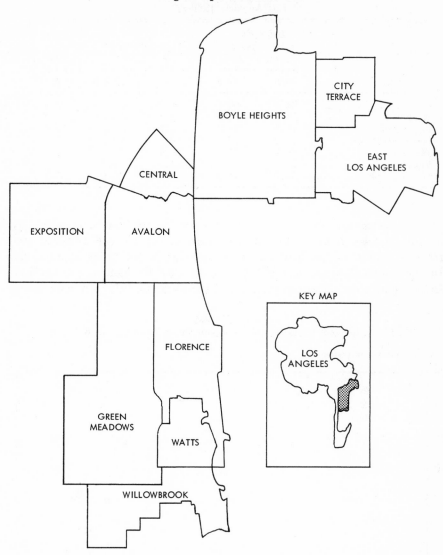

tionship between these variables in both years, but there has been a
shift between 1960 and 1965. The question is what has caused this shift.

A possible explanation is suggested by the theoretical discussion of
the nature of the individual's location decision and its impact on the
process of human decay in urban centers. Specifically, if a declining
labor force participation rate is viewed as one aspect of human decay
in urban areas, it is possible that a selective pattern of population flows

TABLE 14–2
Labor Force Participation, Unemployment, and Population Change, South
Los Angeles, 1960–65

Area	Labor Force Participation Rate (Male)		Unemployment Rate (Male)		Decline in Population (1960–65)
	1960	1965	1960	1965	
Central...............	73.3	60.5	13.6	12.2	38.1
Avalon...............	74.4	64.0	11.9	13.1	26.8
Exposition...........	77.9	71.2	9.9	8.3	19.6
Green Meadows.......	79.9	72.9	10.5	10.2	13.0
Watts................	69.9	57.9	15.6	13.2	16.0
Florence.............	75.7	67.8	11.0	8.5	14.6
Willowbrook..........	76.2	70.3	12.1	10.0	3.9

such as that described earlier will produce this decline. Consequently,
it can be hypothesized that the decrease in labor force participation
rates is related to the flows of population out of the areas in question.
In the simplest form, it might be argued that the greater the outflow
from an area, the greater the loss of the economically competent and

FIGURE 14–2
Unemployment Rates Related to Labor Force Participation Rates

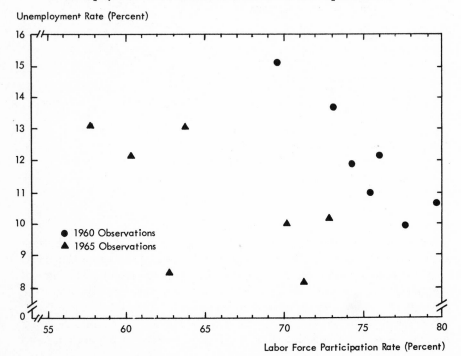

the greater the decline in labor force participation. Accordingly, a least squares regression equation of the form

$$L_i = a + bU_i + cdP_i + u \tag{1}$$

was fitted, where L denotes the male labor force participation rate in the various neighborhoods (denoted by the subscript i), U_i is the area unemployment rate, dP_i is a shift variable which represents the percentage change in population between 1960 and 1965, and u is a random error term. The data for 1960 and 1965 are combined into one set of observations with dP_i having a value of zero for the 1960 information. The results of fitting this regression are[13]

$$L_i = 87.59 - 1.12\ U_i + 0.42\ dP_i,\ R^2 = 0.68 \tag{2}$$
$$(2.24)\qquad (5.25)$$

Clearly, regression (2) does an excellent job of explaining the behavior of male labor force participation rates in the South Los Angeles area. The R^2 of 0.68 is statistically significant at the 0.1 percent level, the coefficient of the unemployment variable is significant at the 5 percent level, and the population change variable's coefficient is significant at the 0.1 percent level. Such evidence is consistent with the thesis that the decline in male labor force participation rates is the product of a selective exodus of individuals from these areas. However, it is entirely possible that the relationship observed in regression (2) is the result of the shift in labor force participation rates being significantly correlated with some other factor which is strongly related to declines in population. An obvious possibility in this respect is the percentage of Negro population in the various areas. This is an intuitively attractive proposition, for it is quite possible that population declines are primarily the result of a substantial exodus of whites from these areas. Such an exodus would produce some lowering of labor force participation rates as the result of the generally lower participation rate found among Negroes. Accordingly, regression (2) was reestimated, with the percentage of Negro population used as an independent variable in place of the population change variable. The results were not significant at the 5 percent level. This suggests that the changes in the percentage of Negroes in the population of the various neighborhoods does not explain the shift in male labor force participation rates.

These results have implications for a familiar argument, namely, that exodus of whites from areas creates ghetto-type conditions which lead to human decay and the like. This is entirely consistent with the results of regression (2) in that the population change variable may well reflect a white exodus from the neighborhoods in question. However, the nonsig-

---

[13] The values in parentheses beneath the regression coefficients are their respective t-values.

nificance of the Negro population variable casts doubt on this, since the proportion of Negroes in a neighborhood apparently does not account for the labor force participation rate shift. Actually, a stronger test of the possibility that the decline in labor force participation in the South Los Angeles area is primarily the product of a white exodus from the area can be conducted by correlating the percentage change in the labor force participation rate between 1960 and 1965 with the change in Negro population in the various areas. If the declining labor force participation rate is the result of whites leaving an area in large numbers and being replaced by Negroes, there should be a significant negative relationship between the Negro population change variable and the change in the labor force participation rate. When such a correlation is calculated, the result is a value of 0.85 which is very surprising. Instead of a significant negative relationshp between Negro population change and the change in labor force participation, there is a significant positive relationship. This argues that the decline in labor force participation rates is greatest in those neighborhoods in which there are the smallest increases in Negro population. Actually, there are declines in Negro population in four of the seven neighborhoods and these show the greatest declines in labor force participation. Apparently, the exodus phenomenon works among Negroes as well as among whites. This suggests that the economically more competent Negroes tend to exit from certain neighborhoods and as they do, signs of human decay begin to appear.

The conclusion that the declining labor force participation rate in the South Los Angeles neighborhoods is primarily the result of a selective exodus of population, both Negro and white, raises the question of the impact of this decline on the economic and social fabric of these neighborhoods. Turning first to the economic side, it is clear that the decline in male labor force participation has a decidedly adverse effect on income levels in the South Los Angeles area. In Figure 14–3, median family income (in real terms) is compared with male labor force participation rates. For both 1960 and 1965 there is a positive relationship between the two variables. Naturally, there is a shift in the relationship between these two years. Such a shift would be expected as the result of economic growth and/or changes in the availability of transfer payment income. The precise character of the relationship between male labor force participation and real median family income can be gauged from the results of fitting a regression of the form

$$Y_f = a + bL + cS + u \qquad (3)$$

where Y_f denotes real median family income, L is the male labor force participation rate, S is a shift variable having a value of one for 1965 and zero for the 1960 observations, and u is a random error term. The results of fitting the regression are

FIGURE 14–3
Median Family Income Related to Labor Force Participation Rates

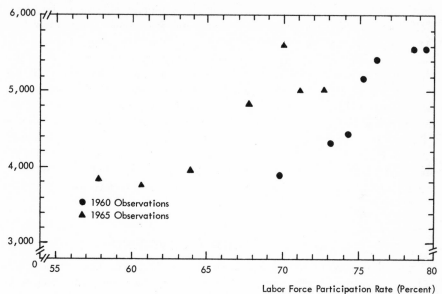

Median Family Income (Dollars)

Labor Force Participation Rate (Percent)

$$Y_f = -5{,}275 + 135\,L + 861\,S, \; R^2 = 0.75 \qquad (4)$$
$$(6.14) \qquad (3.15)$$

which show a highly significant relationship for both the independent variables. This provides some insight into the causes of the general decline in real median family income in South Los Angeles. Between 1960 and 1965 there was actually a decrease in real median family income from $5,122 to $4,736 (in 1965 prices). The major reason for this decline was the decrease in male labor force participation rates. In fact, the decline in incomes would have been even greater than it actually was, were it not for the unusual amount of "shift" in the relationship between median family income and labor force participation between 1960 and 1965. The coefficient of the shift variable in regression (4) is approximately two-thirds larger than that which would be expected if family incomes had increased at the same rate as real per capita national income.[14] It is possible that the primary source of this unusually large shift was the availability of transfer payment income. If this is the case, it appears that such payments eliminated about one third of the income loss resulting from the decline in male labor force participation

---

[14] At current rates of increase in real per capita income, median family income should have increased by about $500 in the South Los Angeles area between 1960 and 1965.

rates. In the absence of such payments, it can be estimated that family income would have been approximately $350 a year lower.[15]

The declines in income attributable to the shift in male labor force participation rates have more than only economic effects. It has been well documented that low-income levels are frequently accompanied by signs of social and personal disorganization. The South Los Angeles area is no exception in this respect. Some very simple comparisons suggest that the process of human decay proceeded apace in this area and that it is highly correlated with the decline in labor force activity. For example, the percentage of females separated from their husbands is negatively related to male labor force participation rates and the percentage of children under age 18 living with both of their parents is positively related to male labor force participation.[16] Consequently, the decline in labor force participation among males between 1960 and 1965 has been accompanied by strong indications of a deterioration in family organization.

III.   CONCLUDING COMMENTS

The discussion of the problems that seem to plague both the agricultural and central urban areas of our society seem to reach the same conclusion in the two cases, namely, that patterns of migration within the economy tend to produce an adverse selection of the population along economic lines. First, there seems to be a systematic movement of people out of the rural toward the urban areas with the net effect being a transfer of the more economically competent to the nonagricultural areas. Further, within the urban areas it can be argued that the more economically able are more prone to move out of the central city areas into the suburbs. The end result is a movement toward a substantial degree of social stratification on an economic basis. With the increased trend toward urbanization (and suburbanization), groupings of people tend to be much more homogeneous than was the case, say, prior to World War II. This is particularly true within the large urbanized areas. Anyone who has lived in such an area is acquainted with the familiar litany which complains about the "flight to the suburbs" of the relatively affluent. Frequently, there is not only a movement to

---

[15] This is roughly the difference between the value of the coefficient of the shift variable and the expected value of that coefficient based on normal increases in real per capita income.

[16] The correlation coefficient between the male labor force participation rate and the percentage of females separated from their husbands ($N = 14$) is -0.73 and the correlation between labor force participation and the percentage of children under age 18 living with both parents is $+0.78$. Both are significant at the 1 percent level.

the suburbs but within the suburbs people live in areas in which individuals are very similar in terms of their economic status. An area such as Los Angeles, for example, is very prone to this type of population grouping. Frequently, there may be as little as a 10 percent range in the market value of houses in a Los Angeles area and if an individual's income increases, he simply moves to an area where homes are more expensive.

The increased economic stratification of our society in terms of their living locations has produced substantial problems, some real and some imagined. The real problems it generates are those that accompany having larger numbers of the less economically able clustered together rather than being more widely dispersed throughout the society. Such clustering causes individuals to have a distorted view of economic reality, particularly when the economic status with which they most identify is contrasted with the mass media version of "middle-class" America. The differential between their reality and their stereotype of average economic status is frequently so great that it is little wonder that so-called "ghetto" attitudes develop. To these groups, it is understandable to interpret the world as consisting of two groups—the "haves" and "have-nots." Similarly, young people reared in a highly stratified suburban economic environment are likely to react in a similar fashion when they chance to encounter poverty for the first time. With their whole idea of what is a typical way of life being somewhat narrow, it is no wonder they are shocked by encountering true poverty. On the other hand, at a time and place when residential areas were much more heterogeneous in their makeup, one tended to have a better perspective as to what the gradations in economic accomplishment were and, also, perhaps, a better appreciation of the reasons for those gradations. However, when one only knows people as a group and not as individuals, there may well be a tendency to assign to them qualities they do not possess. Thus, depending on one's status in life, it is possible to overstate or understate the ability of other groups to function successfully in the labor markets of the economy. When this happens, the actual performance economically of a group is likely to deviate substantially from what one expects of them. Unfortunately, a common response to this frustration of expectations is to assume that the expectations are correct and that some external factor (such as discrimination or exploitation) has intervened to produce the disparity. On occasions this is correct but, if our reasoning about an adverse economic selection of the population of rural and central city areas is valid, it is probably frequently incorrect.

One other by-product of the increased economic stratification in the society is the greater "visibility" of the low-income groups in the economy. With less stratification the relatively poor were more randomly distributed throughout the population. However, in today's world, they tend to be much more obvious because of their concentration. This has probably contributed to the concern that has been manifested over poverty and to our "discovering" the presence of poverty in the very early 1960's despite the fact that the evidence indicates tremendous progress in its elimination.

Be that as it may, what is the solution to the problems of low-income levels in rural areas and urban decay in the central cities. Unfortunately, there is no easy solution if the arguments presented here are correct. If essentially the source of these difficulties is the patterns of migration of the American population, short of arbitrarily controlling that migration, all that can be done is to attempt to channel it through altering the incentives for such migration. For example, if it is desirable to discourage people from moving to the suburbs, there should be no subsidy of commuter railroad lines and no freeways should be built to ease the transit of suburbanites into and out of the cities. All these do when they exist is lower the objective and subjective costs of suburban living. Another alternative is to make the interior city more attractive physically. Some attempts along these lines have been carried out through "urban renewal." However, the net contribution of these projects is debatable. Frequently, they seem to have accomplished little but the displacement of the relatively poor. In fact, this is the general problem in all such solutions to the newly discovered problem of urban poverty. If the flight to the suburb is reversed, there may be nothing more than a displacement of the central city dweller to somewhere else. Instead of the U.S. version of the "ghetto," the central city, there might then exist the Latin-American version, the "barrio," located on the outskirts of the city. The problem is simply this: if people choose to live in economically stratified areas, it may be difficult to keep them from doing it. This is particularly true given the amount of time which people now have available to them to spend in traveling to and from their work. A very good argument can be made that probably the most effective way to counteract this trend toward economic stratification would be to increase the work day to 10 or 12 hours and the workweek to 6 days. That would tend to tie people very closely to their place of work and limit the range of living locations they could consider. However, it is also a patently unfeasible solution on political and social grounds. Beyond this, one can turn to schemes to redistribute income so that the more economically competent cannot afford suburban life. The amount of redistribution necessary to achieve that objective would probably be substantial and that may be even less feasible politically and socially than increasing the workday and week.

chapter FIFTEEN

Policy Considerations: How Well Do American Labor Markets Work?

T_{HE} essential framework of this book has been built around an explanation of the working of the American labor market with a view toward evaluating how well that market operates in solving certain problems that face the American nation. Those problems fall into two categories: the efficient employment of the manpower resources of the society, and the equitable distribution of the rewards to those resources. All that remains to be done is a general assessment of our findings and their policy implications.

I. MACROECONOMIC PROBLEMS OF ECONOMIC EFFICIENCY

Turning first to the matter of efficiency, a number of rather significant generalizations emerge from the discussion of various issues that has been presented in the course of this volume. At the macroeconomic level the major problem is how to promote a consistent full-employment level of manpower usage. The primary barrier to achieving this objective is coping with the tradeoff between unemployment levels and price inflation that seems to be characteristic of the economic experience of the United States.[1] The presence of such a tradeoff means that the society must periodically choose between higher unemployment rates and higher levels of price inflation, a choice which is made more difficult by the presence of the institution of trade unionism. Apparently, trade unions have produced a consistent bias toward higher levels of money wage rates and price levels in our economy. At least, there is evidence of a sizable upward shift in the rate of change in money wage rates that coincides with the enactment in the 1930's of the legislation establishing collective bargaining as an instrument of national policy for resolving industrial disputes. From the public policy standpoint the unemployment-inflation tradeoff poses substantial problems. Given the nation's present tolerance for price inflation it seems that we are systematically prone to incur periodic deviations from full employment in an attempt to counter the inflationary pressures that mount as the unemployment rate falls. These departures from full employment impose a cost on the economy in terms of lost income and output and, in the broadest sense, the part of them that is attributable to the activities of trade unions is one portion of the price we pay for embracing the collective bargaining concept.[2] Devising an appropriate public policy to deal with this problem is quite difficult for one of the basic sources of the dilemma is an institution which is virtually politically untouchable. Ideally, you might wish to deal with this problem by attacking it directly, i.e., by limiting the scope of collective bargaining. However, in this case this is probably not possible. On the other hand, perhaps the problem of the unemployment-inflation tradeoff can be treated by dealing with its chief effects, higher rates of change in money wage rates and prices. In recent years in the United States there has been substantial agitation for some type of wage and price control to be exercised by the Federal government. The mildest suggestion has been the establishment of wage guidelines which would call for percentage money wage rate increases equal to the percentage increase in labor productivity in the United States.[3] Several objections may be raised to such a policy proposal. First, there is the problem of enforcing the guidelines. But, beyond this, some of our earlier analysis would seem to argue that the basic concept underlying

---

[1] The United States is not unique in facing the inflation-unemployment tradeoff. Phillips' curves similar to that developed in Chapter Six have been estimated by Koshal and Gallaway (104–106) for Austria, Belgium, Denmark, Finland, Germany (West), Italy, Korea, the Netherlands, South Africa, Sweden, and Switzerland with generally similar results. The position of the various Phillips' curves varies but the general shape is the same.

[2] There may also be positive benefits from the presence of collective bargaining which counterbalance the costs. For example, the elimination of the recognition dispute as a source of work stoppages has probably reduced the level of time lost due to work stoppages as the result of industrial disputes.

[3] For a discussion of the guidelines concept, see Shultz and Aliber (28).

the guidelines proposal is questionable. In Chapter Seven it was maintained that in a competitive labor market the wage differential between two labor market sectors would be constant in absolute terms rather than in relative terms. The guidelines proposal, though, calls for maintaining the same relative wage structure in the economy. Thus, it may simply perpetuate the basic problem rather than solving it.[4] In a stronger vein the Congress has recently enacted legislation giving the President of the United States the authority to establish direct wage and price controls. Perhaps this is an appropriate solution to the inflation dilemma. However, our past experience with respect to such controls during situations when we have not been engaged in an all-out war has been something less than satisfactory. Admittedly, such controls can hold wages and prices below the levels that they would otherwise reach, but only at the risk of substantial misallocation of resources in the economy. The basic difficulty is avoiding a distortion of the relative structure of prices in factor and commodity markets. The probable tendency will be for the agencies exercising the wage and price control authority to simply extend the existing relative price structures, which means that the longer we employ wage and price controls the more likely we are to have distortions in the structure of relative prices and resource misallocation.[5] Consequently, as a permanent solution to the inflation problem, wage and price controls would seem to have more in the way of liabilities than assets. What other avenues remain, though? Very few. Perhaps the best that can be done is to attempt to steer a middle course between extremely low and very high levels of unemployment, which may be easier said than done. On the positive side, there are some hopeful signs—namely, the evidence that through time the unemployment-inflation relationship has been shifting in a fashion which makes it less and less costly in terms of price inflation to achieve a given level of unemployment.

Also at the macroeconomic level, we have dealt with the question of whether there has been any persistent tendency toward higher unemployment rates in the United States with the passage of time. The verdict is that there has been an upward drift in the aggregate unemployment rate since 1953 amounting to about 1 percentage point. However, the drift has not been a general one. Quite the contrary: it has been concentrated among teen-agers and females. Of the greatest significance is

---

[4] At the extreme it can be argued that for the guidelines policy to have any meaningful impact on money wage rate increases there must be an element of demand inflation present in the economy.

[5] It might be argued that these effects could be minimized by imposing wage and price controls in a selective fashion in problem areas of the economy. My own suspicion in this respect is that having a "little bit" of wage and price control is akin to being a "little bit" pregnant. If the controls are really effective in certain areas, pressure is likely to mount to either abandon them or to broaden them to include other areas.

the fact that with the exception of nonwhite teen-agers there is nothing to indicate that the source of the increased unemployment rates is a decline in the demand for the labor market services of the groups involved. This reflects adversely on the sometimes heard argument that increasing automation and rising skill requirements will progressively operate to produce higher and higher unemployment rates in the United States and will eventually necessitate a drastic revision in our system for distributing income since the labor market will no longer be able to perform this function.[6] In fact, the conclusions reached here indicate that there is little cause for alarm concerning the drift in these unemployment rates. Fairly reasonable real growth rates over the next decade are quite capable of reversing this drift with the one exception of nonwhite teen-agers. Consequently, it would seem that the behavior of the structure of American unemployment does not pose any general long-term problems for the American economy.

II. MICROECONOMIC PROBLEMS OF EFFICIENCY

A number of problem areas which have their roots in the microeconomic behavior of individuals participating in the labor market have been explored. Basically, they involve the labor supply responses of members of the population under differing market conditions. First, at the level of the total labor force, the available data suggest that generalizations to the effect that it is a relatively constant proportion of the working age population are not valid. Rather, there is some reason to believe that there is a good deal of responsiveness of individual labor force participation patterns to variations in the economic rewards which are offered by the marketplace—both in the short and long run. The evidence to support this contention is varied but quite consistent. The expected labor supply responses are found among the aged when they have been faced with changes in the constraints affecting their labor force participation. They are found across all age-groups when individuals are faced with a general decline in economic activity and various researchers have identified these responses among females.[7] Finally, data describing the relationship between prospective earnings levels and the proportion of individuals working suggest the appropriate reactions.[8] Collectively, these examples of people responding to labor market conditions in the directions predicted by formal economic theory indicate that any simplistic notions about constancy in the overall labor force participation rate are not warranted. Whatever constancy may exist

---

[6] See Theobald (**187**).

[7] Cain (**24**) and Mincer (**136**).

[8] Several other studies also suggest this type of response. For example, see Chapin (**27**), Brehm and Saving (**18**), and Kasper (**96**).

is simply the product of changes in labor force participation in various sectors of the total labor force canceling each other in a chance fashion.[9]

The conclusion that labor force participation rates are sensitive to the economic rewards offered to people augurs well for the ability of labor markets to efficiently allocate labor resources in the economy. As labor markets tighten, rising wage rates have the capacity to pull additional labor inputs into productive activities if individual labor force participation is responsive to differences in economic rewards. Consequently, it would appear that existing labor market mechanisms in the United States possess the ability to contribute to a more efficient use of the economy's resources by increasing the supply of labor whenever the demands of the economy call for an increased use of resources. In short, observed behavior in American labor markets in this respect is quite consistent with the operation of an efficient labor market.

Once in the labor market the behavior of people also seems to be of a type that promotes economic efficiency. Labor markets that are performing in the fashion expected of them by conventional economic theory will shift labor resources towards those areas of employment in which wage levels are relatively high. Clearly, individual movement patterns between various types of employment conform quite closely to this model. Regardless of the type of movement—geographic, interindustry, or occupational—differences in earnings levels are a prominent factor in determining the distribution of mobile individuals among various employment opportunities. Further, this force appears to operate both in relatively short and long periods of time. Not only does this argue that American labor markets are efficient in their operation but where information is available the evidence indicates that they have been becoming more efficient with the passage of time.

From the standpoint of broad economic policy this means that a more efficient use of economic resources can be promoted by permitting market mechanisms to function as freely as possible. It is certainly appropriate to attempt to create an environment which promotes this by improving the flow of labor market information and the like but notions to the effect that we need some sort of centralized "manpower" planning would not seem to be supported by the research results reported in this volume. Granted, there may be some "side effects" or "externalities" associated with allowing labor markets to function freely, such as urban crowding, congestion, the flight to the suburbs, etc. However, if it is truly felt that the social problems created by the existing pattern of migration flows are intolerable, an appropriate policy approach to reshaping those migration patterns would be to use the sensitivity of people to market conditions to achieve the desired goals rather than try-

---

[9] Easterlin concurs in this view in (44).

ing to suppress this responsiveness.For example, if a certain geographic redistribution of population is desired by the society, simply offer people a bounty or premium in the form, say, of a special tax exemption if they choose to live in certain areas. Or, to discourage people from living in some sections a special scheme of tax rates could be designed to increase the costs associated with having a residence in those areas.[10] In short, given that the market forces do appear to work, use them instead of resisting them.

III. THE LABOR MARKET AND EFFICIENCY: A SUMMARY

From the efficiency standpoint American labor market institutions seem to deserve fairly high grades. With rare exceptions the existing market mechanisms appear to be functioning in the fashion envisaged by formal economic theory and thus are contributing to a more efficient utilization of available manpower resources. When problems do exist they are frequently either produced or exacerbated by attempts to tinker with the market devices. For example, at the macro level the problems generated by the magnitude of the unemployment-inflation tradeoff are certainly more substantial as the result of the observed shift in the Phillips' curve relationship that appears to have accompanied the adoption of collective bargaining as conscious national policy. Or, take the familiar problem of the upward drift in unemployment rates among nonwhite teen-agers. There is some strong evidence that our preoccupation with enacting minimum wage legislation has greatly contributed to making this problem more acute by "pricing" nonwhite teen-agers out of the labor markets in which they participate.[11] These are but two examples of how tampering with existing labor market arrangements can have undesirable effects on the efficiency with which they accomplish the task of allocating labor resources. Thus, the conclusion seems to be an obvious one: where at all possible rely on the normal functioning of market mechanisms to achieve the objective of efficient manpower utilization.

IV. SOME EQUITY CONSIDERATIONS: AN AGGREGATE VIEW

While the performance of the American labor market in generating an efficient pattern of use of the nation's labor resources appears to

---

[10] Most externalities are subject to attack through this approach. For example, I suspect that placing a substantial tax on automobiles which produced air pollutants in excess of prescribed standards would do more to promote the development of effective pollution control devices than all the rhetoric we now hear ever will accomplish.

[11] For example, see Adie and Chapin (30). Also, see Barth (4) and Gavett (76).

be quite good, it is less clear that its end product in the realm of economic equity is of a similar quality. The problem here is that when we pass from a discussion of economic efficiency to one of economic equity, the focus shifts from observing how markets perform compared to some theoretical norm which will produce efficiency to dealing with how markets perform relative to a somewhat vague and often nebulous concept of how income in the society ought to be distributed. Consequently, a reasonably objective analysis of how equitably labor markets distribute income to individuals is difficult to develop. What has been done in the chapters devoted explicitly to this problem falls short of a complete analysis of the equity issue. However, it does afford some useful insights into some of the basic questions which have been raised in recent years in American society regarding the extent to which all members of the society are sharing in the fruits of economic progress. This is the fundamental problem which is embodied in the now familiar "backwash" concept.

At the level of the society as a whole the evidence which is available does not lend substantial support to the "backwash" notion. There are several ways to evaluate this proposition. One is to accept the standard approach to defining poverty which involves employing some absolute level of income and to then determine the extent to which the normal operation of labor market mechanisms moves people across that boundary. The record during the 1960's indicates that substantial progress has been made in reducing poverty as defined in this sense. However, it is possible that progress of this type could be made while the lower tail of the income distribution was not sharing proportionally in the benefits of economic growth. Probably the simplest and most straightforward approach to testing for this possibility embodies the concept of "neutrality" of shifts in the income distribution which was advanced in Chapter Ten. Implicitly, this takes as a norm for determining how economic gains are shared the existing distribution of income in society. If there is no change in the equality of the income distribution as it shifts, the shift can be considered to be neutral with respect to all income groups. On the basis of this criterion it seems clear that there is little to recommend the "backwash" hypothesis. Consequently, it does appear that the existing system of income distribution with its emphasis on the labor market parcels out the gains in income resulting from economic growth in at least a proportional fashion. In fact, during the 1960's it may even have been biased in the direction of favoring the lower tail of the income distribution. Be that as it may; it could be argued, however, that strict neutrality of income shifts is an inappropriate criterion because it assumes that the existing pattern of income distribution is an acceptable one. This is a very difficult contention to evaluate since it necessitates passing judgment as to what is or is not the desired distribution of income. There simply are no criteria for this that are universally accepted. Consequently, we cannot say how much progress is or is not being made in dealing with the poverty problem when it is interpreted in this fashion.[12] All that can be said at this juncture is that it is clear that the existing pattern of income distribution has not been becoming more unequal in recent years and that relative to it the "backwash" hypothesis does not appear to be valid.

V. THE ECONOMIC PROBLEMS OF
POPULATION SUBGROUPS

While in general the evidence does not support the backwash proposition, there still appear to be problems of an equity type associated with particular subgroups of the population. The most pronounced difficulties seem to arise in the cases of nonwhites and females. Both of these groups suffer from low levels of income relative to the society as a whole and the problems seem to be extremely intractable ones. Among nonwhites the available information indicates that they seem to share at least proportionally in the benefits of economic growth. However, at the same time, the rate of progress in closing the income differential between whites and nonwhites is painfully low. This would seem to imply that such public policy approaches to the problem of the white-nonwhite economic differential as equal employment opportunity legislation, exhorting businessmen to hire nonwhites, and equalizing the quality and quantity of white and nonwhite education have been relatively unsuccessful. A possible explanation for the apparent lack of progress in closing the white-nonwhite income gap may be found in the tentative evidence which has been presented to the effect that there may well be a rationale for this differential in the form of objective economic costs which must be met by employers if they hire nonwhites. If this is the case, dealing with the problem of the disparity between the economic well-being of whites and nonwhites will be extremely difficult. Put bluntly, this dilemma is probably not susceptible to attack by programs aimed at removing alleged imperfections from labor markets. This ignores what seems to be the real possibility that these differentials have their roots in the normal functioning of labor markets and that the current policy approaches amount to asking employers participating in those markets to behave in an unusual fashion.

A somewhat similar situation exists for females in the United States except that, if anything, the problems for this subgroup are even more acute. First, there are fairly strong indications that in some instances their relative economic position has actually deteriorated over time.

---

[12] A relativistic criteria for measuring progress in eliminating poverty has been suggested by Fuchs (**55**). For a good discussion of this problem, see Bowman (**16**), pp. 49–107.

Thus, family units headed by a woman can properly be classed as a group among which there is evidence of the operation of the backwash phenomenon. Second, the available data point much more strongly toward the existence of pure market discrimination against women. Granted, there do appear to be significant real economic costs which employers must bear when they hire female labor. However, in addition, it seems that they exact an extra advantage which is reflected in wages for females that are lower than those which would be warranted on the basis of productivity considerations. From the economic policy view, this means that there is more room for antidiscrimination legislation and the like to function in the case of economic treatment of women. Nevertheless, it also seems reasonably clear that the potential usefulness of such public policy approaches is limited and that once that limit is reached a fundamental problem of income inequality between males and females will remain. There does not appear to be any reason to feel that this basic income differential would prove to be any more amenable to the standard public policy approaches than has the white-nonwhite differential.

Clearly, the greatest problems we face are those of relative income levels of nonwhites and women. Among other subgroups of the population comparatively minor difficulties seem to exist. With teen-agers there is the upward drift in unemployment levels while aged income levels have not increased as rapidly as general income levels during the post-World War II period. However, in both cases there appear to be special circumstances which have produced the phenomena with little indication of long-run problems. In fact, among the aged it can actually be argued that the changes reflect an improvement in their level of general well-being as they voluntarily substitute leisure for income.

VI. SOME POLICY ALTERNATIVES

The overall impression one obtains, when the wide range of problems involving the distribution of income is considered, is that there are some areas of the economy where substantial difficulties exist, difficulties which may not be easily solved through the present policies which are being employed. But, what are the alternatives? A number of suggestions have been made recently which involve some type of direct income supplementation on a more regular basis than that which is provided by the current general welfare system. For example, there have been several variants of something called a negative income tax.[13] The basic principle of these proposals is that there should be some extension of the tax

---

[13] One of the major advocates of the negative income tax proposal is Tobin (190). For a survey discussion of the negative income tax concept, see Green (80).

schedule to include "reverse" tax payments when income levels of individuals and families fall below a certain level. In this fashion low-income people would automatically receive income supplements whenever their income fell below a prescribed level. In its broadest form the negative income tax has been proposed as a full substitute for all other governmental programs which provide nonwork related income to various sectors of the economy.[14] Thus, it could conceivably replace all forms of general welfare, the social security system, unemployment compensation, and programs designed to provide the agricultural portion of the economy with greater amounts of income, among others. Conceptually, the negative income tax proposals are closely related to the guaranteed annual income advocated by Robert Theobald (**187**). He has argued for placing a floor under income on the grounds that the existing course of American economic development is progressively isolating people from contact with the labor market so that we face a crisis of income distribution. Again, this is the "backwash" concept and it has already been pointed out that the evidence which is available does not support Theobald's contention as a general proposition. However, this does not mean that some such proposal as his might not be adopted simply because the society felt it just and proper to do it.

Another current policy proposal is the Family Assistance Plan (FAP) suggested by the Nixon administration. It is similar in some respects to the negative income tax and guaranteed annual income approaches except that it is narrower in scope and (with some exceptions) requires recipients of benefits to demonstrate a certain willingness to work by making themselves available for employment.[15] The proposed legislation embodying the FAP proposal also has provisions for (1) improving the quality of labor market information available to those in need of assistance, and (2) retraining of individuals to enhance their employment opportunities. For the most part, the Family Assistance Plan would replace the present Aid for Dependent Children (AFDC) program which has been subject to substantial criticism. Finally, it is entirely possible that the society might decide to simply stay with the present system of supplementing the income of the poor through a mixture of programs at various levels of government. Consequently, the range of possible policy proposals to deal with the question of income supplementation for the poor is quite wide. And, it can be made even wider by including certain proposals that have not received as much attention as the ones that have been mentioned here. For example, it has sometimes been suggested that employers should be encouraged to hire and train disadvantaged workers through a system of tax credits and subsidies or some

---

[14] This is Friedman's proposal in (**53**).

[15] For example, many female heads of households would be exempted from the work registration provisions.

combination thereof. Another suggestion has the federal government supplying employment to the low-income sectors by functioning as an employer of last resort.[16]

Given the variety of possible policy approaches that have been discussed, how can we choose between them? To answer that question it is necessary to establish beforehand exactly what a system of income supplementation is designed to accomplish. This will involve making some important value judgments and the final policy one selects will reflect those judgments. Since I cannot anticipate the full range of objectives which various people might define as being the appropriate set of goals for a program of income supplementation, I will simply state what my own criteria are, attempt to justify them, and then evaluate the various alternatives in light of those criteria.

Basically, two criteria will be employed to evaluate the various policy options available to us. These are (1) whatever policy is adopted should provide some immediate relief for the economic problems of low-income groups, particularly in the troublesome areas of nonwhites and females, and (2) the policy should encourage participation in the mainstream of American economic life on the part of the people affected.

The rationale of these criteria is fairly obvious. First, given the degree of dissatisfaction and unrest that currently exists in our nation, any meaningful policy approach must be designed to provide immediate aid and not merely the promise of "better things in the future." Second, the criterion that the policy solution encourage an entry into the usual patterns of economic activity is based initially on a belief that a long-run solution to our present problems will only occur through drawing the various parts of the society into similar modes of activity. What we must avoid is an approach that can be interpreted by the low-income population as saying, in effect, "There does not appear to be any way in which you can participate fully in the normal economic activity of the country but, since this bothers our conscience, we will 'pay' you for this affront." The potential for creating a feeling of alienation among the poor by pursuing policies which ignore this criterion could be immense. Further, the criterion of encouraging participation in the normal economic activities of the society would seem to be consistent with the evidence which indicates that with only a few exceptions variations in the income levels of people are closely tied to variations in the aggregate level of economic activity. If the backwash proposition has any validity at all as a criticism of American economic life, whatever policies we adopt should be designed to lessen the scope of its operation rather than serving to perpetuate it where it now exists or encouraging it in

---

[16] One suggestion along the employer of last resort line is contained in Minsky (138). Several proposals involving wage subsidies have been advanced. For example, see Buchanan and Moes (21), Bowman (16), pp. 99–103, and Muth (142).

other areas. Clearly, this would seem to suggest that an appropriate policy ought to encourage participation in labor market activities by the poor.

On the basis of these criteria, what can be said about the various policy alternatives that have been described? Consider initially the existing system for dealing with the problem of income supplementation. Its record is at best somewhat spotty. To begin, the fact that there is evidence of problem areas such as nonwhites and females would suggest that the existing system has not been particularly effective in dealing with these critical areas. This may well be due to the fact that the basic mechanisms for providing income supplementation frequently include constraints which actively discourage labor force participation by the recipients of assistance by attaching penalties to the receipt of work-related income. On that ground alone, the existing system does not satisfy the criterion of encouraging behavior which will tend to pull people into the mainstream of the economy's activities. Consequently, it would seem to fall short of satisfying what I have defined as an appropriate set of objectives for an income supplementation policy.

What about the negative income tax or guaranteed annual income proposals? In some respects they represent an improvement over the present approach to providing the disadvantaged with income. For one thing, they would not impose as substantial a set of restraints on labor force activity by individuals. Any of these proposals have lesser penalties attached to the receipt of work-related income than does the present system. Also, they do have the virtue of providing immediate relief for the disadvantaged. However, while representing an improvement over our present way of doing things, these proposals still have the shortcoming of tending to discourage participation in the labor force by lowering the effective wage rate which is earned through labor market activity.[17]

Next, we may consider the Nixon Family Assistance Plan. It attempts to deal more explicitly with the problem of work incentives by requiring most recipients of assistance to make themselves available for employment while providing assistance in locating jobs and possible retraining. In this sense, it faces up more directly to the work incentives question. However, there are still difficulties inherent in the proposal. First, the penalty associated with earning income remains substantial—50 percent on income amounting to more than $60 per month. Second, some argue that it amounts to having to "work for relief" and that this is nonenforceable. How do you determine when a person has made an adequate attempt to find work? How do you define what is suitable work for the person in question? Must he be forced to take just any job that

---

[17] That workers will respond in this fashion to such shifts is indicated by the previously cited studies of Brehm and Saving (18), Kasper (**96**), and Gallaway's findings (**64**).

appears? These are problem areas in any such program but we are not entirely without experience in dealing with them. The very same questions arise in connection with the unemployment compensation system that presently exists and, while the answers we have developed to these questions are not perfect, the system does seem to be reasonably workable. Consequently, this would not seem to be an insurmountable obstacle.

Beyond the matter of the feasibility of the work registration provision, other aspects of the Family Assistance Plan are mildly bothersome. While one would seem to be " on the side of the angels" in advocating job retraining programs and the like, they do not always lead to the results which are anticipated. In fact, in some cases they have been only slightly better than total failures in enhancing the employability of individuals. Part of the difficulty seems to be in making the decisions as to what types of job training to provide. Obviously, the best judge of what kind of job training would be useful in a particular line of economic endeavor is the employer himself. However, by and large, he does not conduct the job training in most of the programs which have been devised. Consequently, the problem of relating the content of job training programs to the needs of employers arises and, unfortunately, the record of performance in this area is quite varied. Accordingly, a skeptical view of the possible effects of the job retraining provisions may be appropriate. One last problem associated with the Family Assistance Plan is the gaps in coverage of low-income individuals which would remain if it were enacted. The plan is limited in its applicability to family units of two or more persons where at least one of them is a child.[18] While this covers a large number of those who may require income supplementation, it does not deal with economic problems of groups such as unattached individuals and couples without children.[19] To summarize, the Family Assistance Plan seems to have a number of small nagging shortcomings and certainly lacks the grandeur and simplicity of the alternative proposals. At the same time, it represents a substantial departure from the existing approach to income supplementation and, in spite of its shortcomings, it might prove quite workable. In fact, to the extent that the failings of the proposal represent the art of political compromise it may well have a better chance of ultimate success than its competitors. If it is enacted into law, though, don't expect an overnight transformation of our society. Certain very obvious problems in the area of income supplementation will remain.

[18] A child is defined as a member of the household under the age of 18 or under the age of 21 if attending school.

[19] The omission of these groups is not so critical in the case of childless couples where only 8 percent were considered as being in poverty in 1968. Among unrelated individuals, however, the poverty rate was 34 percent in 1968. Source: U.S. Department of Commerce (199).

In the earlier discussion two other policy alternatives were mentioned in passing—the payment of subsidies to employers to hire the economically disadvantaged and having the federal government function as an employer of last resort. Both of these proposals differ in varying degrees from the others we have discussed by placing a greater emphasis on work activity as a source of income for the poor. The employer of last resort proposal attempts to do this by having government provide jobs where none exist in the private sector while the subsidy approach attempts to channel income supplements through the labor market in the form of making jobs available to low-income people by providing an economic incentive to hire the economically disadvantaged. The employer of last resort proposal has the disadvantage that labor resources are employed in the production of goods and services which have not met the test of the marketplace. Of course, this is always the case with public goods as contrasted to private goods, but it may be compounded in the employer of last resort scheme by the obvious intent of the program, viz, to supply income to the poor. Under these circumstances the motivation to examine closely the nature of the activity which people are hired to perform is less compelling than it is when the end product of government-produced services must be justified in terms of utility of the product to the populace as a whole.[20]

The employer subsidy approach to income supplementation is much less objectionable on these grounds since the objective of the economic activity in which workers are employed has been determined in the markets for goods and services and, thus, presumably reflects the relative preferences of individuals for various goods and services. On the other hand, the argument that employers should not be "paid" to employ people simply because those people are economically disadvantaged can be anticipated. The answer to that objection is a simple, "Why not?" Two basic reasons can be advanced for explaining the unwillingness of employers to hire the economically disadvantaged: (1) lower levels of productivity (both marginal and average) and/or (2) discrimination against the low-income groups. In the first of these cases, the subsidy to the employer (assuming it is properly set) simply compensates him for the productivity difference. In the second case an economic reward is offered to overcome the employer's taste for discrimination by increasing the value to the employer of the product produced by the discriminated against worker to something large enough to overcome the discrimination. On the basis of the broad conclusions reached earlier, a case can be made for workers in low-income groups being low income

---

[20] If the alternative were no jobs at all for these people, clearly the society would be better off to employ them in this fashion rather than having them lie idle even though the end product of their labor had not been validated by the market for goods and services.

because they are low productivity. To the extent that this is true, compensating employers for the costs they incur (in terms of lower output) in hiring low-income workers has a strong logic to it. And, in those cases where a pure discrimination effect may be operative (such as against women) compensating employers for the subjective costs associated with hiring the low-income groups could prove to be an effective way of reducing the discrimination element. Again, the objection may be voiced that employers should not profit from discrimination. But, are they really profiting? If their subjective taste for discrimination has been so strong that they have been engaging in hiring practices which involve their incorrectly viewing the labor input of certain minority groups as being less desirable, they must feel strongly about this issue. Thus, if as a society we feel that these preferences must be overridden, it may be more appropriate to distribute the monetary equivalent of these subjective costs among the entire society by paying the employer a subsidy instead of insisting that he bear these costs in their entirety.

As yet, nothing has been said concerning how these last two alternatives measure up to the criteria for evaluating income supplementation devices suggested earlier. It should be fairly obvious that they both attempt to draw individuals into work activity which would seem to satisfy the criterion of integrating individuals into the mainstream of American economic life. On the whole, though, the employer subsidy plan is superior in this respect in that the economic activity is clearly located in the private sector of the economy and has little connotation of being a "public works," "makework," or "work relief" type activity. As to the other criterion, providing immediate short-run relief for the income problems of the poor, the employer of last resort approach may have an edge in that it may be possible to employ people more quickly when there need be less concern about the economic validity of the activity they are employed to conduct. However, on balance, I suspect the subsidy plan would have the net advantage when both criteria are considered although both of them have the shortcoming of not being able to deal completely with the income maintenance problems of groups with traditionally weak attachments to the labor force.[21]

The rather natural question to raise at this point is, "What policy proposal is best for the American economy at present?" My own preference in this respect is a mixed "bag" of policy proposals designed to meet the criteria I have established and the special needs of various subgroups in the economy. First, certain of the existing programs for income maintenance are really quite satisfactory. Among these are the Old Age Survivors Disability Health Insurance (OASDHI) or social

---

[21] Women are a case in point in this respect.

security system for providing income to the aged and the disabled.[22] For reasons advanced in Chapter Twelve, I cannot join in some of the widespread criticism of that system as being inadequate for the needs of the aged.[23] Also included in this group would be the unemployment compensation system which seems to perform reasonably adequately for the limited purposes for which it was designed. The most suspect of existing income maintenance programs are those that fall under the rubric of "general welfare" and for these my inclination would be to substitute some type of program embodying subsidies to employers for hiring the economically disadvantaged.[24] This could be particularly effective among the poor in those areas where labor force participation is the normal mode of activity. Also, some of the evidence which has been presented to the effect that there may be objective economic costs to employers associated with hiring some of the economically disadvantaged indicates that employment stimulating programs which do nothing to compensate for these costs may have little success. The subsidy program has the advantage of attracting the poor into lines of economic activity which are in the mainstream of economic life in the United States and offering them an opportunity to participate in "normal" society. By contrast, many of the alternatives rely on straight direct income grants which we have already remarked amount to little more than charity to those we consider to be incapable of being a member of the mainstream of American life. One further advantage of the subsidy plan is that it could be used to encourage employment of new entrants into the labor force, particularly teen-agers, and would function as a counterweight to the adverse employment effects of legislation such as the minimum wage laws. On the negative side, it may not be particularly effective in areas where labor force attachment is weak or where society feels

---

[22] This does not mean that there is no room for improvement in this system. For one thing, I would recommend extending the early retirement provisions to younger and younger age groups with appropriate actuarial reductions in benefits until almost no one availed themselves of this option at the earliest age at which it was available. Similarly, actuarial increments could be provided for those who postponed retirement beyond age 65. These also could be offered up to an age at which few people availed themselves of the opportunity. In this fashion, a benefit structure which was optimal from the standpoint of the beneficiaries of the system could be developed.

[23] For a detailed statement of my reasons for this position, see (67).

[24] The details of such a subsidy plan involve some considerable work. However, suggestions can be found in Muth (142) and Bowman (16). My own thinking runs along the lines of subsidies to employers for hiring low-productivity workers which decline over time in order to encourage employers to upgrade worker skills. For example, the subsidy schedule could be set so as to be zero after five years. If, at that time, a worker was still not self sufficient in the market, he could simply be "recycled" through the program. Some more detailed thoughts along these lines are presented in an appendix to this chapter.

it is in its best interest to discourage labor force participation. This could be the case, for example, with families headed by a woman. In instances such as this, some variant of the other income supplementation schemes could be used such as the Family Assistance proposal with voluntary work registration provisions.

A possible complaint about the policy menu I have proposed is that it is a "mixture," a "mishmash," and lacks the elegance and simplicity of some of the other schemes. This is true and deliberately so. The problems and needs of the economically disadvantaged in American society are varied and a public policy which is sweepingly simplistic is not likely to fit the complexities of these problems and needs. For example, among the aged there is no need to encourage labor force participation: But, among the young or those in the prime working years this may be quite desirable if people are truly to be incorporated into contemporary American society. And with women, we may wish to pursue a course of action intermediate between these approaches. In short, the problems may simply have too much variety to be adequately dealt with by one single income maintenance proposal.

One final *caveat* is in order concerning the policy proposals which have been made. In no way do they deal with the problem of majority-minority group economic differentials except at the lower end of the income distribution. At least, though, they absorb the impact that such differentials have in terms of creating severe economic dislocation. However, in the intermediate and higher income ranges such differentials would be likely to remain. Of course, this is true for all the alternatives we have discussed. As to a policy approach to eliminate these differentials in their totality, I must confess that no obvious one seems to be available. This is easily the most intractable problem we face.

VII.   A FINAL SUMMATION

The evidence is in and the arguments have been made. What more can be said about the functioning of American labor markets in solving various manpower problems? In the best of all possible worlds we would have been able to conclude with one sweeping panacea-type recommendation which would have instantaneously produced an optimal set of labor markets. That this is not the situation in which we find ourselves should be reasonably obvious by now. All we can do is say that there is room for improvement here and there and that by a careful and reasoned approach we can make progress in mitigating the effects of certain social problems. Perhaps the lack of some final overwhelming set of policy recommendations stems from the fact that we have made no sweeping indictments of things as they are. Far from it; by and large, it has been found that given half a chance American labor markets will do a reasonably effective job of accomplishing the objectives that economic theory assigns to such markets. In this respect there has been a central theme, a broad sweep, implicit in the discussion, namely, that the market does work and that if society will clearly define its goals and objectives it is possible to use market mechanisms, precisely because they do work, to achieve these ends. This is the positive side of things. From another view, that theme also implies that if you attempt to suppress the workings of the marketplace, the prospects for successfully achieving a given goal are substantially reduced. If these basic notions were only better understood among policy makers, a good deal of social mischief could be rather simply avoided. With that, enough said!

APPENDIX

A More Detailed Proposal for Income Supplementation Through Employer Subsidies

In this appendix, I will outline the essentials of a plan involving the federal government paying employers a direct subsidy for employing individuals who can be classified as having "low" levels of productivity.[25] Exact details will be filled in but they are merely illustrative (although realistic) and could be modified. On the basis of federal income tax returns it is possible to determine from W-2 reports the level of wage related income of any individual. Let us set a delimiting standard of $3,200 for determining whether individuals are "low" productivity. This is simply the present federal minimum wage rate multiplied by 2,000 (the number of hours of work that corresponds to full-time employment). Now, suppose a worker reports only $3,000 of W-2 type income for a year. On the basis of 2,000 hours of work this means an average wage of $1.50 an hour. In this situation, the federal government would pay an employer a subsidy of say $0.15 an hour for employing this worker ($0.10 to fill the gap between his present wage and the minimum and $0.05 to cover administrative costs and provide an incentive to the employer to hire the worker).

A number of questions immediately occur, such as "How do you administer such a system?", "How do you ensure that workers receive the benefits of the subsidy?", "What is the maximum subsidy which

---

[25] I have used the term productivity somewhat loosely here. Low productivity includes such things as inadequate work performance due to lack of education or skills as well as discrimination against workers because of race or sex. In fact, it really covers any factor which makes a worker less desirable to employers in the labor market.

would be paid?", "How long does the subsidy last?", "Who should be eligible for the subsidy?", "What does this do for individuals who traditionally have little access to the labor market?", and "What would be the cost of such a program?"

Actually, the administration of the system should be relatively simple. It has already been suggested that classification by productivity status could be accomplished through the Internal Revenue system. It would be simple enough to issue a worker classification card which would distinguish low productivity from other workers and at the same time indicate the hourly subsidy which anyone who employed him would be eligible to receive. All that would then be necessary is to provide a vehicle through which the employer could collect his subsidy. This could rather effectively be done by allowing the employer to deduct his subsidy payments from either his periodic income tax or social security tax payments. One advantage of the latter would be that subsidized workers could be rather easily noted on the quarterly employer's report and it would be an easy task to verify (through social security account numbers) whether the worker was, in fact, a low-productivity one. Of course, it is presumed that the social security system would be reimbursed by the federal Treasury for the deducted subsidy payments.[26]

The next question is how to ensure that individual workers receive the benefits of the subsidy which is being paid by the federal government. Since the amount of the subsidy is geared to the level of the federal minimum wage this can be accomplished by requiring that the employer pay that minimum. This handles instances where the employer is in an activity not covered by the federal minimum wage law. If this is the case, the employer can actually "opt" into the minimum wage system. But, what about those cases where employers are already covered by the federal minimum wage? Presumably, they would not presently be employing any low-productivity workers by this definition unless they worked only part time. In this case, the requirement for the employer to receive the subsidy would be that the worker be employed full time.[27]

"How large a subsidy should be paid?" We already have indicated that it should be a sliding scale type subsidy based on the difference between actual earnings and an accepted level for defining low-productivity status. A sample of the type of subsidy schedule which might be adopted is shown in Table 15–A–1. In that table a maximum subsidy of $0.50 an hour has been set. This is merely a judgment on our part and some experimentation might be required to determine what the ap-

---

[26] In case of subsidies exceeding the total tax payment a refund would be necessary, of course.

[27] Some provisions would have to be included to make allowances for workers not being employed due to sickness. What is envisioned here is that the worker would not be employed part time for economic reasons.

propriate maximum subsidy should be. The criterion for determining this would be whether the present subsidy schedule was achieving the desired level of income supplementation. Clearly, though, there is no fixed formula for setting this maximum.

We can now turn to the matter of how long the subsidy should last. The ultimate objective of a program such as this is to draw individuals into the mainstream of American economic life. Consequently, it is hoped that through the process of paying the subsidy individuals will be able to acquire sufficient work experience and on-the-job training to enable them to become self-sufficient over time.[28] To encourage employers to

TABLE 15–A–1
Suggested Subsidy Schedule for
Implementing Employer Subsidy
Income Supplementation Plan

Reported W-2 Income	Hourly Subsidy
$3,100–$3,199.............	$0.10
3,000– 3,099.............	0.15
2,900– 2,999.............	0.20
2,800– 2,899.............	0.25
2,700– 2,799.............	0.30
2,600– 2,699.............	0.35
2,500– 2,599.............	0.40
2,400– 2,499.............	0.45
Less than 2,400............	0.50

train and upgrade these individuals it is suggested that the subsidy be designed to disappear gradually over, say, a period of five years. Thus, an initial subsidy of $0.25 an hour would decline $0.05 a year until it disappeared. Hopefully, at that time workers would have progressed sufficiently in terms of work skills and the like to be able to perform competitively in our economy. But, what about the worker who does not progress in this fashion? What happens to one who after the subsidy expires falls back to low-productivity income levels? Very simple. Just re-certify him as a low-productivity worker on the basis of his earnings in, for example, the first year after his subsidy expires and start the cycle of subsidy payments once more.

Next, who should be eligible to have a subsidy paid to his employer as the result of his being a low-productivity worker? Actually, there is no reason for excluding anyone, regardless of age and sex, from being

---

[28] Hopefully, getting Negroes employed in this fashion would also have the impact of breaking down discrimination type barriers through the process of "education" of employers concerning the capabilities of Negro workers.

eligible for certification. This is one of the virtues of such a system. It can be employed to deal with a wide range of problems. For example, new entrants to the labor market (particularly teen-agers) would be eligible for certification and this would encourage employers to hire them. Or, more housewives might be induced to enter the labor market by the higher wages employers could offer due to the subsidy which employing these workers would mean. This would lead to a greater level of total employment and, presumably, higher levels of national product.

An almost natural question to raise with respect to this scheme is how to handle the matter of individuals who traditionally have little association with the labor market or who are unable to find a job even with the subsidy that the government is willing to pay. As a case in point, consider female heads of households. For the most part these represent widows and those who are either separated or divorced from their husband. Frequently, they have dependent children and frequently they are also recipients of some type of public assistance (such as Aid for Dependent Children). What does the wage subsidy proposal do for this group? The answer to that depends on what priority is placed on drawing individuals into labor market activity. If the society feels that this group should be encouraged to enter into the labor force, the subsidy can be adjusted appropriately and alternative sources of transfer payment income can be limited in such a fashion as to encourage labor force participation. However, it may well be that as a society we do not feel that this is desirable.[29] If this is the case, we are still at liberty to continue such programs as Aid for Dependent Children. Of course, the same applies to our existing social security system. Thus, the wage subsidy proposal differs from the Friedman negative income tax scheme by not being a complete substitute for all other federal transfer payment programs. Therefore, it is possible to tailor a "mixed" program depending on whether we feel that various subgroups of the population should be encouraged to participate in the labor market.

This still leaves to be resolved the problem of how to deal with individuals who are unable to find a job even with certification as a low-productivity worker. If an individual is unable to locate a job, he has the option of registering with the local office of the U.S. Employment Service. If he does this and it is determined that he is a family head, some allowance similar to unemployment compensation could be paid while the job-seeking process takes place. If at the conclusion of a specified period (say, 13 weeks) the individual has not found a job, he would then be certified by the employment service as eligible for the receipt of some form of general assistance payments. Thus, the subsidy system,

---

[29] For example, we might feel that it is desirable to keep female family heads at home in order to provide a better environment for the rearing of their children.

the employment service function, and the general assistance program could be integrated.[30]

One further question remains, namely, "What might the potential cost of such a program be?" We can only make rough estimates but assume that its net effect was to create 3,000,000 new jobs which did not exist before and that this led to a reduction in unemployment of 1,500,000.[31] Further, assume that 10,000,000 individuals who are already employed have their income levels upgraded by the subsidy to some minimally acceptable level. If the subsidy involved in each of the new jobs which is created is, say $0.50 an hour, this would amount to $1,000 per year per job or a total of $3 billion. To this must be added the cost of the subsidy for the other 10,000,000 previously employed workers. If this subsidy averages $0.25 an hour, the cost would be $500 per job or a total of $5 billion. Thus, together these two aspects of the program would cost $8 billion annually under these assumptions. But, what about the additional output resulting from the extra 3,000,000 jobs which have been created? If, on the average, these generate an additional $4,000 of output per year, the resultant increase in output would be $12 billion.[32]

To summarize, it has been argued that a scheme of income supplementation can be designed which will provide immediate income increases for low-productivity, low-income individuals and at the same time more intimately involve those individuals in the normal workings of the American economy.

---

[30] Individuals who attempt to participate in the labor market and are unsuccessful but who are members of a family unit with a primary wage earner would not be certified for general assistance. They would also not receive the unemployment compensation type allowance while job seeking.

[31] It is assumed here that two new jobs must be created in order to reduce unemployment by one worker. This is based on the findings of Dernburg and Strand (37).

[32] Any increased output due to increased labor force participation is a pure net gain in that the "cost" we have talked about is merely a transfer of income from one sector to another and not a "real" cost as such.

References

1. Aaron, Henry. "The Foundations of the 'War on Poverty,' Re-examined," *American Economic Review,* December, 1967, pp. 1229–40.
2. Aronson, Robert L. *Components of Occupational Change in the United States, 1950–1960.* Technical Monograph Series, No. 1. New York: New York State School of Industrial and Labor Relations, 1969.
3. Bancroft, Gertrude. *The American Labor Force: Its Growth and Changing Composition.* New York: John Wiley & Sons, Inc., 1958.
4. Barth, Peter S. "The Minimum Wage and Teenage Unemployment," *Industrial Relations Research Association Proceedings,* 1969, pp. 296–310.
5. Barth, Peter S. "Unemployment and Labor Force Participation," *Southern Economic Journal,* January, 1968, pp. 375–82.
6. Batchelder, Alan B. "Decline in the Relative Income of Negro Men," *Quarterly Journal of Economics,* November, 1964, pp. 511–24.
7. Batchelder, Alan B. "Occupational and Geographic Mobility: Two Ohio Area Case Studies," *Industrial and Labor Relations Review,* July, 1965, pp. 570–83.
8. Becker, Gary S. "A Theory of the Allocation of Time," *Economic Journal,* September, 1965, pp. 493–517.
9. Becker, Gary S. *Human Capital.* New York: Columbia University Press, 1964.
10. Becker, Gary S. *The Economics of Discrimination.* Chicago: The University of Chicago Press, 1957.
11. Bhatia, R. J. "Unemployment and the Rate of Change of Money Earnings in the United States, 1900–1958," *Economica,* August, 1961, pp. 286–96.
12. Blumen, Isadore; Kogan, Marvin; and McCarthy, Philip J. *The Industrial Mobility of Labor as a Probability Process.* Vol. VI. Cornell Studies in Industrial and Labor Relations, Ithaca, N.Y.: Cornell University, 1955.
13. Bowen, William G. *Wage Behavior in the Postwar Period.* Princeton, N.J.:

Princeton University Industrial Relations Section, Department of Economics, 1960.

14. Bowen, William G., and Berry, R. Albert. "Unemployment Conditions and Movements of the Money Wage Level," *Review of Economics and Statistics*, May, 1963, pp. 163–72.

15. Bowen, William G., and Finegan, T. A. "Labor Force Participation and Unemployment," in A. M. Ross (ed.), *Employment Policy and the Labor Market*. Berkeley, Calif.: University of California Press, 1965, pp. 115–61.

16. Bowman, Mary Jean. "Poverty in an Affluent Society," in Neil W. Chamberlain (ed.), *Contemporary Economic Issues*. Homewood, Ill.: Richard D. Irwin, Inc., 1969, pp. 49–107.

17. Brechling, Frank P. "The Trade-Off Between Inflation and Unemployment," *Journal of Political Economy*, July/August, 1968, Part II, pp. 712–37.

18. Brehm, C. T., and Saving, T. R. "The Demand for General Assistance Payments," *American Economic Review*, December, 1964, pp. 1002–18.

19. Bronfenbrenner, Martin. "A Contribution to the Aggregate Theory of Wages," *Journal of Political Economy*, December, 1956, pp. 459–69.

20. Bronfenbrenner, Martin. "Aggregate Wage Theory and Money Illusion: Reply," *Journal of Political Economy*, October, 1957, pp. 445–47.

21. Buchanan, James M., and Moes, John E. "A Regional Countermeasure to National Wage Standardization," *American Economic Review*, June, 1960, pp. 434–38.

22. Bunting, Robert L. "A Test of the Theory of Geographic Mobility," *Industrial and Labor Relations Review*, February, 1961, pp. 432–45.

23. Bunting, Robert L. "Labor Mobility: Sex, Race, and Age," *The Review of Economics and Statistics*, May, 1960, pp. 229–31.

24. Cain, Glen G. *Married Women in the Labor Force*. Chicago: The University of Chicago Press, 1966.

25. Cairnes, J. E. *Some Leading Principles of Political Economy Newly Expounded*. New York: Harper & Bros., 1874.

26. Cartter, Allan M. *Theory of Wages and Employment*. Homewood, Ill.: Richard D. Irwin, Inc., 1959.

27. Chapin, Gene L. "Unemployment Insurance, Job Search, and the Demand for Leisure," *Western Economic Journal*, March, 1971, pp. 102–7.

28. Shultz, G. P., and Aliber, R. Z. *Guidelines, Informal Controls, and the Market Place*. Chicago: The University of Chicago Press, 1966.

29. Chapin, Gene L., and Adie, Douglas. "Teenage Unemployment Effects of Federal Minimum Wages," *Research Paper No. 47*. Athens Ohio: Department of Economics, Ohio University, 1970.

30. Adie, Douglas, and Chapin, Gene L. "Teenage Unemployment Experiences and Federal Minimum Wage Regulation," *Industrial Relations Research Association Proceedings*, 1970.

31. Coleman, J. S. *et al. Equality of Educational Opportunity*. Washington, D.C.: U.S. Office of Education, 1966.

32. Council of Economic Advisors. *Economic Report of the President*. Washington, D.C.: U.S.G.P.O., 1964.

33. Council of Economic Advisors. *Economic Report of the President*. Washington, D.C.: U.S.G.P.O., 1964–67.

34. DeLeeuw, F. "A Revised Index of Manufacturing Capacity," *Federal Reserve Bulletin*, November, 1966, pp. 1605–15.
35. Demsetz, Harold. "Structural Unemployment: A Reconsideration of the Evidence and the Theory," *Journal of Law and Economics*, October, 1961, pp. 80–92.
36. Denison, E. F. *The Sources of Economic Growth in the United States.* Supplementary Paper No. 13. New York: Committee for Economic Development, 1962.
37. Dernburg, T. F., and Strand, K. T. "Hidden Unemployment, 1953–62: A Quantitative Analysis by Age and Sex," *American Economic Review*, March, 1966, pp. 71–95.
38. Dewey, Donald. *Selected Studies of Negro Employment in the South.* Washington, D.C.: National Planning Association, 1955.
39. Dow, Louis A. "On Choice in Labor Markets," *Industrial and Labor Relations Review*, October, 1957, pp. 96–102.
40. Duncan, Otis Dudley. "Inheritance of Poverty or Inheritance of Race?" in Daniel P. Moynihan (ed.), *On Understanding Poverty.* New York: Basic Books, 1968, pp. 85–110.
41. Dunlop, J. T. *Wage Determination under Trade Unions.* New York: Augustus M. Kelley, Publishers, 1944.
42. Durand, John D. *The Labor Force in the United States, 1890–1960.* New York: Social Sciences Research Council, 1948.
43. Easterlin, Richard A. "Interregional Differences in Per Capita Income, Population, and Total Income, 1840–1950," *Trends in the American Economy in the Nineteenth Century*, Vol. 24, *Studies in Income and Wealth.* Princeton, N.J.: National Bureau of Economic Research, Princeton University Press, 1960, pp. 73–140.
44. Easterlin, Richard. *Population, Labor Force, and Long-Swings in Economic Growth.* New York: National Bureau of Economic Research, Columbia University Press, 1968.
45. Easterlin, Richard. "Labor Force Participation and Unemployment: A Review of Recent Evidence: Discussion," in R. A. Gordon and M. S. Gordon (eds.), *Prosperity and Unemployment.* Berkeley, Calif.: University of California Press, 1966, pp. 126–134.
46. Easterlin, Richard A. "The American Baby Boom in Historical Perspective," *American Economic Review*, December, 1961, pp. 869–911.
47. Eckstein, Otto. "Money Wage Determination Revisited," *The Review of Economic Studies*, April, 1968, pp. 133–43.
48. Eckstein, Otto, and Wilson, Thomas A. "The Determination of Money Wages in American Industry," *Quarterly Journal of Economics*, August, 1962, pp. 379–414.
49. *Economic Report of the President.* Washington, D.C.: U.S.G.P.O., 1964–67.
50. *Economics of Aging: Toward a Full Share in Abundance.* Hearing before the Special Committee on Aging, U.S. Senate, 91st Cong., 1st sess., Part 1—Survey Hearing. Washington, D.C.: U.S.G.P.O., 1969.
51. Fein, Rashi. "Relative Income of Negro Men: Some Recent Data," *Quarterly Journal of Economics*, May, 1966, p. 336.

52. Fellner, William. *Competition among the Few.* New York: Augustus M. Kelley, Publishers, 1949, pp. 252–76.

53. Friedman, Milton. *Capitalism and Freedom.* Chicago: The University of Chicago Press, 1962, chap. XII.

54. Friedman, Milton. "The Role of Monetary Policy," *American Economic Review*, March, 1968, pp. 1–17.

55. Fuchs, Victor. "Toward a Theory of Poverty," in *The Concept of Poverty*, a report of the Task Force on Economic Growth and Development, Washington, D.C.: Chamber of Commerce of the United States, 1965, pp. 69–92.

56. Galbraith, J. K. *The Affluent Society.* London: Hamilton, 1958, chap. XXIII.

57. Gallaway, Lowell E. "Age and Labor Mobility Patterns," *Southern Economic Journal*, October, 1969, pp. 171–80.

58. Gallaway, Lowell E. "Geographic Flows of Hired Agricultural Labor: 1957–1960," *American Journal of Agricultural Economics*, May, 1968, pp. 199–212.

59. Gallaway, Lowell E. *Geographic Labor Mobility in the United States 1957 to 1960.* Research Report No. 28. Social Security Administration, Washington: U.S.G.P.O., 1969.

60. Gallaway, Lowell E. "Industry Variations in Geographic Labor Mobility Patterns," *Journal of Human Resources*, Fall, 1967, pp. 461–74.

61. Gallaway, Lowell E. *Interindustry Labor Mobility in the United States: 1957 to 1960.* Research Report No. 18. Social Security Administration, Washington: U.S.G.P.O., 1967.

62. Gallaway, Lowell E. "Labor Mobility, Resource Allocation, and Structural Unemployment," *American Economic Review*, September, 1963, pp. 694–716.

63. Gallaway, Lowell E. "Mobility of Hired Agricultural Labor: 1957–1960," *Journal of Farm Economics*, February, 1967, pp. 32–52.

64. Gallaway, Lowell E. "Negative Income Tax Rates and the Elimination of Poverty," *National Tax Journal*, September, 1966, pp. 298–307.

65. Gallaway, Lowell E. "Negative Income Tax Rates and the Elimination of Poverty: Reply," *National Tax Journal*, September, 1967, pp. 338–43.

66. Gallaway, Lowell E. "Proposals for Federal Aid to Depressed Industrial Areas: A Critique," *Industrial and Labor Relations Review*, April, 1961, pp. 363–78.

67. Gallaway, Lowell E. "Remarks on Economics of Aging: Toward a Full Share in Abundance," in *Economics of Aging: Toward a Full Share in Abundance.* Hearings before the Special Committee on Aging, U.S. Senate, 91st Cong., 1st sess., Part 1—*Survey Hearing.* Washington, D.C.: U.S.G.P.O., 1969.

68. Gallaway, Lowell E. "The Aged and the Extent of Poverty in the United States," *Southern Economic Journal*, October, 1966, pp. 212–22.

69. Gallaway, Lowell E. "The Foundations of the War on Poverty," *American Economic Review*, March, 1965, pp. 122–31.

70. Gallaway, Lowell E. "The Foundations of the 'War on Poverty' Reexamined: Reply," *American Economic Review*, December, 1967, pp. 1241–43.

71. Gallaway, Lowell E. *The Retirement Decision: An Exploratory Essay,* Social Security Administration, Research Report No. 9. Washington, D.C.: U.S.G.P.O., 1965.

72. Gallaway, Lowell E. "Unemployment Levels among Non-White Teen-Agers," *Journal of Business,* July, 1969, pp. 265–76.

73. Gallaway, Lowell E.; Chapin, Gene L.; and Vedder, Richard K. "The Effect of Geographic Mobility on Regional Income Differentials: A Test of the Steady-State Equilibrium Process," *Proceedings,* Business and Economics Section, American Statistical Association, 1970.

74. Gallaway, Lowell E.; Gilbert, Roy F.; and Smith, Paul E. "The Economics of Labor Mobility: An Empirical Analysis," *Western Economic Journal,* June, 1967, pp. 211–23.

75. Gallaway, Lowell E., and Scully, Gerald W. "An Economic Analysis of Minority Group Discrimination in the United States," Midwest Economic Association, Chicago, Ill., April, 1969.

76. Gavett, Thomas W. "Youth Unemployment and Minimum Wages," *Monthly Labor Review,* March, 1970, pp. 3–12.

77. Gilman, H. J. "Economic Discrimination and Unemployment," *American Economic Review,* December, 1965, pp. 1077–96.

78. Gilman, H. J. "The White/Non White Unemployment Differential," M. Perlman (ed.), *Human Resources in the Urban Economy.* Baltimore: Resources for the Future, Inc., 1963, pp. 75–113.

79. Gilpatrick, Eleanor G. *Structural Unemployment and Aggregate Demand.* Baltimore: The Johns Hopkins Press, 1966.

80. Green, Christopher. *Negative Taxes and the Poverty Problem.* Washington: Brookings Institute, 1967.

81. Greenwood, Michael J. "An Analysis of the Determinants of Geographic Labor Mobility in the United States," *Review of Economics and Statistics,* May, 1969, pp. 189–94.

82. Hansen, W. Lee. "The Cyclical Sensitivity of the Labor Supply," *American Economic Review,* June, 1961, pp. 299–309.

83. Harrington, Michael. *The Other America: Poverty in the United States.* Baltimore: Penguin Books, 1964.

84. Hathaway, Dale E. "Migration from Agriculture: The Historical Record and Its Meaning," *American Economic Review,* May, 1960, pp. 379–91.

85. Heaton, Herbert. *Economic History of Europe.* Rev. ed. New York: Harper, 1948, p. 481.

86. Hiestand, Dale L. *Economic Growth and Employment Opportunities for Minorities.* New York: Columbia University Press, 1964.

87. Hildebrand, G. H. "Structural Unemployment and Cost-Push Inflation in the United States," in George Horwich (ed.), *Monetary Process and Policy: A Symposium.* Homewood, Ill.: Richard D. Irwin, Inc., 1967, pp. 15–29.

88. Hobson, John. *Evolution of Modern Capitalism: A Study of Machine Production.* London: W. Scott and New York: C. Scribner's Sons, 1894.

89. Hobson, John and Albert F. Mummery, *Physiology of Industry.* New York: Kelley and Millman (Reprints of Economic Classics), 1956.

90. Holt, C. C. "Job Search, Phillips' Wage Relation, and Union Influence,"

in *Macroeconomic Foundations of Employment and Inflation Theory*, E. S. Phelps (ed.), New York: W. W. Norton, 1970, pp. 53–123.

91. Jaffe, A. J., and Carleton, R. O. *Occupational Mobility in the United States, 1930–1960*. New York: Kings Crown Press, 1954.

92. Johnson, D. Gale. "Policies to Improve the Labor Transfer Process," *American Economic Review*, May, 1960, pp. 403–12.

93. Johnson, President Lyndon B. *War on Poverty*. Committee Print, Selected Subcommittee on Labor and Public Welfare. U.S. Senate (Washington, D.C.: U.S.G.P.O., 1964).

94. Junk, P. E. "A Macroeconomic Theory of Wages: Comment," *American Economic Review*, September, 1957, pp. 679–82.

95. Kalachek, E. D. "The Determinants of Higher Unemployment Rates, 1958–60," unpublished doctoral dissertation, Massachusetts Institute of Technology, 1963.

96. Kasper, Hirschel. "Welfare Payments and Work Incentive: Some Determinants of the Rates of General Assistance Payments," *Journal of Human Resources*, Winter, 1968, pp. 86–110.

97. Katzner, Donald W. "Theory and Cost of Racial Discrimination," unpublished paper.

98. Kaun, David, and Fechter, Alan. "Metropolitan Area Intercounty Migration Rates: A Test of Labor Market Theory," *Industrial and Labor Relations Review*, January, 1966, pp. 273–79.

99. Kerr, Clark. "The Balkanization of Labor Markets," in E. Wight Bakke et al., *Labor Mobility and Economic Opportunity*. Cambridge: The M.I.T. Press, 1954, pp. 92–110.

100. Keynes, J. M. *The General Theory of Employment, Interest and Money*. London: Macmillan & Co., Ltd., 1936.

101. Killingsworth, Charles. *Nations Manpower Revolution*. U.S. Senate, Subcommittee on Employment and Manpower of the Committee on Labor and Public Welfare, Hearings, Part 5, 88th Cong., 1st sess. Washington, D.C.: U.S.G.P.O., 1963.

102. Klein, L. R., and Gallin, D. M. "Wharton Index of Capacity Utilization," *Wharton Quarterly*, Vol. 1 (1967), p. 21.

103. Klein, L. R., and Kosobud, R. F. "Some Econometrics of Growth: Great Ratios of Economics," *Quarterly Journal of Economics*, May, 1961, pp. 173–98.

104. Gallaway, Lowell E., and Koshal, Rajindar K. "An International Comparison of Phillips' Curves," *Western Economic Association*, 1971.

105. Koshal, Rajindar K., and Gallaway, Lowell E. "The Phillips' Curve for Belgium," *Tijdschrift voor Economie*, No. 3 (1970).

106. Koshal, Rajindar K., and Gallaway, Lowell E. "The Phillips' Curve for West Germany," *Kyklos* (forthcoming).

107. Krueger, Anne O. "The Economics of Discrimination," *The Journal of Political Economy*, October, 1963, pp. 481–86.

108. Kuh, Edwin. "A Productivity Theory of Wage Levels—An Alternative Approach to the Phillips Curve," *The Review of Economic Studies*, October, 1967, pp. 333–60.

109. Kuznets, Simon; Miller, Ann Ratner; and Easterlin, Richard A. *Population Redistribution and Economic Growth, United States, 1870–1950*,

Vol. 2. *Analyses of Economic Change*. Philadelphia: American Philosophical Society, 1960.

110. Lampman, R. J. "On Choice in Labor Markets," *Industrial and Labor Relations Review*, July, 1956, pp. 629–36.

111. Lansing, J. B. *The Propensity to Move*. Labor Mobility Publication No. 3, Area Redevelopment Administration, U.S. Department of Labor. Washington, D.C.: U.S.G.P.O., 1964.

112. Lansing, J. B., and Morgan, J. N. "The Effect of Geographic Mobility on Income," *Journal of Human Resources*, Fall, 1967, pp. 449–60.

113. Lansing, J. B., and Mueller, Eva. *Residential Location and Urban Mobility*. Ann Arbor, Mich.: Survey Research Center, University of Michigan, 1964.

114. Lansing, J. B., and Mueller, Eva. *The Geographic Mobility of Labor*. Ann Arbor, Mich.: Institute for Social Research, University of Michigan, 1967.

115. Lebergott, Stanley. *Manpower in Economic Growth: The American Record since 1800*. New York: McGraw-Hill Book Co., 1964.

116. Lee, E. S.; Miller, A. R.; Brainerd, C. P.; and Easterlin, R. A. *Population Redistribution and Economic Growth, United States, 1870–1950*, Vol. 1. *Methodological Considerations and Reference Tables*. Philadelphia: American Philosophical Society, 1957.

117. Lerner, Abba. "Problem of Achieving and Maintaining a Stable Price Level: Discussion," *American Economic Review*, May, 1960, p. 217.

118. Lester, Richard A. "Marginalism, Minimum Wages, and Labor Markets," *American Economic Review*, March, 1947, pp. 135–48.

119. Lester, Richard A. "On Choice in Labor Markets: Comment," *Industrial and Labor Relations Review*, July, 1956, pp. 641–42.

120. Lester, Richard A. "Shortcomings of Marginal Analysis for Wage-Employment Problems," *American Economic Review*, March, 1946, pp. 63–82.

121. Lewis, H. Gregg. *Unionism and Relative Wages in the United States*. Chicago: The University of Chicago Press, 1963.

122. Liebling, H. I., and Cluff, A. T. "U.S. Postwar Inflation and Phillips Curve," *Kyklos*, Vol. 22, No. 2 (1969), pp. 232–50.

123. Lipsey, R. G. "Structural Unemployment Reconsidered," in A. M. Ross (ed.), *Employment Policy and the Labor Market*. Berkeley, Calif.: University of California Press, 1965, pp. 210–55.

124. Lipsey, R. G. "The Relation between Unemployment and the Rate of Change of Money Wage Rates in the United Kingdom, 1862–1957: A Further Analysis," *Economica*, February, 1960, pp. 1–31.

125. Anderson, W. H. Locke. "Trickling Down: The Relationship between Economic Growth and the Extent of Poverty among American Families," *Quarterly Journal of Economics*, November, 1964, pp. 511–24.

126. Long, Clarence D. "A Theory of Creeping Unemployment and Labor Force Replacement," *Annual Meeting*, Catholic Economic Association, 1960. Reprinted in 107 Cong. Rec. 12455 (daily ed. July 25, 1961).

127. Long, Clarence D. "Impact of Effective Demand on the Labor Supply," *American Economic Review*, May, 1953, p. 460.

128. Long, Clarence D. *The Labor Force under Changing Income and Employ-

ment. Princeton, N.J.: National Bureau of Economic Research and Princeton University Press, 1958.

129. Lowry, Ira S. *Migration and Metropolitan Growth.* San Francisco, Calif.: Chandler Publishing Co., 1966.

130. Machlup, Fritz. "Marginal Analysis and Empirical Research," *American Economic Review,* September, 1946, pp. 19–54.

131. Machlup, Fritz. "Rejoinder to an Antimarginalist," *American Economic Review,* March, 1947, pp. 148–54.

132. Maher, J. "Union, Non-Union Wage Differentials," *American Economic Review,* June, 1956, pp. 336–52.

133. Malthus, Thomas R. *The Principles of Political Economy considered with a View to their Practical Applications.* Boston: Wells and Lilly, 1821.

134. Michelson, Stephan. "Incomes of Racial Minorities," unpublished manuscript.

135. Miller, Herman P. *Income Distribution in the United States.* U.S. Bureau of the Census. Washington, D.C.: U.S.G.P.O., 1966.

136. Mincer, Jacob. "Labor Force Participation among Women," in National Bureau of Economics Research, *Aspects of Labor Economics.* Princeton, N.J.: National Bureau of Economic Research and Princeton University Press, 1962.

137. Mincer, Jacob. "Labor Force Participation and Unemployment: A Review of Recent Literature," in R. A. Gordon and M. S. Gordon (eds.), *Prosperity and Unemployment.* Berkeley, Calif.: University of California Press, 1966, pp. 73–112.

138. Minsky, Hyman. "Effects of Shifts in Aggregate Demand upon Income Distribution," *American Journal of Agricultural Economics,* May, 1968, pp. 328–39.

139. Mooney, J. D. "Urban Poverty and Labor Force Participation," *American Economic Review,* March, 1967, pp. 104–19.

140. Mortensen, Dale T. "A Theory of Wage and Employment Dynamics," in *Macroeconomic Foundations of Employment and Inflation Theory,* E. S. Phelps (ed.), New York: W. W. Norton, 1970, pp. 167–211.

141. Moynihan, Daniel P. "Employment, Income, and the Ordeal of the Negro Family," *Daedalus,* Fall, 1965, pp. 745–70.

142. Muth, Richard. *Federal Poverty Programs,* Report R-166. Washington: Institute for Defense Analysis, Economic and Political Studies Division, January, 1966.

143. Muth, Richard. *The Evaluation of Selected Present and Potential Poverty Programs.* No. IDA/HG66-5594. Washington: Institute for Defense Analysis, Economic and Political Studies Division, January, 1966.

144. Oi, Walter Y. "Labor as a Quasi-Fixed Factor," *Journal of Political Economy,* December, 1962, pp. 538–55.

145. Organization for Economic Cooperation and Development. *International Trade Union Seminar on Active Manpower Policy, Supplement to the Final Report.* Paris: Secretariat, Organisation for Economic Co-operation and Development, Manpower and Social Affairs Directorate, Social Affairs Division, 1964.

146. Ornati, Oscar. *Poverty amid Affluence: A Report on a Research Project.*

The New School for Social Research. New York: The Twentieth Century Fund, 1966.

147. Orshansky, Mollie. "Counting the Poor: Another Look at the Poverty Profile," *Social Security Bulletin*, January, 1965.

148. Parnes, Herbert S. *Research on Labor Mobility: An Appraisal of Research Findings in the United States*, Bulletin No. 65. New York: Social Science Research Council, 1954.

149. Perry, George L. *Unemployment, Money Wage Rates, and Inflation*. Cambridge, Mass.: The M.I.T. Press, 1966.

150. Phelps, Edmund S. "Money Wage Dynamics and Labor-Market Equilibrium," *Journal of Political Economy*, July/August, 1968, Part II, pp. 678–711.

151. Phelps, Edmund S., *et al. Macroeconomic Foundations of Employment and Inflation Theory*. New York: W. W. Norton & Co., Inc., 1970.

152. Phillips, A. W. "The Relation between Unemployment and the Rate of Change in Money Wage Rates in the United Kingdom, 1862–1957," *Economica*, November, 1958, pp. 283–99.

153. Pigou, A. C. *The Theory of Unemployment*. New York: Augustus M. Kelley, Publisher, 1933.

154. President's National Advisory Commission on Rural Poverty. *The People Left Behind*. Washington, D.C. U.S.G.P.O., 1967.

155. Raimon, Robert L. "Interstate Migration and Wage Theory," *Review of Economics and Statistics*, November, 1962, pp. 428–38.

156. Raimon, Robert L. "Labor Mobility and Wage Inflexibility," *American Economic Review*, May, 1964, pp. 133–55.

157. Rayack, Elton. "Discrimination and the Occupational Progress of Negroes," *Review of Economics and Statistics*, May, 1961, pp. 209–14.

158. Rees, A., and Hamilton, Mary T. "The Wage-Price-Productivity Perplex," *Journal of Political Economy*, February, 1967, pp. 63–70.

159. Reynolds, Lloyd G. "The Impact of Collective Bargaining on the Wage Structure of the United States," in J. T. Dunlop (ed.), *The Theory of Wage Determination*. New York: St. Martin's Press, Inc., 1957.

160. Ross, A. M. "The External Wage Structure," in G. W. Taylor and F. C. Pierson (eds.), *New Concepts in Wage Determination*. New York: McGraw-Hill Book Co., 1957.

161. Ross, A. M. *Trade Union Wage Policy*. Berkeley, Calif.: University of California Press, 1953.

162. Rothschild, K. W. "Aggregative Wage Theory and Money Illusion," *Journal of Political Economy*, October, 1957, pp. 442–45.

163. Rothschild, K. W. "Aggregative Wage Theory and Money Illusion: Rejoinder," *Journal of Political Economy*, October, 1957, pp. 447–48.

164. Rottenberg, Simon. "On Choice in Labor Markets," *Industrial and Labor Relations Review*, January, 1956, pp. 183–99.

165. Rottenberg, Simon. "Reply," *Industrial and Labor Relations Review*, July, 1956, pp. 636–43.

166. Rottenberg, Simon. "Reply," *Industrial and Labor Relations Review*, October, 1957, pp. 102–3.

167. Rowan, Richard L., and Northrup, Herbert R. *Readings in Labor Eco-*

nomics and Industrial Relations. Homewood, Ill.: Richard D. Irwin, Inc., 1968, pp. 21–24.

168. Samuelson, P. A., and Solow, R. M. "The Analytics of Anti-Inflationary Policy," *American Economic Review,* May, 1960, pp. 177–94.

169. Schultz, T. W. "Investment in Human Capital," *American Economic Review,* March, 1961, pp. 1–17.

170. Scully, Gerald W. "Interstate Wage Differentials: A Cross-Section Analysis," *American Economic Review,* December, 1969, pp. 757–73.

171. Scully, Gerald W., and Gallaway, Lowell E. "A Spectral Analysis of the Demographic Structure of American Unemployment," *Research Paper No. 55,* Department of Economics, Ohio University, Athens, Ohio, 1970.

172. Shriver, Sargent. "Statement to Congress," in *The War on Poverty.* Committee Print, Selected Subcommittee on Poverty of the Committee on Labor and Public Welfare, U.S. Senate. Washington, D.C.: U.S.G.P.O., 1964.

173. Simler, N. J. "Long Term Unemployment, the Structural Hypothesis, and Public Policy," *American Economic Review,* December, 1964, pp. 985–1001.

174. Simonde De Sismondi, Jean. *Nouveaux principes d'economie politique ou de la richesse dans ses rapports avec la population.* Paris: Chez Delaunay, 1819 and 1827.

175. Sjaastad, Larry A. "The Cost and Returns of Human Migration," *Journal of Political Economy,* October, 1962, Supplement, pp. 80–93.

176. Sobotka, S. "Union Influence on Wages: The Construction Industry," *Journal of Political Economy,* April, 1953, pp. 127–43.

177. Solow, R. M. "A Skeptical Note on the Constancy of Relative Shares," *American Economic Review,* September, 1958, pp. 618–31.

178. Stigler, George. "Information in the Labor Market," *Journal of Political Economy,* October, 1962, pp. 94–105.

179. Stigler, George. "The Economics of Information," *Journal of Political Economy,* June, 1961, pp. 213–25.

180. Stoikov, V. "Increasing Structural Unemployment Re-examined," *Industrial and Labor Relations Review,* April, 1966, pp. 368–76.

181. Strand, K. T., and Dernburg, T. F. "Cyclical Variation in Civilian Labor Force Participation," *Review of Economics and Statistics,* November, 1964, pp. 378–91.

182. Tarver, James. "Metropolitan Area Intercounty Migration Rates: A Test of Labor Market Theory," *Industrial and Labor Relations Review,* January, 1965, pp. 213–22.

183. Tarver, James. "Metropolitan Area Intercounty Migration Rates: Reply," *Industrial and Labor Relations Review,* January, 1966, pp. 279–81.

184. Taussig, Michael. "Negative Income Tax Rates and the Elimination of Poverty: Comment," *National Tax Journal,* September, 1967, pp. 328–37.

185. Tella, A. "Labor Force Sensitivity to Employment by Age and Sex," *Industrial Relations,* February, 1965, pp. 69–83.

186. Tella, A. "The Relation of Labor Force to Employment," *Industrial and Labor Relations Review,* April, 1964, pp. 454–69.

187. Theobald, Robert. *Free Men and Free Markets.* New York: Clarkson N. Potter, Inc., 1963.

188. Throop, A. W. "The Union-Non-Union Wage Differential and Cost-Push Inflation," *American Economic Review*, March, 1968, pp. 79–99.

189. Thurow, Lester C. "The Causes of Poverty," *Quarterly Journal of Economics*, February, 1967, pp. 39–57.

190. Tobin, James. "On Improving the Economic Status of the Negro," *Daedalus*, Fall, 1965, pp. 878–898.

191. Turner, Frederick Jackson. *The Frontier in American History*, New York: Henry Holt and Co., 1937.

192. U.S. Congress. *Economic Opportunity Act of 1964*. Hearings before the Subcommittee on the War on Poverty Program of the Committee on Education and Labor, House of Representatives, 88th Cong., 2d sess. Washington, D.C.: U.S.G.P.O., 1964.

193. U.S. Congress. Subcommittee on Economic Statistics of the Joint Committee. *Higher Unemployment Rates, 1957–1960: Structural Transformation or Inadequate Demand*. Washington, D.C.: U.S.G.P.O., 1961.

194. U.S. Department of Commerce. *Survey of Current Business*. Washington, D.C.: U.S.G.P.O., July, 1969.

195. U.S. Department of Commerce. Bureau of the Census. *Census of Population, 1960, United States Summary, General Social and Economic Characteristics*. Washington, D.C.: U.S.G.P.O., 1961.

196. U.S. Department of Commerce. Bureau of the Census. *Estimates of the Population of the Largest Standard Metropolitan Statistical Areas: 1960 to 1964*, Current Population Reports, Population Estimates, Series P-25, No. 330. Washington, D.C.: U.S.G.P.O., 1966, p. 2.

197. U.S. Department of Commerce. Bureau of the Census. "Income in 1968 of Families and Persons in the United States," *Current Population Reports*. Series P-60, No. 66. Washington, D.C.: U.S.G.P.O., December 27, 1969.

198. U.S. Department of Commerce. Bureau of the Census. "Lifetime Occupational Mobility of Adult Males, March, 1962," *Current Population Reports*, Series P-23, No. 11. Washington, D.C.: U.S.G.P.O., May 12, 1964.

199. U.S. Department of Commerce. Bureau of the Census. *Poverty in the United States 1959 to 1968, Current Population Reports*, Series P-60, No. 68. Washington, D.C.: U.S.G.P.O., December 31, 1969, Tables 1 and 2.

200. U.S. Department of Commerce. Bureau of the Census. *Special Census Survey of the South and East Los Angeles Areas*, November, 1965, *Current Population Reports*, Technical Studies, Series P-23, No. 17. Washington, D.C.: U.S.G.P.O., 1966.

201. U.S. Department of Commerce. Bureau of the Census. *Statistical Abstract of the United States, 1962*. Washington, D.C.: U.S.G.P.O., 1963.

202. U.S. Department of Commerce. Bureau of the Census. *Survey of Current Business*, July, 1969. Washington, D.C.: U.S.G.P.O., 1969.

203. U.S. Department of Commerce. Bureau of the Census. *Trends in the Income of Families and Persons in the United States, 1947–1960*, Technical Paper No. 8. Washington, D.C.: U.S.G.P.O., 1963.

204. U.S. Department of Commerce. Bureau of the Census. *U.S. Census of Population*, Vol. 1, *United States Summary*. Washington, D.C.: U.S.G.P.O., 1961.

205. U.S. Department of Commerce. Bureau of the Census. *U.S. Census of*

Population: 1960, Detailed Characteristics, U.S. Summary. Washington, D.C.: U.S.G.P.O., 1961, pp. 1–578 and 1–734, 1–735, and 1–736.

206. U.S. Department of Labor. "A Report on Manpower Requirements, Resources, Utilization and Training," in *Manpower Report of the President.* Washington, D.C.: U.S.G.P.O., 1967, Statistical Appendix.

207. U.S. Department of Labor. *Employment and Earnings for the United States, 1909–68,* Bulletin No. 1312-6. Washington, D.C.: U.S.G.P.O., 1968, Table 5, p. xxvii.

208. U.S. Department of Labor. *Manpower Report of the President.* Washington, D.C.: U.S.G.P.O., March, 1966.

209. U.S. Department of Labor. *Manpower Report of the President.* Washington, D.C.: U.S.G.P.O., March, 1970.

210. Gallaway, Lowell E., and Vedder, Richard K. "Mobility of Native Americans," *Journal of Economic History* (forthcoming).

211. Vedder, Richard K., and Gallaway, Lowell E. "Settlement Patterns of American Immigrants, 1850–1968," *Proceedings, Fifth International Congress of Economic History.* Leningrad, 1970 (forthcoming).

212. Weintraub, Sidney. "A Macroeconomic Approach to the Theory of Wages," *American Economic Review,* December, 1956, pp. 835–56.

213. Weintraub, Sidney. "A Macroeconomic Theory of Wages: Reply," *American Economic Review,* September, 1957, pp. 682–85.

214. Woytinsky, W. S. *Additional Workers and the Volume of Unemployment.* Committee on Social Security of the Social Science Research Council, Pamphlet Series No. 1. Washington, D.C.: Social Science Research Council, 1940.

215. Woytinsky, W. S. *Employment and Wages in the United States.* New York: The Twentieth Century Fund, 1953.

216. Woytinsky, W. S. "The Labor Force," in *Employment and Wages in the United States.* New York: The Twentieth Century Fund, 1953, chap. 23.

217. Zaidi, Mahmood. "Structural Unemployment, Labor Market Efficiency, and the Intrafactor Allocation Mechanism in the United States and Canada," *Southern Economic Journal,* January, 1969, pp. 205–13.

Index

This book has been set in 10 and 9 point Lino No. 21, leaded 2 points. Chapter numbers are in 14 point Ultra Bodoni and chapter titles are in 24 point Bodoni Bold. The size of the type page is 27 by 45½ picas.